Bhutan

Chomolhari

N

THE TURQUOISE MOUNTAIN

- THE TURQUOISE MOUNTAIN -
BRIAN BLESSED
— ON EVEREST —

With additional material by
JOHN-PAUL DAVIDSON

BLOOMSBURY

First published in Great Britain 1991
Bloomsbury Publishing Limited, 2 Soho Square, London W1V 5DE
Copyright © 1991 by Brian Blessed
Additional material © 1991 by John-Paul Davidson

The moral right of the authors has been asserted

PICTURE SOURCES
All photographs by John-Paul Davidson except
page 1 *top:* from the author's collection
page 1 *bottom:* Judy Goldhill
page 3 *bottom:* Adrian Rigelsford
pages 22 *bottom*, 23, 24: David Breashears/Veronique Choa

Maps in picture section and on endpapers: Fen Field

A CIP catalogue record for this book
is available from the British Library

ISBN 0–7475–1046–6

10 9 8 7 6 5 4 3 2 1

Typeset by Parker Typesetting Service, Leicester
Printed by Clays Ltd, St Ives plc

CONTENTS

This book is dedicated to
Captain John Noel,
the embodiment of the spirit of adventure

Let us probe the silent places, let us seek what luck betide us,
    Let us journey to a lonely land I know,
There's a whisper in the night wind, there's a star, a gleam to guide us,
    And the wind is calling … calling … let us go!

RWS

I

Galahad of Everest

From my earliest days epic stories of great adventure would stir my imagination, and leave me begging for more. Home was 30 Probert Avenue, Goldthorpe, near Rotherham, South Yorkshire. The avenue itself was part of a circle that contained a hundred houses or more. The whole place was full of trees and high hedges, containing an intricate labyrinth of hidden dens and pathways.

The small road was festooned with old-fashioned gas lamps, casting their mysterious shadows in the gathering dusk. On opposite sides of the circle of houses ran two railway lines, one rusty and disused, the other part of the Great North Eastern Railway, which boasted such engines as the Mallard and the legendary Flying Scotsman.

The whole landscape served as the perfect setting for a million escapades, for these were the early exciting years of the 1940s, and I was seven years old. Spanning the rusty, broken-down railway line was a large iron bridge. This magnificent structure was the focal point of our frenzied activity.

The gang of lads I belonged to was second to none. Our leader, Calden Williams, with his open face, blue eyes, curly blond hair and graceful bearing, was to us all that was heroic and noble.

His sense of fair play inspired us to feats of great courage, as we embarked on our daily 'dasties' – the Yorkshire term for acts of daring. These included jumping off the bridge at various heights, somersaulting over fences and hedges, getting as close as possible to the wild dogs that guarded Earnshaw's orchard, holding your breath till you were blue in the face, and finally, placing yourself within range of the dreaded, sinister dwarf Lennie and his big white stick. Blows from this strange Rumpelstiltskin were fast and furious, and to avoid them required speed and agility, not to mention a certain degree of madness in the first place.

They were smashing days, full of unlimited adventure. Attached to the girders under the railway bridge were dozens of ropes, swaying in all directions. There were rails underneath, but no one had ever seen a train pass through.

This was our fantasy land, full of fire-breathing dragons, swamps infested by savage crocodiles, man-eating sharks and flesh-hungry piranhas. There were bloodthirsty vampires, rotting zombies, invaders from another planet, and armies of green Treen Warriors from the Dan Dare picture strip in the *Eagle* comic.

Then there were cowboys like Johnny Mack Brown, Tex Ritter, Zorro and my personal favourite, Hopalong Cassidy; fortress-like castles and knights in shining armour, majestic kings and invisible entities; and Arthur Conan Doyle's *The Lost World*, with the adventures of Professor Challenger.

We would crawl up the embankment, all choking, dying of thirst in the sweltering heat of the Sahara, or gasp, exhaling our last breath, frozen in the snows as Scott of the Antartic. Our games were as unending as they were inventive. We had no toys – we simply shaped our hands into what we were pretending to play with. We could only dream of having a six-shooter like Hopalong Cassidy.

Gradually, like war-worn warriors with energies totally spent, we would make our way home and relax in the back garden of my friend Geoffrey Green. He was a stocky, cheerful, dark-haired boy about a year older than me. He was neat and tidy, and possessed numerous scrapbooks: a veritable treasure-house of photographs, football programmes and articles from the *Daily Herald* and *Reynolds' News*.

Our whole gang of fifteen or more would sit agog as Geoffrey flashed through the pages with pride or pointed to some unique autograph. Mouth-watering stuff, it would make me swoon with longing. By contrast, my scrapbook, with two pieces of cardboard on the outside, was held together with coarse string.

Though none of us could measure up to Geoffrey, we each

could, on occasion, produce some original surprise that would fill even his eyes with envy. On one such afternoon I proudly presented a matchbox in good condition, with a few matches in it, and the channel swimmer, Captain Webb, on its front. The effect was instantaneous, and each lad related his admiration for the noble captain.

'Imagine swimming all them miles!' remarked Colin Picton, his small, wiry frame tense with awe and concentration.

'I can't even swim a yard,' said another lad.

There was no doubt at all that Captain Webb was a great favourite, and this was substantiated by the fact that I received three good clay marbles for the matchbox. The conversation did not stop there, for everyone started to sound forth on the subject of heroes. Emphasis fell on Scott of the Antarctic, as Gerald Affey painstakingly took us through every mile of that famous expedition.

Surprisingly, Gerald was fifteen years old, twice our age, but somehow he fitted in perfectly with the gang and acted as mediator with our parents whenever they questioned our way-out activities. By nature, he was calm and tolerant, with a wisdom beyond his years that everyone respected. We christened him the 'Wise Owl'.

Gerald's sensitive voice conveyed dramatically all the characters and events from that ill-fated expedition, and when he finally finished with Scott's own words: 'I do not regret the journey; we took risks, we knew we took them, things have come against us, therefore we have no cause for complaint ...', we sat quietly with tears in our eyes.

In an instant the rapt mood had evaporated, and we pressed on further in our quest for the great ones. I must have seemed rather like Toad of Toad Hall as I took centre stage, expounding passionately on the amazing strengths of Hercules and Samson. I raged up and down the garden, uninhibitedly acting out scenes from their lives, forcing rounds of applause from the appreciative lads.

Gerald himself applauded and laughed good-naturedly at my exaggerations. It was only when I insisted that Strang the Terrible, the giant with a club who was in the *Beano* every week, was a friend of mine and lived in a cave beneath my house, that he kindly steadied me. Raising his hand in gentle authority, he silenced the disbelievers by maintaining that what I had said could possibly be true. His soothing voice embellished the theme, and he went on to suggest that certain comics did indeed tell the truth.

'Bear with me, lads,' he begged. He then disappeared into his house, reappearing minutes later with a copy of the *Hotspur*. Sitting down, he effortlessly turned the pages, and quietly beckoned us to join him.

There, in the centre pages, was a real-life picture of two fine-looking men, with old-fashioned clothes and tidy hair styles.

'Who are they, Gerald?' we all clamoured at once. 'We can't read it 'cos the words are too long!'

Softly, he uttered the words, 'Mallory and Irvine ...'

'Never heard of 'em,' said Gary Simmons, the youngest of our gang. Gerald smiled at this and continued.

'Well, lads. The title at the top says, "The Mystery of Mallory and Irvine". It's about two men who disappeared in the mists in 1924, about 800 feet from the top of Mount Everest ...'

We hadn't a clue what he was talking about.

'Mount Everest?' we asked. 'What is it? Where is it?'

'Everest is a mountain,' Gerald replied. 'The highest in the world, standing 29,002 feet high.' (It was some years later before it was discovered that it was even higher, at 29,028 feet.)

This was still double Dutch to us. The figure was quite beyond our understanding. More light was shed on the subject when Gerald mentioned the figure of five and a half miles.

'Crikey! That's abaht as far as Donny,' I gasped, meaning Doncaster. 'It must go right up into the sky, higher than the clouds!'

'It does indeed, Brian,' confirmed Gerald.

The magnitude of it all stunned us into a long silence that eventually ended when we broke into a series of whoops and shouts.

It was impossible to contain our excitement as expressions of 'Bloody 'ell!', 'Blinkin' 'eck!' and 'He must be tellin' fibs!' rent the air.

Gerald viewed it all with a contented smile, at the same time pretending to quieten us as the neighbours shouted their disapproval of our foul language.

'Come on, lads. Stop the swearing!' ordered Calden, like some army officer.

Dutifully, we obeyed and silence was the order of the day. Bunched tightly round the 'Wise Owl', we earnestly begged him to read the whole page to us. His voice conveyed vividly the abridged version of the story in the comic.

Fantastic images of a wild landscape full of vast ridges, arêtes, couloirs, deep, yawning crevasses and intimidating precipices penetrated our minds. Visions of men in Norfolk jackets and Homburgs, battling in sub-zero temperatures against blizzards and winds of a hundred miles an hour or more, filled our hearts with trepidation and fired our imaginations.

The final sentences describing how the support climber, Odell, last saw the two heroes, Mallory and Irvine, so near the summit, gradually disappearing into the mist, never to be seen again, left us dumbstruck.

Our bodies, which had been contorted with tension, collapsed like a pack of cards as we fell against each other, totally perplexed by the mystery of it all. From the depth of our silence, there came soft entreaties, urging Gerald to explain.

In response, the young man presented his most enigmatic face, and refused to say another word. We broke up and made our separate ways home, each convinced in his own mind that the intrepid mountaineers had succeeded.

Days later, swinging on our garden gate, I eagerly awaited the arrival of my favourite hero: no less a person than my father, who worked as a coal miner in the local Hickleton Main Pit. Darkness was beginning to fall, and the rusty lamps that lined the streets spluttered into life, casting twisting and curling shadows across the pavement. Soon, through the ghostly darkness, a noise could be heard: nails and steel scraping across the road; hob-nailed boots setting off sparks in the dusk, heralding the arrival of my father.

He was an amazing sight, and it always thrilled me to see him. Attached to the front of his mining helmet, a small light beamed through the blackness of the night, occasionally catching the whites of his eyes and making them glint brightly. He looked like some mystical Greek god, his face stained black as pitch by the ingrained coal dust.

Always at this point he would stoop down and lift me up above his head, resting me on his shoulders. Once inside the house, the light from the fire heightened the blackness of his eyes and the whiteness of his teeth as he smiled.

When he had climbed into the chipped enamel bath, eroded through years of constant use, he would let me wash his back. His skin was hard and covered in lumps and bumps, cuts and bruises that he had received from small roof-falls. It looked like some vast purple landscape. Hard scrubbing was the only way I could get him clean. Then he would stand up and wash the rest of his body himself.

It was easy for sun-tanned bodies to look good, even when they are in poor shape, yet he stood there like white marble, looking chiselled and muscular; very impressive. As he vigorously rubbed himself dry, I rambled on about Gerald's story of Mallory and Irvine.

'What do you think happened to 'em, Dad?'

'It's hard to know, lad,' he replied. 'Pass my vest, will yer? I remember it very well and read about it in all the newspapers. We all felt very sad, but they died, and that were that. It were a brave effort, Brian, lad … And I doubt if it'll ever be known if they climbed it or not. Gerald's right, it's a mystery … I'd like to think they did it. Best leave it at that.'

'I bet you could climb it, Dad,' I choked out.

'No, lad. I couldn't, and even if I were capable, I wouldn't choose to go up there.'

'Why, Dad … Why?' I continued, surprised.

'Because, lad … That mountain is so high … It's forbidding, wild and lonely. Hell on earth, you might say … I wouldn't want to be up there for all the tea in China!'

'Do you think I could climb it one day?' I shouted. He smiled at this, and as the smile evaporated, he muttered, 'I doubt it, lad. There's nowt up there. I feel about it the same way I feel about you going down the coal mines … I don't want it for you, and never in a million years would I want you going up Everest!'

An air-raid shelter that my father had built in the back garden had fallen into disuse, partly because the German menace was negligible in the area, and also because the shelter tended to fill with water. Dad also felt that our sturdy brick house could easily withstand the Hun's occasional attacks. Therefore, that small, half-hidden corrugated fortress became my domain. It goes without saying that any member of our gang was allowed to visit my mysterious lair.

When Calden himself appeared at the entrance, with his floppy blond hair shining in the sun and his laughing, vibrant blue eyes searching my face for an invitation, he was cordially admitted. Sitting himself comfortably on a box, he produced a large, fat, green book from behind his back. Consumed with excitement, he whispered, 'This is a book abaht them two fellers!'

'Who's tha mean, Calden?' I asked.

'Mallory and Irvine!' he shouted back. 'Tha knows, Brian, who died on Everest ... Well, this is the 1924 book!'

'Crikey! Where's tha got it from?'

'From a friend of me dad's,' Calden smiled.

After several seconds of paralysing silence, I gently stroked the emerald tome. Eventually, I whispered, 'I bet it's worth a bob or two?'

'Thousands and thousands!' Calden replied forcefully.

'Bloody 'ell!' I said softly. 'Calden ... Are you allowed to open it up? Maybe there are some pictures.'

'There are,' he said in a choked voice. 'Look, Brian. Look at this, I've slotted pieces of paper in to mark the best spots. This picture 'ere is the last one taken of the two men before they set off for the top!'

'Bloody 'ell!' I said, over and over.

With trembling fingers Calden painstakingly pointed out all the different landscapes and characters.

'Look at this, Brian. Look at the size of the North Col, with climbers looking like spots at the bottom ...'

After an hour or so my visitor concluded and we sat back musing at the wonder of it all.

'Oh, Calden,' I gently beseeched. 'Please let me 'ave the book for a couple of days.'

Calden's reaction to this was extreme caution, as he had already loaned me a book about wildlife, which I had not yet returned.

'Just for a day?' I urged. 'Please, only a day? ... I'll take good care of it, I promise ...'

In the end, his face twisted in doubt, the fine young lad nodded his consent, and we carried the precious book into the house.

Calden's trust in me was, I'm afraid, woefully misplaced, as I offered up all kinds of excuses for holding on to the book. My decision to keep it in the air-raid shelter, where it was subjected to wind, rain and damp, proved disastrous. Eventually I didn't dare show it to anybody. The binding started to deteriorate, and consequently the pages and the map at the back became loose. Finally, the cloth cover became detached, and the whole book ended up a sorry heap of paper in the corner.

The dreadful thing was that Calden had been so trusting and patient. Now he simply had to have it back, as his uncle had insisted on its being returned. When the moment arrived, and the dreaded knock came at the door, I visibly shrank back into the kitchen and collided with my mother. In a flash, I explained the situation and begged her to give the remains to Calden. My voice was cowardly and piteous.

'Oh, please, please, Mammy, give it to him. I can't do it ... Oh, please, please ... I like him so much, and he'll be so upset ... Tell him I don't know how it got in such a pickle ...'

It is the only time in my life that I ever say my mother look at me contemptuously. Picking up the remains of the book, she sped to the door and opened it. Instantly, I hid. Not mincing words, she came straight to the point.

'Here is your book, Calden, and it's in a fine old mess. I'm sorry you should get it back in this state. Brian can be very irresponsible.'

The poor boy was thunderstruck, and walked in a daze down the path and on to the road. My mother's voice trailed after him: 'In future, lad, don't lend him anything. He doesn't know how to look after things ...'

With my face hidden behind the lace curtains, I watched him, his shoulders sagging, gradually disappear. Falling back, I slowly slid down into the corner of the sitting room into a dead huddle. I never felt so ashamed in all my life.

Days later I found myself uncomfortably in his company by a

fast-moving stream on the edge of a thick wood named the Wind Cover. Not a single word had he said to me since the episode of the book. I stared up at the trees to avoid his gaze. There was no wind, and apart from the energetic stream, all was perfectly still.

From time to time swallows cut through the air in graceful patterns, squeaking delightfully in celebration. Their frolics entranced us both, and we leapt up and down with glee. After a while I was aware of Calden's arm around my shoulders, then his hand gently turned my head round to face him.

'By gum! Yer know, Brian,' he said. 'You're a right rum lad, but I can't help likin' thee ...'

Years later, when I was sixteen, it was Coronation year, 1953, and throughout the land there was a feeling of expectancy, a sense of destiny, the start of a new Elizabethan age. An amateur dramatic society that I belonged to, the Mexborough Theatre Guild, was putting on Walter Greenwood's *The Cure for Love,* in which I was playing my first lead role. The door of my dressing room burst open and Harry Dobson, my mentor and director, breathlessly poured out the news that Mount Everest had been climbed by the British expedition led by Colonel Hunt.

'Hillary and Sherpa Tenzing have climbed it, Brian, lad! Perfect timing, eh? Just in time for the Coronation!'

The next day the newspapers were full of it. The *News Chronicle*'s headline read, 'The Crowning Glory: Everest Is Climbed'.

Further down the front page it said, 'The news came late last night that Edmund Hillary and the Sherpa guide, Tenzing, of Colonel Hunt's expedition, had climbed to the summit of Earth's highest peak, 29,002 feet high. Queen Elizabeth the Second, resting on the eve of her crowning, was immediately told that this brightest jewel of courage and endurance had been added to the British crown of endeavour. It is understood that a message of Royal congratulation was sent to the climbers.'

It was interesting to note that Hillary later said, 'Wouldn't Mallory have been pleased?' Indeed, the great New Zealander confessed to having the briefest look on the summit for possible traces of the early Everesteers. The fact is, Everest was climbed in

June 1953, and what a colossal achievement it was.

Everyone everywhere was swept up in the emotion of it all. From the early brave expeditions on the mountain had come experience and knowledge, which had been imparted to Colonel Hunt's magnificent team. Their jubilation and success rested firmly on the efforts of these early pioneers. Hunt and his men had performed brilliantly, and the world thrilled to their accomplishment.

In due course the film of the expedition, entitled *The Conquest of Everest*, was shown worldwide to critical acclaim. There is no doubt at all that it sensitively and splendidly conveys the mammoth task that had faced the British expedition. The final moments showing Colonel Hunt receiving news of success at the base of the Lhotse face and embracing the two summiteers are profoundly moving.

On the building site where I worked as a plasterer, my fellow workers talked of nothing else. They were amazed at the difficulty of breathing at high altitudes, finding the idea particularly frightening. One broad-shouldered, fair-haired young man named Ted Pearce, opening and closing his eyes with disbelief at the memory of it all, his voice trailing away with shock, whispered, 'Their breathing! Did you hear their breathing? My God!' As for me, the whole epic overwhelmed and frightened me. My father's words of years before reverberated in my head: 'That mountain is so high! … It's forbidding, wild and lonely. Hell on earth! … I wouldn't want to be up there for all the tea in China!'

This was exactly the way I felt. The very prospect of ever being on Mount Everest made me shudder with horror.

Over the years the image has stayed with me of Everest and, inevitably, of Mallory and Irvine's last, fatal expedition. Time and time again it has invaded my waking thoughts and surfaced in powerful dreams. Many years ago my work as an actor took me to the Austrian Tyrol, where I walked, spell-bound, in the mountains; to Sicily, where I scaled Mount Etna; and to France, where Mont Blanc became my goal. From the day that I climbed that peak I vowed to go to Everest and follow in the footsteps of Mallory and Irvine and their magnificent team, and to tell their story. For, as Mallory himself said, 'To know there's no dream, that mustn't be dared.'

Throughout the seventies and eighties I plagued film producers, directors and anyone who would listen to my idea. I was patronized, fobbed off, turned down flat, encouraged by leads that went nowhere. The project was eating me up, as my wife, Hildegard, was only too aware. Then, in the mid eighties, I was offered a part in a television version of the William Tell story. The idea did nothing for me – until I learnt that it was to be shot in France, near Chamonix. I wasted no time and one late autumn afternoon there, so close that I could almost touch it, was Mont Blanc once again. What memories it brought back.

Surprisingly, too, the filming proved to be fun. The director was a young Canadian, Allan Goldstein, whose fresh, open face and cheerful personality made work a joy for everyone. He was a brilliant director, with a string of fine documentaries to his name, and, to cap it all, he loved mountains.

One day Allan and I stood on the Aiguille du Midi, looking across that wonderful panorama. Needless to say, I gave him the full Everest treatment. After all, here was a fellow mountain-worshipper. Throughout that evening and into the night we covered all aspects of Everest until at last tiredness got the better of us. As I reached the door Allan quietly said, 'The finest producer I know is John-Paul Davidson, who works for the BBC. If anybody can get this off the ground, he can.'

Months later, after many frustrating attempts to reach John-Paul Davidson, I was at last about to meet the man. As I stood outside London's Kensington Hilton Hotel on 23 December 1986, in my mind there was a quiet fantasy in which George Leigh Mallory, dressed in the black armour of King Arthur's knight Sir Galahad, sat tall on a white horse. I mused on how deeply I and my project needed such a knight.

As I looked up, the lights of the steady stream of cars seemed to dim a little and there, on the brow of the hill, appeared the single clear light of a lone steed. I focused intently on it as it drew nearer and then entered the forecourt of the hotel. The rider reined in, in full control of the magnificent beast, which snorted out uneven breaths before at last its eye faded and died. The tall, slim figure in black dismounted from his charger, and removed his black helmet, his dark eyes viewing me all the while with quiet amusement.

'Hello, I'm John-Paul Davidson,' a clear, young voice announced.

Here was the Sir Galahad I had been looking for. We shook hands warmly and made swiftly for the eating-place suggested by my new-found champion. My thoughts and emotions were in a state of happy chaos. Quite unable to control myself, words exploded from my lips. My excitement tore to shreds my usual well-rehearsed patter. As Mallory himself once said of Everest: 'Lord, when I think of it, something bubbles up inside me. The effervescence is sternly repressed, of course ... And then a bubble outs and bursts!'

This was precisely what was happening to me. My bizarre behaviour affected the rhythm of our walking, as I stopped time and again to focus on some point. All this Davidson bore patiently, although he did appear quite bemused by the constant stops.

Soon we were seated comfortably in a snug corner of the restaurant. Davidson's eyes feasted on the varied menu, and after ordering for both of us, he lit up a cigar and relaxed. It was obvious that he enjoyed eating, which he described as 'chomping', a term born of his numerous group expeditions. His filming with the BBC, for such programmes as *Everyman* and *The World About Us*, had taken him far and wide. As the Fairy in *A Midsummer Night's Dream* says:

>   Over hill, over dale, thorough bush, thorough brier,
>   Over park, over pale, thorough flood, thorough fire.

Likewise, Davidson. You name it – he had done it! As I talked nineteen to the dozen, he gently interrupted me with a smile, asking me to call him 'J.P.'.

'Everybody else does,' he said. 'It's short for John-Paul.'

'Okay. J.P. it is!'

In the soft, clear light of the table lamp, I was able to observe him in greater detail. He was about six feet, though his slimness made him appear taller. His face was delicately pale, full yet devoid of excess weight, and his sharp cheek bones highlighted his ultra-sensitive expression. The eyes, high-set brows and slightly thinning hair all seemed black. His deep eyes were the clue to his nature, alternating between mature intensity and the look of a child of five.

My extravagant expressions seemed to delight J.P., yet instinctively I felt he was observing how he could control and harness me. After a couple of hours I had imparted to him every single detail of the Mallory project, pausing only now and then to hear with eager elephant ears his measured comments.

J.P. felt that, despite all my hard efforts, I had perhaps been going about it the wrong way. Relishing his brandy and drawing deeply on his cigar, he ruminated aloud.

'The problem is, is it a drama or is it a documentary?'

'Neither!' I laughed. 'It's something new ... Something completely original!'

He chuckled infectiously.

'It doesn't quite work out that way, Brian. Still ... who knows? ... Maybe! ... Maybe!'

During the rest of our conversation we were delightfully relaxed as the ambience of the place and our enjoyment of each other increased. Leaning back in his big chair, staring at the ceiling and blowing smoke rings, J.P. lazily asked, 'What is Everest really?'

After an intake of breath, I began: 'Once upon a time, there was a large sea, called Tethys, that gently lapped the shores of Asia — Tibet — fifty million years ago. This idyllic land was clothed in magnificent forests, which contained an infinite variety of wildlife, one such example being the moth Edward's Atlas, with a wingspan of twelve inches or more, which still exists today.

'This tranquil landscape was to change dramatically. Over many centuries, a vast continent known as Gondwanaland sailed almost imperceptibly across Tethys, and collided with this ancient shore, thus forcing the soft sedimentary rock of Asia dramatically upwards, as the harder granites, basalts and gneisses of Gondwanaland bit into it. With the tremendous force of it all, this squeezing, wrenching and twisting and pressure resulted in the highest, yet youngest of the world's greatest mountain ranges — the Himalayas — being created.

'It stretches, without interruption, across the top of India in a gentle curve for fifteen hundred miles from East to West, between the Brahmaputra and Indus rivers ... At the core of this colossal squeeze is Everest!

'In 1849 it was known as Peak XV. Observations of it were recorded by the various stations of the Trigonometrical Survey of the plains of India. Then, in 1852, the Bengali Chief Computer rushed into the room of the Surveyor-General, Sir Andrew Waugh, breathlessly saying, "Sir, I have discovered the highest mountain in the world!"

'Sir Andrew named it after Sir George Everest, his predecessor as Surveyor-General of India, under whose directions the triangulations had been started, but afterwards the Everest expeditions discovered that the Tibetan name is Chomolungma, which means "Goddess Mother of the Earth".

'On the Nepalese side it is called Sagarmartha. It also has many other names, including Kangchen Lemboo Geudyong and the Turquoise Mountain.'

Throughout this description J.P. nodded happily, like a child listening to a bedtime story, and continued to nonchalantly blow smoke rings. After an hour or so I finally ground to a halt. I was mildly surprised to see that other humans still existed. Once more I focused closely on the deep, thoughtful face opposite me. From the dark pupils of J.P.'s eyes emanated flashes of hope, giving wings to my thoughts. In a flash he stubbed out his cigar and quietly expressed his conviction that it was possible.

The convivial atmosphere of Julie's Restaurant spilled out with us into the still night air of Notting Hill Gate as we started back to the Kensington Hilton. There, Sir Galahad placed his black helmet firmly on his head, mounted his steed and extended his hand to me in knightly friendship. He then gracefully spurred his charger into motion, reined it in slightly, threw me a handsome salute and sped off into the night.

From that moment on I felt we were on our way. J.P.'s maturity and pragmatism filled me with renewed hope, though I realized there was still a long way to go. Being the good knight that he was, he charged on all fronts and encountered many obstacles. He handled it all with quiet detachment, displaying all the hallmarks of a producer-director who had seen it all before. Yet even for him it was new territory.

To mount the film was going to cost about £500,000, a lot of money considering it was a so-called documentary. In fact this classification was one of the main problems. Prospective investors felt it was too expensive for a documentary, but too cheap for a drama. They insisted that the uniqueness of the enterprise made it impossible to place it in any known category.

When I suggested that it was a 'happening', they instantly became confused and alarmed. On such occasions J.P.'s face would pale slightly as his eyes burned into mine, signalling that I should shut up. The failure of such meetings always drove me potty, whereas J.P. merely took it all with a pinch of salt. The irritating aspect of it all was that he felt the BBC would be prepared to provide half the budget, if some obliging party would come up with the rest.

We were constantly on the point of succeeding, only to see our hopes fade away each time. Still, we were firing on all cylinders and our spirits were high. Our endeavours took us far and wide, including an enjoyable working lunch at Pinewood Film Studios, with the reknowned film producer Peter Snell. He had set up headquarters there, and we were informed that he was enthusiastically forging ahead with plans to develop British Lion Films. This meeting with him had been arranged by a jolly giant named John Rubin.

Rubin was not a man to give up. He had himself opened offices at Pinewood, and had just made his first commitment by buying the rights of the book *A Prayer for the Dying*, which was to be made into a film. Certainly these were days highly charged with emotion and activity. Everyone, including a friend of mine called Nick Shearman, Rubin and J.P., was galvanized into action. At the same time Patrick Dromgoole and HTV were making enquiries among potentially interested parties at the Cannes Film Festival. Heady days!

At the conclusion of our lunch, the newly converted Peter Snell, a handsome man with a quiet charm, guaranteed to do his level best to get the thing going. He and J.P. got on famously. Snell's main connections were in the USA, and he felt optimistic about concluding a deal there.

Throughout this period I was fascinated by J.P.'s total concentration. His vision, drive and painstaking attention to detail were a joy to behold. Out would come his fat address book. Rapidly finding the right page, he would instantly impart the relevant information, while deftly applying his free hand to any spare goodies that were on the dinner table. His undivided attention took in all the possibilities offered by the businessmen opposite him. Then, having brought everything to a satisfactory conclusion, he would sit back with a big cigar and blow smoke rings.

All in all, J.P.'s every movement and thought conveyed the impression of a man with a serious mind, and blessed with grace. I loved the feller! So much so that at times I became a bit possessive and overprotective about him; not that he needed protecting. For example, a reputable company who had initially shown interest were giving us the run-around. Their shilly-shallying was beginning to give me the pip. My feelings were understandable, as a friend of mine, Adrian Rigelsford, a researcher, had put in a tremendous amount of work on the treatment for the film.

I had devoted a lot of time to the storyline, and Adrian had mounted it beautifully in the style of the twenties. He had bound it tastefully, producing dozens of copies in black, gold and blue. We also created a shortened, single-page version. The company in question had received at least a dozen copies of this and other relevant information, long before they met J.P. Then, when they did meet him with me, they hummed and hawed and faffed around until I was atrophied with boredom.

Several weeks later we met them again. Their head man appeared as usual, sweating slightly, with his shirt sleeves rolled up and his mind at sixes and sevens. At the end of an indecisive half-hour he suggested that we give him some sort of treatment, with possibly a condensed form, since in these busy times his people had little time to peruse long scripts.

It was then that I gently informed him that these had been given to him weeks ago. He confessed that he couldn't recollect this, and would I give him some more. He had obviously thrown them in the nearest bin. That was the last straw. I didn't mind that they had messed me around, but to treat my colleague in this way incensed me. J.P. was an outstanding man, who was affectionately and deeply respected by the powers that be at the

BBC. As we walked out of the building I firmly insisted that we would never go back there again.

'I won't subject you to it!' I shouted. 'Pillocks! ... All of them! ... Screw 'em!'

As I jumped into a taxi I quickly recovered my good humour on noticing the Bonnington Hotel on my left. Recalling the climber Chris Bonington, it was another signpost pointing the way to the mountain.

For a long time I had yearned to meet Captain John Noel. He, at the ripe old age of ninety-seven, and Noel Odell, ninety-six, the last man to see Mallory and Irvine alive, were the last surviving members of the ill-fated 1924 Everest expedition. Captain Noel is without doubt regarded as one of the finest explorers of all time. If we could arrange to meet him it would be our first real step towards the mountain. The thought filled me with excitement. Until now we had been dealing with committees and talk. Here was the chance to realize something tangible: to actually be with an important member of those glorious twenties expeditions. And yet in truth the prospect of meeting the great gentleman seemed remote.

Throughout many discussions with J.P. we felt that it was vitally important to have the noble captain in our film, forming a bridge between the twenties and today. I don't mean to sound callous, but it was imperative to get a move on, given his age. Yet how were we to go about it? It just so happened that Nick Shearman had formed an acquaintance with Chris Bonington and felt that he could possibly arrange through him to see Captain Noel and also Noel Odell. The prospect of meeting the great Bonington excited me as much as seeing the old Everesteer. My enthusiasm boiled over.

I'm afraid I've jumped the gun a bit. J.P., Nick and I had felt very strongly, for a considerable time, that the combination of Bonington and myself on Everest would be a winner. To put together a master climber and a greenhorn like myself on film would prove irresistible.

Another plus was that Bonington appeared to have a natural flair for the screen, displaying a refined ease as well as a colourful personality. In short, his sophisticated manner perfectly suited the style of the twenties. So, through Nick, we sent Chris the script of *Galahad of Everest*. His immediate reaction was most encouraging, for he informed us in a letter that he would be coming down to London in the near future on his way to Beijing in China, and that he could easily drop in and see us.

I would have none of this, as I felt that it was a fundamental rule that one must always make the effort to spare an esteemed person any inconvenience. We would drive up to Cumbria to see him. Nick and I were blissfully happy at the prospect of it all. Bonington is, without doubt, a legend in his own lifetime. It would be impossible, in the space available, to list his achievements, but these include his tremendous climbs in Britain, the Alps, South America, Antarctica and, finally, the Himalayas.

After his conquest of such giants as Annapurna II (26,041 feet) and Nuptse (25,700 feet), there was his splendid organization and leadership of the British ascent of the South Face of Annapurna in 1970 — the most important Himalayan face climb to that date. Many other climbs followed, and in 1975 he organized and led a British post-monsoon expedition to Everest which succeeded in climbing the massive South-West Face — a staggering achievement. These amazing exploits by Bonington and his companions have thrilled the hearts of millions throughout the world. As Jim Perrin, that respected mountaineer, said of him, 'He is obviously and outstandingly the public face, the ambassador for our sport.'

Like two pilgrims, Nick, my erstwhile companion, and I, on a chilly January morning in 1987, approached the front door of Badger Hill, in the majestic countryside of Cumbria. The door swept open and a beaming Bonington greeted us. He stood six feet or more, and looked predictably lean and fit.

'I'm impressed — you're bang on time,' he said, ushering us in. 'I suppose that's something that comes as second nature in your profession.'

Immediately Chris introduced his wife, Wendy, an attractive dark-haired lady of medium height. A broad smile lit up her face as she beckoned us over to the roaring fire. Mugs of hot coffee were quickly placed in our hands, and our hosts made every effort to make us feel at home. In that cheery atmosphere the conversation flowed freely.

Chris (short for Christian) displayed an impressive fluency and speed of mind. This, combined with his quiet charm and deep nature, added up to a very fascinating personality. From the beginning we got on together splendidly, not least because his sudden emotional outbursts were not dissimilar to mine. It was only when I went overboard about Everest that Chris held his sides with laughter and questioned my judgement. My emotions soared up and down volcanically, and Nick endeavoured to bring me back to reality. All the while, grinning like a Cheshire cat, Wendy astutely observed us, no doubt convinced that here was another 'Conquistador of the Useless'.

Yet despite the passion the meeting was completely practical, with Chris intriguing us with his genius for planning. My questions came thick and fast. For example: 'What is a logistics manager, Chris?'

Patiently, the great climber explained all. When we had finished, he cheerily suggested that we should go for a walk. It was a particular pleasure to see the couple's devotion to each other. Chris's manners were impeccable. Delicately but firmly holding Wendy's hand, he painstakingly helped her over a stile, or guided her carefully around any hole or obstacle on the rough pathway. It was a rare glimpse of old-world charm, never to be forgotten.

As we ascended, the momentum of the walk stimulated our minds to new heights. Despite occasionally sinking up to his knees in a bog, Chris, unperturbed, kept his gaze straight ahead, periodically blowing his nose and kicking his boots clean. I observed that his bare head was sweating considerably.

'Won't you get a head cold?' I asked.

'No,' he replied. 'Never do.'

All the while, the dogs circled round us at a considerable distance, expressing in their speed and motion that special joy that only canines know. Chris's walking speed had me now and then breaking into a slight trot to keep up with him.

'You're a fast walker!' I shouted.

To this Wendy smilingly replied, 'Well, Brian. This is his

"quite slow" out of consideration for me. His normal speed is something else!'

Laughing, Chris added, 'My daily routine of training is either to go for a run around and up the hills, or walk vigorously with a very heavy pack on my back.'

This titbit of information made us all laugh as we climbed higher, towards a distant hill. God, was I enjoying myself! It was a rare experience to be walking side by side with Chris.

'Have you climbed in the Lake District?' he asked.

When I shook my head, he suggested, with feeling, 'You must climb with me ... I'll arrange it.'

'If so,' I shouted back, 'I'll certainly need to be on a tight rope if I'm following you!'

More laughter followed, as our voices were drowned in the wind. Finding some shelter from it leeward of some rocks, I returned to the subject of Mallory. My emotions ran amok, inspiring me to new heights of praise for my hero. Without warning, Chris came down on me like a ton of bricks.

'You are making no sense whatsoever, Brian! What you are saying bears no relation to reality!'

Momentarily taken aback, I insisted that Mallory's last climb, with Irvine, on Everest was heroic and noble. On hearing this, Chris came back at me like forked lightning.

'You are talking absolute rubbish, and ridiculously over-romanticizing! It is crass nonsense to say that Mallory's attempt was noble! He was utterly and completely selfish! What you are saying makes me ill. Noble, my foot! He was selfish! Selfish! Selfish! He had to be to have any chance of getting up. It had nothing to do with being noble. I know exactly what I'm talking about, as I've been in the same position as Mallory time and time again. I am totally selfish too!

'When I am high on a mountain like Everest, all I think about is getting up and surviving – nothing else enters my head. If I had, for one moment, allowed myself the luxury of imagining that I was being some kind of noble creature, it would probably have cost me my life. Dear me, you do talk such arrant nonsense!

'If, by some miracle, we manage to pull off going to Everest, how on earth do you think you will survive on that mountain – by being noble? The very thought pains me. You had better learn that it can be absolute hell up there. The East Rongbuk Glacier itself is hard drill ... '

Throughout this outburst I remained stunned and intrigued. Eventually I choked out, 'At least you must admit that Mallory had great tenacity.'

'Tenacity? Yes,' replied Chris. 'But I beg to differ on many other points. For instance, to my mind, George Finch was a better climber.'

This I totally disagreed with, maintaining steadfastly that climbing contemporaries of both men judged Mallory to be far superior to anyone at that time on rock.

'On ice,' I continued, 'he was equal to Finch.'

The fact that I was speaking so strongly, and as a non-mountaineer, sparked off a sudden good-natured laugh from Chris. Affecting a mock stance of a boxer under siege, he concluded, 'You're quite a firebrand, aren't you, Mr Blessed?'

This had the effect of rendering us all helpless with laughter. It was Wendy, with calmness and wisdom, who restored order, saying, 'I think you should both stop talking about Mallory, and save it for the mountain.'

After a long pause she added with a far-away smile, 'I've never heard Chris speak in this way before. It augurs well for the film – you spark one another off, yet you are at ease with each other.'

Hand in hand with the good-natured fireworks between us, I sensed a basic law. Chris had been in the army, and I in the RAF. Instinctively we recognized this, and it promoted a quiet feeling of discipline. When he described the ascent of the East Rongbuk Glacier as 'hard drill', the term was commonplace to me. It was refreshing to meet someone who was totally honest. In the world of entertainment you come across a great deal of flannel, which can insidiously seduce you into becoming slightly artificial.

Back at the house, with boots and outer garments removed, and dogs contented, my host, enjoyably rubbing his feet, viewed me long and hard. He eventually broke his stare by saying, 'I think we'll get on very well.'

The words filled me with warmth and happiness, and we both grinned boyishly. During a wonderful meal of rustic simplicity,

Chris turned to me and said, 'Nick performed very well, Brian, when he climbed with me a while ago. Well done!'

The praise immediately sparked a radiant smile on the enigmatic face of my quiet companion. In fact, much to my astonishment and amusement, Nick entered passionately into a long discussion about the aforementioned climb, and this led to in-depth observations on our projected Everest expedition.

His ideas, though spoken fervently, were well thought out and stunningly original. He felt that it was imperative that we should follow the exact route of the reconnaissance expedition of 1921. This, he emphasized, would take us through India, Sikkim and Tibet.

'It would be so wonderful,' he enthused, 'if we could take the small "Toy Train" called the Crook-A-Dest, from Siliguri to Darjeeling.'

This was something that Nick and I had discussed for hours.

'The little train still exists,' I added.

Nick then engineered a complete silence by telling us how Mallory had written in 1921, on approaching a great plain in Tibet between Gyangka Nampa and Shiling, that he was 'stepping off the map'.

The magic of the statement hit us all. The conversation gathered further momentum when Chris proposed that we should wear the clothes of the twenties, as well as using the tents and equipment of that era. Incidentally the same idea had been put to me by climbers in Switzerland years before. Chris maintained that we would have to use common sense about this, and back it up with modern gear, tempering the garish modern colours with the subtle shades of green and brown of the twenties. After long consideration, he expressed deep concern about how high we should go on the mountain, pointing out the great dangers of the highest place on earth. He leaned back on his chair, his eyes focused on the ceiling.

Slowly, after what seemed an eternity, he returned his gaze somewhat in our direction. I say somewhat, as he appeared to look through us, or rather round us. The sun periodically shone on to his face as it broke through the clouds, gently forcing him to look slightly sideways. I had the distinct impression that it caused him mild distress – perhaps the result of his many fine expeditions.

Then again, it may have been my imagination, as after a while he held me in a straight, uncomplicated gaze. In those moments I felt his triumphs and tragedies. Here was a seasoned, middle-aged man whose sensitive voice, aquiline features, greying hair and deep eyes conveyed vividly all that was most natural in a man of adventure.

His face was a map of continents, companionship and far horizons. At times it would break out into a childlike grin, as he remembered some humorous anecdote, only to tremble slightly as his self-control struggled with some painful memory. To share this experience with the great man was, for both Nick and me, a rare privilege.

Chris was firmly of the opinion that the North Col of Everest, at 23,000 feet, should be our objective. He candidly said that I would be extremely fortunate to get anywhere near the place, as the highest I had been was Mont Blanc, at 15,700 feet. There is a huge difference, he maintained, between that and 23,000 feet. Grinning from ear to ear, he added, 'You have a tendency to gloss over the terrain of Everest. We'll get to Base Camp at such and such a time, then move up to Camp I, then to Camp II, then on to Camp III at 21,000 feet, etc, etc ... And then on and on ... It doesn't work that way, Brian. A thousand and one things can happen ... Blizzards, plunging temperatures, well below zero. Frightful winds, soaring temperature on the glaciers, glacier lassitude, headaches, nausea, pulmonary oedema, cerebral oedema ... The list is endless! Still, who knows, Brian? You may do well at altitude, I must confess I don't fare very well up high.'

'You could have fooled me,' I replied. 'A little bird told me you climbed the great mountain − not to mention scores of others at altitude.'

Chris waved aside my flattery. He was convinced that if the expedition could reach the North Col, a fine achievement, we would complete an acceptable film on Mallory.

'I shall approach the Chinese Mountaineering Association,' he said, 'and ask permission for us to film on Everest between July and August 1988. I am against us going in March or April-May time, as it will be very cold. In July, the mountain warms up a great deal; this has to be taken into consideration when people are standing around filming. All the non-climbers will have to be carefully monitored and looked after – a tremendous undertaking. We must take the utmost care; in my book, losing fingers and toes is completely unacceptable.'

I suggested that perhaps the climbers, if we got to the Col, could have a go for the summit, following Mallory's route. Chris was firmly against this, explaining, 'I know climbers – once they realize there is a possibility of going for the top, they develop "summititus", which will make them forget all about the filming.'

I nodded my head like a good soldier and shut up. All the while, Wendy had been plying us with delicious coffee, and took advantage of the lull to introduce another attractive lady, Louise Wilson, Chris's secretary.

Louise politely shook hands, obtained Chris's signature for an important document and swiftly took leave of us. This was a timely reminder that we should be on our way, for our hosts had been more than generous and we had no desire to outstay our welcome. Nevertheless they insisted that we should quickly look upstairs where Louise worked.

Computers were very much in evidence, signifying a disciplined, professional team, capable of handling the complex business affairs that are an inevitable part of Chris's life. The shelves contained a veritable treasure of photographic slides, painstakingly compiled. This gift for photography is splendidly revealed in all his expedition books. Chris is constantly sought by various companies throughout the world. Now everyone was working hard on his current expedition, to a daunting, unclimbed Himalayan mountain of 23,560 feet called Menlungtse.

As we made our way to the front door, Chris said he would write at once to the old Everesteers, Noel Odell and Captain Noel, to arrange a filmed interview with them. Graciously he took my hand, and ventured one final question: 'What really is the precise objective of this film?'

'Well, Chris, I can do no better than to quote what I have written in the treatment: "This expedition and film are devoted to conveying as precisely as possible the exact story, as reported in the expedition books of the 1920s. *We are not* attempting to solve the mystery of Mallory and Irvine's last climb. Indeed, we feel mystery is a rare commodity today. Most certainly, we are *not* grave-digging. We simply wish to pay tribute to a great man and his magnificent companions … What better way than to follow in their footsteps?"'

Chris vigorously nodded his head in full agreement, and Wendy and he bid us a hearty farewell.

When I arrived back home I learned that two other good spirits were about to get married in Scotland. It was my Sir Galahad himself, J.P. His bride-to-be was Margaret Magnusson, daughter of Magnus Magnusson of the popular BBC series *Mastermind*. Margaret was as pretty as a picture, having striking natural-blond hair, a fair complexion, dazzling blue eyes and a perfect slim figure to match. She worked for BBC News and was a live wire of energy. Possessed of a no-nonsense, open nature, she didn't suffer fools gladly. The very essence of her personality was honesty. Within seconds of entering a room, she displayed all the clarity of her Icelandic forefathers, combined with that special warmth and colour of Scotland. Aye! She was a force to be reckoned with!

Our mood of celebration was soon dampened by disappointing news from Peter Snell of British Lion Films. His forays in the USA had completely flopped; various film companies and consortiums had turned the project down flat. It was the old story: too expensive for a documentary, too cheap for a drama. Also, they wanted to know, where's the love interest? In addition they felt it was out of the question that a middle-aged actor could get near Everest, let alone climb the mountain. A good original idea, was their verdict, with full marks for enterprise, but in short, forget it!

I have always felt very deeply that if you have a go, no matter what the outcome, you are succeeding. The efforts of the fine people involved in this dream of Everest were making it all worthwhile. At every twist and turn, and every set-back, they each were placing a foot on the mountain. You can only do so much on your own, then you need other people. This simple truth was becoming more and more evident to me.

Soon after Peter Snell's disappointing news, John Rubin found that he was receiving similar treatment. Door after door closed in our faces. HTV, in the guise of Patrick Dromgoole and Ron Evans, were making mammoth efforts to get money for me, from individuals as well as remote companies – so far to no avail, but by God, they were trying.

Each year at the Cannes Film Festival HTV present their new programmes to prospective buyers aboard a colourful ship in the harbour. They kindly agreed to show to all their clientele a message from me on video, about the Everest project. They also emphasized their willingness to show me talking to the old Everesteer, Captain Noel, if I could get it filmed in time.

Chris Bonington was down south, on his way to China to arrange his Menlungtse expedition, and at the same time to seek permission for us to go to Everest. My wife, Hildegard, had not met him before, and she accompanied me to Heathrow to wish him *bon voyage*. Over a beer in the hotel lounge he leisurely described to Hildegard the complexities of mounting big expeditions. He again emphasized that he personally found climbing at great altitudes very taxing. Nevertheless he could scarcely hide his excitement at the prospect of having a shot at unclimbed Menlungtse.

A week later, following a cheerful phone call from Bonington's secretary, I received a copy of a letter she sent to Mr Ying Dao Shui of the Chinese Mountaineering Association in Beijing.

6th March 1987

Dear Mr Ying Dao Shui,

BRITISH MALLORY EXPEDITION 1988

Further to our telex sent today, 6th March, I am just confirming that the registration fee of 8,000 Yuan for the above expedition to Mount Qumolangma in July and August 1988 has been transferred to the 'All China Sports Federation' account at the Bank of China. It will clearly be marked 'Mountaineering', and is being sent from Lloyds Bank of London, England. I do hope it arrives safely, but please let me know if there are any problems, and I shall do my best to sort them out.

I know Chris Bonington is very much looking forward to going to Mount Qumolangma again.

Best Wishes, Yours Sincerely,
Louise Wilson

Eight thousand yuan is about £1,300, and for the first time I was committed to using my own money. Hildegard was most concerned about it, fearing it would trigger off a whole spate of expenses. But the die was cast, and I felt compelled to forge ahead. There were so many irons in the fire, one surely must come up trumps.

The long round of wheeling and dealing continued, and I would return home in the evenings holding my head in desperation. It was the same old story: some company, impressed by the fact that the BBC would go halfway, seemed almost on the point of saying yes, only to recoil in confusion over some silly minor point.

It was terrible. The whole saga was now playing havoc with my home life, and Hildegard was getting absolutely fed up with it all. The never-ending Everest theme drove her up the wall. It was so unfair to subject her to it night and day, but I seemed incapable of casting off my constant identification with it. 'For God's sake!' Hildegard burst out with great passion one day. 'You are losing all sense of proportion. We are here – your family! And you are missing out on us! Your mad obsession is boring us all to death! God in heaven, man! You don't leave it alone for one second! Just look at the girl here, who I'm washing in the bath. She is your daughter, Rosalind, shortly to be a young lady. You don't look at her, you look through her at your damn silly mountain!

'We all love you, including my mother, and you force us to exclude you from our daily activities because of your neglect of us. The other day Rosalind quietly said to me, "Oh, I do wish Daddy would stop talking about Everest, it's spoiling everything!"'

Hildegard's beautiful face contorted with tears as she softly entreated me to give it a rest, and to once more be the loving, simple man they could all relate to. This genuine and sincere outburst completely shook me, and brought back a little sanity, so that we had an evening of stillness and peace.

The next day we walked together hand in hand, with our dogs on Sunningdale golf course, one of our favourite jaunts. The weather was surprisingly warm and calm for March, perfectly in accord with our quiet mood. As we meandered leisurely from green to green, Hildegard gently and kindly pointed out a few home truths.

'As I said yesterday, your loved ones suffer and they are completely innocent. This selfish behaviour makes me feel cold and lonely. Your obsession with Mallory and Everest is verging on the manic ... It is simply getting out of control.

'The Brian that I once knew and loved is virtually unrecognizable. Your sense of humour, which I have always adored, is non-existent ... Then you are constantly tense and over-excited with expectation ... God in Heaven! Protect us from expectation!

'One of the most disturbing aspects that has developed in you is a negative attitude towards people who you think have let you down ... You condemn them out of hand ruthlessly, and in no uncertain terms, ranting and raging like a bull until my senses can't stand it ... You cannot conceive how unattractive you become during these moments.

'I never want to blunt your aspirations. I positively loathe it when any human being imposes on another to the detriment of that person's freedom. It is simply that, to quote your own much-used words, "You are becoming negative and mechanical."

'Brian, quite simply, learn to take things with a pinch of salt, like J. P. As for our home life, join us again. Regarding the expedition, if it's going to happen, it's going to happen ... If not, it's not ... Leave it to J. P. to sort it all out. Finance and organization on this scale, you know nothing about. I remember you telling me that one of your heroes, Ouspenski, once said to one of his pupils, "Be cheerful!" Sensible advice, Brian.

'You know, you really have been stagnating. I seriously think you should go and do something practical. It's about time you stopped talking and climbed a mountain. You still don't know what you would be like at altitude. Why don't you take Geoff Arkless and go to Kilimanjaro. It'll do you the world of good!'

This unexpected suggestion galvanized me into action. Before long, in company with Cathy, my pretty elder daughter from my first marriage, and my long-time friend and climbing mentor Geoff Arkless, I found myself on a flight to the Dark Continent and Kilimanjaro.

It was to prove an amazing adventure. As luck would have it, J. P. and Margaret were over there on their honeymoon. Margaret looked so lovely and happy — a right bobby-dazzler! We all met up at Marangu, at the base of the mountain, and after a short period of preparation we were conducted by Wachagga guides up the tourist route.

After several days of suffering and headaches we proudly reached the summit of the great mountain, at 19,340 feet. We were tickled pink!

Margaret, who had been frightfully sick on the last four thousand feet of the ascent, agreed that going high did something – even if it was only to make you appreciate coming down afterwards! She thought I was absolutely crazy even to contemplate tackling Everest.

Cathy, who had also gamely soldiered on despite a severe pain in the side of her head and a swollen hand, now looked forward to a holiday in Mombasa.

J. P. and Margaret bid us a hearty farewell and continued on their honeymoon trail across Kenya, while Geoff and I spent a week around Mount Kenya, doing various routes before returning to climb Kilimanjaro by the remote and beautiful Great Western Breach Wall route.

I returned to England refreshed and inspired. Hildegard was quite right. It had done me the world of good.

2

Old Soldiers Never Die

Captain John Baptist Lucius Noel: explorer extraordinary, Fellow of the Royal Geographical Society, Associate of the Royal Photographical Society and Honorary Life Member of the American Museum of Natural History. In 1913, with three native porters and disguised as a Muhammadan, Noel made an exceptional journey through forbidden Tibet towards Mount Everest. He got to within forty miles of the mountain, the first Westerner to do so, and exchanged shots with Tibetan troops before being forced to retreat. At a meeting of the Royal Geographical Society on 10 March 1919 he delivered a lecture about his pre-war incursion into Tibet which aroused intense enthusiasm among his audience.

In the discussion that followed, the President of the Alpine Club, Captain Percy Farrar, spoke of reaching the summit itself. This, said the President-Elect of the RGS, Sir Francis Younghusband, was the decisive leap forward. Younghusband determined that Everest would be the main goal of his three years in office. Having proved a catalyst, Captain Noel was an obvious choice as the cinematographer of the 1922 and 1924 Everest expeditions. He had had a distinguished career in the First World War, having fought at Mons, Le Cateau and Ypres.

With the end of the war, Noel was assigned to the Norpa Force, a small army of about six thousand men in northern Persia. His general ordered him to explore the southern shore of the Caspian Sea, to calculate the chances of the Bolsheviks invading Persia through the Elburz Mountains. Noel set out by horse, and since restrictions on photography had been relaxed, he took with him his Debrie motion-picture camera, and made a film about the caviar industry. What a character!

J.P. and I had decided that we simply had to film Captain Noel and finance it ourselves, as no one had yet come forward with the money for the complete project. All such worries were thrown aside as we eagerly anticipated our meeting. Noel was ninety-seven and the sole surviving member of the twenties expeditions. Sadly, a few weeks earlier, Noel Odell had passed away.

As Nick Shearman, my wife's niece Ingrid and I drove down to the captain's home in Kent in March 1988, thoughts of his exploits sang in my brain. His fascinating films of the 1922 and 1924 expeditions had filled the Scala Theatre in London. He followed this with numerous coast-to-coast tours of the USA, where he proved himself to be an outstanding lecturer. His photo-graphic plates, taken on a primitive frame camera and colour-tinted by hand, are miraculous images of the remote, mysterious Tibetan landscape.

Again, Noel's achievement of taking a 35-mm camera to the top of the North Col of Everest, at 23,000 feet, beggars belief. He also developed his film on that col in a makeshift darkroom consisting of a specially designed tent. Nothing was too much for him, for high on that mountain he constantly provided tea and soup in his wicker flask for the climbers returning wearily from the North Ridge. On one occasion he even sacrificed some of his film by setting it alight at night to show the way for Mallory and his companions.

My brain was now burning with impatience. At last, there was the signpost pointing the way to the small village of Brenzett, where Captain Noel lived with his daughter Sandra. It was intriguing that a man who had spent most of his life devoted to the mountains and Mount Everest should have chosen the flat country of Romney Marsh as a home. J.P. had already arrived at the pretty weatherboarded cottage, and the film crew was much in evidence, adjusting cables and setting up lighting.

Through the window, in the shadowy recesses of the sitting room, I could make out a pale face with glowing eyes that stared straight back at me. A huge hand beckoned, and I made my way inside. As I entered the old-world atmosphere of the room, a smiling J.P., magician-like, moved sideways with a graceful flourish to reveal a venerable old English gentleman.

'My dear fellow,' I whispered softly, 'I've wanted to meet you all my life. What a privilege to shake your hand, dear sir. My goodness me, you look in fine fettle.'

I found myself automatically assuming the gracious manners of the twenties. Captain Noel's great hands, reminding me of an orang-utan's, encircled mine as he drew me to him.

The burning eyes I had observed outside blazed with intensity as he studied my features. Those deep pools of observation, semi-weeping with old age, shone with rare humour as his whole face lit up with a smile.

The brow was wrinkled like delicate lattice-work. Two deep, furrowed lines plunged down alongside his sharp nose, leading to a whisper of a moustache and thin lips that trembled with sensitivity and emotion. A dark-blue woollen bonnet rested on his full head of hair. Despite his age, his skin was in good condition, emphasizing his sound constitution.

'I know why you've come to see me ... You think I'm going to conk off!'

'You're damn right!' I replied.

'They've named a star after me,' the captain proudly stated, reaching out and showing me the certificate of the Inter-Planetary Society.

'They should have named a universe after you!' I laughed.

'Now then, Daddy. Before you and Mr Blessed get further involved, let's all have coffee and a bite to eat.'

The voice belonged to Captain Noel's daughter, Sandra, a very attractive lady in her early forties. Her lovely dark eyes and clear complexion indicated a healthy constitution like her father's. Her voice was pleasant and cheerful. It was a pleasure to see the old boy knock back the biscuits and sandwiches. Here was a man who had not forgotten how to enjoy life – that is, except when Sandra nagged him about his left leg.

'Oh, Daddy ... Please remember to exercise your leg ... Keep bending and stretching it ... '

The captain sighed and grumbled under his breath.

'Never mind, old boy,' I said. 'You're alive and well, and can help us enormously with our film.'

I then outlined the project to him. Much to my delight, he passionately approved of the whole thing, gripping my shoulders with emotion as I arrived at certain points, and smiling and nodding encouragingly as he heard titbits of information that fired his marvellous memory. I ended by saying, 'People generally don't know anything about these wonderful expeditions, Captain Noel. J.P., Nick, myself and other admirers wish to rectify this. We would love it if you would consider being Honorary Deputy Leader of the expedition.'

'Good heavens, Blessed!' gasped the captain. 'Or should I call you Long John Silver?' he whispered conspiratorially, with a wicked smile. 'I really don't think I could get up Everest now, though I must confess, one is rather tempted by the prospect. Nevertheless, I do feel that it is only fair to point out to you, young fellow, that I'm not as young as I was, and feel that I would prove more of a hindrance than a help if I attempted to come any part of the way with you. Bearing this in mind, I am more than ready to offer any advice and information that can assist you in this fine enterprise, deeming it a privilege to be part of your team.'

We filmed the captain on and off for about eight hours. It was a *tour de force* by the great man. His zest and energy, as he conveyed the great spirit of those early days of exploration in the Himalayas, astonished us all. It made my fanciful mountain stories trite; he dwarfed me with his experience and grasp of reality.

The affinity between us grew deeper during the day; so much so that I was able at times to be as insistent as Sandra. I would hold him firmly by the shoulders, maintaining forcefully that he was giving me a pat reply that he had given to numerous interviewers before. I would urge him to dig deeper into his memory.

'Good heavens, Long John!' he smiled. 'I've never been taken to task so strongly before. You're quite a tartar!'

'Well, Captain Noel,' I replied, 'you are driving me potty about Mallory. Every time I ask you about him, you describe him as "wiry".'

'Yes, he was thin ... wiry!'

'That tells me nothing about him!' I shot back.

'Didn't you like him?' I pursued.

'Yes, I liked him immensely ... Of course!' replied the old boy stoutly. 'But he was always on his knees in my tent, writing love letters ...'

'Ah, now we're getting somewhere.'

Ingrid was helping us out by doing the odd job here and there. Now she sweetly took over my position in the chair, and was holding the old boy's hands, listening to his tales. I had the distinct impression that he found the change most refreshing, and it allowed me to take in the room.

A fire burned brightly in the small, old fireplace, its atmospheric flames blending with the subtle light of two period table lamps. Although the walls badly needed a lick of paint, their slightly faded quality seemed a perfect background for the many pictures that absorbed our attention, the most riveting being the captain's famous painting of Everest Base Camp. The intricate colours of the rocks, with little coloured tents of yellow, green and blue contrasting with the Central Rongbuk Glacier, and the gigantic, dominating North Face of Everest, created a stunning picture.

The whole room was full of history. Shelves were crammed with historic *objets d'art*, books of clearly monumental importance and hundreds of newspapers from the early part of the century.

'These are the boots I wore on Everest, Blessed ... You can have them for your film, and also this wicker flask that I used,' said the captain, bringing me back to the present. 'I used to fill this flask with hot water, then proceed to the ice cliff, the North Col, and when I needed to fix a wooden piton, I'd dig out a small hole in the ice, pour the hot water in, and stick the piton in it. Because of the extreme cold, it would quickly freeze, giving you a perfect anchor.'

When I returned to the picture, saying that I hadn't realized that the captain painted, he explained: 'I was sent to art school in Florence, but my father was a soldier. He didn't want me to be an artist; he wanted me to be a soldier. When I failed to get into the Indian Army, I asked for the British Army and chose a regiment in North India, so I could be near the Himalayas. Of course, it is history, my achievement in 1913 of getting within forty miles of Everest. What is not commonly known is that I made three attempts before this, over the space of three years ...'

This statement left me speechless. As the filming continued, we moved to the captain's study, a treasure-house of archives. A dark-red curtain hung in one corner, protecting a large, gold-coloured, magic-lantern-like slide projector. The captain pointed to it proudly.

'I'll have it working for you when you come next time with Bonington,' he promised.

On an equally large old table were displayed numerous coloured photographic slides that took my breath away. There, in the very centre, side by side, were Mallory and Irvine, their features pristine and pure, yet made full-blooded and real by the captain's ingenious use of aniline dyes. Sitting there alongside him, I felt I was on hallowed ground. For the next two hours his ancient features smiled and wept by turns, as he lived through the memories of those staggering expeditions. Then, contorted with emotion, he dragged out the story of his realization that Mallory and Irvine were dead.

'Captain Norton was standing alongside me. He was snow-blind and his eyes were covered in bandages. I had my camera automatically focused and filming the Sherpas high above us on the North Col. At the same time I was free to look through my powered telescope. Then, what we all feared took place. I perceived the Sherpas place blankets, and their own bodies, in the snow in the shape of a cross. I just couldn't believe it. I placed my eyes repeatedly back to the telescope in the hope that the signal would change ... But it didn't.

'Of course, Norton, who was blind, was relying on me informing him ... But I simply hadn't the heart to tell him. "What does it say?" he kept asking. The Sherpas eventually told him it was a cross, and they were dead.'

Poor Captain Noel. For a few moments I held him close and consoled him. Sandra entered with some tea for us.

'He has a tendency to cry a great deal these days. Anyway, drink up, Daddy, and give it a rest.'

As he drank and the colour returned to his cheeks, I bluntly changed the subject.

'Have you ever seen a yeti, Captain Noel?'

His eyes lit up like flash bulbs.

'No, I've never seen one, but the lamas and Sherpas informed me that they existed, and that they were very vicious, being capable of eating a man or horse. They advised me, if I saw one, to turn and, if possible, run downhill, as they had long, red hair and it would fall over their face, therefore preventing them from seeing you.

'With female yetis it was slightly different, as they had long, sagging breasts, and by the time they'd thrown them over their shoulders, you could escape … But, I've never myself seen one.'

I doubt whether in the history of film-making any other company has used as much film as we did that day. As the evening wore on, we were in danger of running out.

It had also become evident what an amazing entrepreneur Captain Noel had been in his time. When he assembled his film of the 1922 expedition, *Climbing Mount Everest*, the Wardour Street film trade showed no interest.

'You know, Blessed. I told the Geographical Society that we should hire the Philharmonic Hall. They said it would cost a lot of money. I said, we've got to find it. We rented the hall for ten weeks, we had a fine operator and we installed two Ross film projectors, and we had a big lunch at Frascati's restaurant for the newspapers, and we gave them a private showing.

'We opened up and lost £400 the first week. The Geographical Society got frightened. I said, "Don't bother, the press reports are marvellous, just you wait till people read them, then they'll come." From that moment on, the board outside the hall said "No Seats" … We took £10,000 at the door over a period of ten weeks, then it was released at theatres all over the country.'

The captain took another swig of tea and collapsed with laughter.

'You've got to hold on, Blessed. Never, never give in. That's what I did with my film. My second film, of the '24 expedition, did even better. I formed a company, Explorer Films. The backers included Archibald Nettleford, Engineer Charles Merz, Lord Salveson of the Scottish Geographical Society, the Aga Khan and Professor Chalmers Mitchell. Sir Francis Younghusband was President of the company.

'You know, Blessed, you must not listen to film experts. They said to me, without a love interest your second film is bound to fail. They asked, could we not bring out actors and actresses and make a romance in the snow? They were all proved wrong. On the opening night at the Scala Theatre in London I persuaded seven Tibetan monks, from a monastery in the interior of Tibet, to come to England and to appear in the prologue. The orchestra included members of the Goossens family: father conducting, Sidonie playing harp, Leon the oboe.

'The opening night was presided over by Prince Henry, the Duke of Gloucester, and Sir Francis Younghusband. The press notices were exceptionally good, although the *Kinematography Weekly* complained about the London weather. How could the critic be expected to judge the quality of the photography when the theatre was full of fog?

'George Bernard Shaw was there, and said to me afterwards, "The Everest Expedition was a picnic in Connemara, surprised by a snowstorm!"'

These last words caused the captain to spill his tea, as he collapsed again in a fit of giggles. I joined him, and we became a pair of giggling five-year-olds. Sandra laughed too, saying, 'You're just like Daddy. You'll never grow up!'

After a further hour our audience was almost at an end. I found myself nodding away, with a glazed look in my eyes, while the old boy continued talking with ever-increasing intensity. Sandra had, during the course of the day, made up the fire several times, and the flames were now once more highlighting the ancient features of the noble explorer. Then suddenly, and quietly, his mood changed. His blue eyes fixed on me with a haunting concentration, all the more compelling as they were highlighted by the senile red of the lower rim. His whole manner became remote and introspective, the voice faint and barely audible.

'I know what happened to Mallory and Irvine,' he said.

Captain Noel had a habit of rocking back and forth in his chair, and was at this point in danger of falling backwards. To counter this, my toe, unknown to him, was hooked under the wooden seat. The strain on my toe was murderous, and at the same time I was praying that the camera wouldn't run out of film. Thankfully, it didn't. The captain continued.

'Several days after they had died, I was at the Rongbuk Monastery, below Base Camp, with a monk in a dark chamber. By the power of his mind, he had the ability to focus a film-like apparition of their last hours on a blank wall. It gave the appearance of a faded black and white film.

'There, quite clearly, were Mallory and Irvine with their backs to the summit, which was a small distance above them ... They were coming down. Mallory, just below the final pyramid, fell into a crevasse and died. Irvine continued down as best he could and fell, due to exhaustion, and died.

'I must say, Blessed, that the vision we were looking at made no sense to me. I have filmed every part of the final pyramid, and I have never seen anything resembling a crevasse. Yet, I completely believed in what I had seen. Comparing it with my film, I recognized that the crevasse was between the yellow band and the final pyramid. That's where Mallory is, with Andy Irvine further down.

'At all events, it still doesn't prove that they climbed it, as they were coming down, though the summit looked very close. Then, of course, this was a vision shared by the monk and myself, not what you would call scientific. I ask you, Blessed ... Who is going to believe it?'

After a pause, the old boy concluded, 'If you had lived as they had lived, and died in the heart of nature, would you, yourself, wish for any better grave than the pure white snow of Everest?'

Back in London, J.P. moved at the speed of light to develop the film of Captain Noel, as I was hoping that it would be ready in time to show to likely investors at the Cannes Film Festival. Half the time he hadn't a clue what I was up to, nor had he on this occasion. He simply transferred a copy of the film on to a simple VHS video cassette for convenience, and I raced to Heathrow in the hope that I could catch Derek Clarke of HTV *en route* to Cannes.

Ron Evans, a lovely man who was Director of Programmes at HTV West, was endeavouring, with all the means at his disposal, to get our project off the ground. He and Derek had been exploring every angle, as they felt it was such a strong idea, and bound to get going sooner or later.

I had also filmed myself on Video 8, enthusiastically explaining the storyline, and I carefully placed this before Captain Noel's film, where it fitted perfectly. Now I found myself frustrated again, as I was informed by British Airways that Derek was already on the plane, and it was shortly to take off. I explained my predicament to the staff, and they were kindness itself. Nothing was too much for them as they ran hither and thither to help me.

The actual running was done by two pretty, young, breathless stewardesses, who smiled and bent the rules in their effort to deliver my package. Round corners they ran, as fast as their high heels would allow them, down long corridors to the departure gate. All I could do was sit down on a vacant trolley and wait. Fifteen minutes later their excited faces appeared at the desk above me.

'We found them, Mr Blessed! We got there in time. They were just about to close the doors. You can put your mind at rest. We only hope it works out for your film.'

I gave them kisses galore and thanked them profusely.

'We are only too glad to help, Mr Blessed,' they replied. 'And thank you for the hours of entertainment you've given us ... Could we have your autograph?'

It seemed such a simple request after their splendid effort. Of all the events that became part of the Everest story, this was by far the sweetest.

Life at home had now returned again to a much happier atmosphere. Everest was still around, but in its proper place. However, I had not yet learned to take setbacks with a pinch of salt, like J.P. There were, nonetheless, distinct signs that I was learning to count to ten. Everywhere, smiles were much in evidence.

'You'll find peace one day, darling,' said Hildegard, laughing. 'You're such a silly knucklehead.'

My daughter Rosalind was now thirteen, and was already developing into a fine young lady. She was going to the Marist Convent School in Sunninghill, and was very happy there, possessing, like her mother, a very high IQ. One glance at her homework was enough to make me shriek and run for cover. My sense of humour has never really developed beyond the nursery stage, and it is when I am being particularly silly that Rosalind finds me the most appealing. Sitting by my large koi-carp pond drinking tea one day, she joined me for a chin-wag.

'You know, Rosalind …' I beamed at her. 'Surprise, surprise! Would you believe it? I've had my Everest programme turned down again today. I felt really sorry for myself. I thought, poor old Brian – rejected again. So I thought I'd help myself to a good, old-fashioned helping of self-pity … It was absolutely lovely! I must do it again sometime.'

Her reaction to my rambling was to chuckle quietly, assume the air of a long-suffering headmistress and pat me encouragingly on the head.

Then we stood quietly looking at the large koi, which are so tame and greedy that they will actually stick their necks many inches out of the pond to be fed. How pretty Rosalind looked, with her long, light-brown hair reaching to her shoulders, and her rich, dark-brown eyes dancing with fun. Yes, things were much better. Spring was bursting out everywhere, and God was in his heaven.

What is more, we had moved into a new home. It was a simple, single-storey cottage, more like a villa really, with lots of windows where the light poured in from every direction. Never have I known such a happy place. It was surrounded by about an acre of lawns, including my twelve-thousand-gallon koi pond, which incidentally I have dug and built for the umpteenth time. Beyond this lay about three acres of paddocks, where Hildegard kept her many ponies.

Delightfully, the phone would ring once a week, with helpful information from Captain Noel. He took his position as the expedition's Honorary Deputy Leader very seriously. The phone calls were short and always to the point. On one occasion the old boy remarked that he had read that I was going to Corfu to film the BBC production *My Family And Other Animals*. He expressed his unreserved admiration for my co-star Hannah Gordon.

Some weeks later I found myself in Corfu, standing on the beach outside the Astia Palace Hotel with that fine actress. We were both peering up at the island's highest mountain, Pando Krato. Hannah, with a look of concerned amusement, asked, 'Are you really taking them up there?'

She was referring to Anthony Calf, Guy Scantlebury and Christopher Godwin, who were also starring in the serial.

'Yes, indeed,' I replied. 'Ah, it's easy. They'll have no problems.'

It was all part of a charity climb. Pando Krato means 'Place of God', and is about 3,500 feet high. Its East Face, if you can call it that, is gently inclined with forty-degree sandstone rocks leading to the summit. I had been climbing it every day after filming, as part of my fitness programme. Although it was only a scramble – Chris Bonington and Doug Scott could climb it blindfolded *and* in tuxedoes – it did pose a few amusing problems.

The scree on the lower slopes was incredibly loose, so I would find I'd gained a hundred yards, only to lose it and create a minor landslide, ending up back where I started. I never did quite master it, particularly when moving horizontally. Also, I discovered that I was a bit of an interloper, for the mountain really was the domain of a wild and woolly goatherd. Each evening as I approached the halfway mark, he would appear slightly above me with his large herd. Goats on mountains can be ridiculously curious, and these were no exception, their inquisitiveness bringing them close above me, forcing me to find any shelter available to avoid the numerous small rocks they dislodged. Throughout this they made funny farting noises, desisting only when the goatherd growled out a command that convinced me that he probably ate rusty nails for breakfast. Then, with a suggestion of a salute, he turned away.

What really intrigued me was the way he appeared to float across the scree slopes. His rhythm and motion were effortless, and only rarely did he delicately touch the slope with his rustic stick. I had the haunting sensation that I was observing a scene that had been enacted from the time of Homer. Approaching the distant ridge, the ragged figure could easily be mistaken for a centaur leading his proud stallions. The far-off sounds of the goats bleating, rasping and farting restored my senses. I love fantasizing. Not difficult on Pando Krato.

The climb was arranged, and the appointed day was still, with not a whisper of a breeze. The sun was bright and fierce, and as it continued to ascend the brilliant blue heaven, the heat grew ever more intense. We had experienced several hot days, but this was without doubt much more extreme. Added to this, the bright sandstone rocks seemed to be incapable of dissipating the rays. Instead, they heated up rapidly, reflecting back both light and heat.

To our right the sizzling coastline stretched for miles, pointing the way to the island of Ithaca. Finally, it petered out to the naked eye in a shimmering haze of hot mist. The vast, calm sea surrounded all with its magnificence. As we gained height the coastline of Albania could clearly be seen. It would be fair to say that, apart from the first hour, the climb was sheer hell. That bright orb burnt us to a crisp.

In anticipation of this we had calculated that our generous supply of bottles of mineral water would easily answer all our needs. It proved hopelessly inadequate. With about a mile of rough terrain still to go to the monastery on the summit, we completely ran out. The fact that the lads were fit and strong convinced me that all would be well, but it really was horrendous.

In all my experience on mountains I have never known anything so dangerous. All my previous ascents on this route had taken place during the late afternoon, when the heat had subsided. I never for a moment thought that we would suffer from dehydration. The idea crossed my mind of descending 2,000 feet to a rustic hut belonging to my old friend the goatherd. He kept a good supply of water in old plastic bottles and pots there, and I had once used this facility, despite the fact that scores of dead spiders populated the water. Who gives a damn when you're thirsty!

Anyway, I decided against going down. Quite apart from the fact that it would take too long, the lads would be so disappointed about failing. This was their very first climb, and they were determined to press on. Now that we had scrambled up the gullies of the cliff on to the gently sloping plateau, I felt sure that we would find the odd pond or pool somewhere. It was not to be, and our condition became serious. For a while I had noticed that we had stopped perspiring, everyone's lips began to swell and speech was becoming increasingly difficult. Yet the lads remained in good spirits, with the odd attempt at humour breaking through, such as when Chris Godwin cried out, 'Who do I have to sleep with to get off the mountain?'

An hour or so passed, and it was now midday. The sun was virtually overhead and unrelenting in its ferocity. I was leading them on a circular route; this was slightly longer but far less strenuous than going straight on, which would have entailed descending and ascending valleys. Suddenly Guy and Anthony sighted an old, broken-down well that contained a tiny amount of brackish water, which Chris was convinced contained goat's piss.

'Beggars can't be choosers,' I said. 'Get it down you.'

Not only did it taste vile – it was also hot.

The benefits of this stop were debatable, and we pressed on. After another couple of hundred yards we sank down on our knees in the half shade of some boulders. We were cooking like roast chickens. To breathe the air among the rocks was torture – it burnt your tongue and throat. Our suffering lungs, as if rebelling against the fiery air we were subjecting them to, blew out disgustingly, making a sound like a blacksmith's antiquated bellows.

Our faces and lips were now covered in salt, and speech was almost impossible. We had just one large boulder-strewn hill to surmount to reach the summit, and then I promised them a room full of taps, where they could drink to their hearts' content. All three affected a smile, motioning me on. Another twenty yards and we collapsed again in utter agony.

'Giss a kiss, darling,' Chris rasped out.

'Only when you get up, you great poof!' I replied. 'Then I'll give you all a kiss. Keep going – Nanny knows best!'

Anthony, his face strained and tense, came alongside me, determined to force his way up the last section. Guy, who was still capable of a broad smile, joined me too.

'Then, D'Artagnan, we are four!' breathed Chris, and the last fifty feet were completed.

Ten minutes later Four Musketeers drank deep from the promised taps of the Pando Krato Monastery. It was a tremendous, gutsy effort by the lads. Their endeavours had realized £4,000 for a bereaved Greek family who badly needed it. In the gardens near the centre of Corfu, there is a single statue of the great prince and hero, Achilles. In my mind's eye, in that magical, sun-drenched island, surrounded by wine-red seas, I see three large sandstone rocks bearing the names Scantlebury, Calf and Godwin.

Months later I was back in fair England again, of which Mallory said:

'Never mind Everest and its unfriendly glories. I'm tired of travelling and travellers, far countries and uncouth people, trains and ships and shimmering mausoleums, foreign ports, dark-skinned faces and a garish sun. What I want to see is faces I know, and my own sweet home; afterwards, the solemn facades in Pall Mall, and perhaps Bloomsbury in a fog, and then an English river, cattle grazing in Western meadows. ... '

Of course, Mallory was referring to Asia. I don't think he ever visited Corfu. I'm sure that if he had he would have been quite captivated by it. He most certainly would have climbed Pando Krato, and drunk from the long line of taps in the monastery, though I very much doubt that he would have attempted it during the heat of the day. It really was very stupid of me to take those men up there in such a furnace – they might have died. Still, even great climbers have, on occasion, made questionable decisions.

I've had a sporadic relationship with mountains and climbers, and the world of acting has constantly interrupted this process. Geoff Arkless has often ticked me off for saying that I am not a climber. His hackles rise, and even his Geordie musicality is lost when he says, 'Please don't say you're not a climber. You've been up some of the world's great mountains ... Climbed them, Mr Blessed. You didn't float up! You had to climb them, therefore you are a climber, so you're talking rubbish.'

Acting is a great art, requiring absolute discipline and total commitment. For me, acting is a must. Actors really have no choice, and that is all there is to it. If acting is not essential for an actor, then he should seriously consider packing it in, and allow his place to be taken by someone who *is* dedicated. Yet acting has rarely given me happiness. Apart from the odd production, and my amateur days in Yorkshire, I have found it rather distressing. Mountaineering, on the other hand, makes me happy, yet there is no doubt at all that I have very little talent for it.

Over the years, I have had the good fortune to observe many climbers at close quarters, enjoying their bonhomie, attending their fascinating lectures, and watching them, on film and live, ascend awesome and inspiring routes that thrilled my soul to the core. And yet, even though they have all the same weaknesses and frailties as the rest of mankind, I can't begin to understand these fine ladies and gentlemen.

In mountaineering there are absolute laws. If you break them, you inevitably risk life and limb. It is amazing, at ground level, how much we get away with. Flirting with the law constantly, and breathing a sigh of relief when we think we've got away with it ... Not so on a mountain.

High up there, the starkness, the reality of your situation forces you to dig in and listen to the ancient voice. Glaciers move, weather conditions fluctuate. You don't abuse the mountain. That it is alive is self-evident. When you climb with a partner the rope between you is an umbilical cord; you look after him, he looks after you. Frequently, in the most appalling conditions, climbers have to attain stillness of mind and employ sound judgement to find the correct solution to the immediate problem. Because of the dangers, the climber must respect the ancient wisdom that says absolute discipline is freedom.

People frequently ask me why climbers keep on going from mountain to mountain. It is a question that I am woefully unable to answer. I cannot pretend to know the innermost thoughts of the entire climbing fraternity. At bottom it remains a mystery. People often argue that climbing is a drug. This point of view, to me, is naïve, worthless. Maybe it is the freedom I mentioned that drives climbers on.

Freedom is not a static state, but appears to grow and grow, without limits. Possibly this feeling accumulates and continues to develop within the climber, from mountain to mountain. Whatever it is, in that world of high winds, cold, heat, joy, sadness, tents, ridges and foul-smelling latrines, the climber deems that state of mind sacred and quietly protects it. They have my unstinting admiration.

I've often felt that if I had met Mallory, my relationship with him would not have been dissimilar to the one that he recorded in 1919, on a railway platform in St Gervais, on his way to Chamonix:

'The whole of the Mont Blanc group was surprisingly white, and even on the west side of the valley, great patches of snow were visible below the precipices. I found myself discussing these phenomena with a young Frenchman, as we stood upon the platform. I soon found out that he was very well informed about everything we saw. He was able to name every point which I had forgotten or never knew, and seemed to know every ascent on this side. I had little doubt that he had an ambitious programme and, though I had no intention of referring to my own performances, I began to question him about his. He made no difficulty about telling me. The story of his conquests came tremendously forth, his eyes shining with enthusiasm. It was not a long story; and it was a modest record, incredibly modest − Lore, as he evidently possessed, should be expended on so little.

'His party, he confided, if they could get really fit, intended as a crowning glory, to ascend Mont Blanc from the Grands Mulets. I have said that I intended not to speak about my own achievements or projects, because I usually find that I dislike myself when I do. However, it seemed necessary to break my resolution, and I mentioned that I had twice been to the top of Mont Blanc. The Frenchman questioned me eagerly, and insisted upon hearing everything. I felt that I had never met so passionate a mountain lover ... '

Of all Mallory's stories, I always find this the most amusing.

3

An Uphill Struggle

When I returned to England from Corfu in mid-summer 1988, with body brown and expectations high, I eagerly sought out the latest news on the Everest project. It wasn't too encouraging; in fact it was a total thumbs down. The Cannes film showing had yielded plenty of interest, but precious little else. It was the same old story. Ron Evans was persisting, and Derek Clarke had been lobbying his contacts at National Geographic Television. The outcome of this was that, though they were very enthusiastic about the concept, they were not forthcoming with any co-production dollars or outlets. This was definitely the worst time in the whole campaign. It rather reminded me of one of the Chorus speeches in Shakespeare's *Henry V*:

> Now entertain conjecture of a time,
> When creeping murmur and the pouring dark,
> Fills the wide vessel of the universe.

The exciting campaign, which had gathered so much momentum over the years, finally petered out and ground to a halt in early October 1988. Even Ron and Derek, despite their heroic efforts, ultimately had to admit that it was time to call it a day. I shall never forget their kindness and industry. Ron's letter says it all:

Dear Brian,
We've been trying to give Everest a final push – or, more accurately, Derek has – here in Bristol this last week amongst the world's wildlife/environmental/adventure channels, who've

had their top people in the city for the 'Wildscreen Festival'.

Unfortunately, however, there haven't been any takers. People say, 'What a marvellous idea, but ... '

Derek has also worked on the Discovery Channel in the USA, National Geographic and the UK Channel Four, but again has drawn blanks.

So, sadly, I think we've got to arrive at the conclusion that we've taken it as far as we can at HTV and reluctantly pull away from the project.

It is a marvellous idea, but we can't see an ITV placing for it. It's obvious home, as we've discussed, would seem to be via the BBC's output in this programme area.

I'm sorry we're stepping aside, but I don't think there's anything further we can usefully do to help the project along. What a shame.

As ever, best of wishes

Yours sincerely, Ron Evans.

There were now no more irons in the fire. Nothing. Whichever way I looked. Yet strangely enough, I didn't feel sad. How could I, when everyone had tried so hard? You can't ask for any more than that.

My days were occupied with filming and long, long walks with the dogs, as if in a dream. You could see the confused look in the dogs' eyes – they were used to me jogging, or sprinting in my lumbering way; I had become quite fit in preparation for the climb. Now, my introspective state went cap in hand with my uninspired motion. There was no feeling of depression – simply a relaxed acceptance of the situation. Hildegard quite liked it this way, stroking my forehead as I quietly smiled. To all outward appearances, the volcano was dormant.

Sitting in my study at night, with my old wizened ginger mongrel Jessie wrapped round my feet, I viewed with detached humour the scores of books I had accumulated about Everest. Did I really read all those? I mused. Extraordinary to have allowed oneself to become so self-obsessed, to the exclusion of everyone and everything around me. Now my long-cherished dream seemed far away, and the image of the mountain appeared to be fading at the edges, yet inwardly I felt that all was not lost. The candle was still burning ... albeit faintly. In this quiet, meditative state, somewhere I felt as sure as I did of spring that the dream would be realized.

Patience was now what was required. 'All roads lead to Rome ...', the saying goes, but not for me. There was only one road, one that led all the way to the ancient East Rongbuk Glacier. My heart yearned for it, but where was my Sir Galahad now?

What an ego, to think that I owned J.P. He was much in demand, as befits a knight. From hither and yonder, people sought his services. His lance was now toiling with the Thunder Dragon: he was making a film about the Kingdom of the Thunder Dragon, that fascinating country Bhutan. He was planning to follow this by making a film with Chris Bonington about the yeti and the un-climbed mountain, Menlungtse.

Chris, as I expected, was, with a strong team of climbers, again returning to the fray, determined to succeed this time. His depar-ture left me feeling numb and lonely. He had quite rightly pulled out of our project, having done everything in his power to help us, including taking part in some extra filming with me and Captain Noel. Chris and the old boy had delighted in each other's com-pany. Chris had also attended several meetings in London, meet-ing a rich variety of people in the entertainment world and commerce. Throughout it all, his conduct was practical, deter-mined and gentlemanly.

I particularly remember one meeting in a Mayfair hotel, when we sat down for an hour with J.P. and John Rubin and meticul-ously endeavoured to scale down the size of the expedition, to make it more palatable to investors. It was a considerable effort for Chris, as he was deeply involved with a lecture tour. Near the end of the meeting he rounded on me quite strongly. Not mincing his words, he made it quite clear that any notion I had of bringing surplus people to Everest was out of the question. His voice grew in intensity, and his index finger flashed in my face emphatically, as he announced, 'If cuts have to be made, then we must all make sacrifices.'

That evening I was at home relaxing, when the phone rang. It was Chris; his voice sounded robotic.

'If I sound a little strange, it's because I'm phoning from the back of a car, *en route* to my next lecture ... I'm phoning up to say how sorry I am that I was so outspoken today.'

'Oh, not at all, Chris,' I replied. 'You were absolutely right and justified ... '

'No!' protested Chris. 'I was out of order. You're such a kind chap, and I was a little insensitive ... '

'There's nothing to apologize about, Chris,' I insisted. 'I always find you totally kind, honest and charming.'

He then started to laugh.

'Brian, I think you should consider joining the diplomatic service ... Anyway, my best wishes to you ... See you soon ... '

I was deeply impressed. What a splendid fellow, I thought, he didn't have to make that phone call. It was another fine example of the stature of the man. It was a sad day when he was forced to make the decision to leave us.

With Chris gone, and J.P. away in the Bhutanese forests, I found myself on my way once again to see Captain Noel. He was now ninety-nine, and I was joining him and Sandra for lunch. After a marvellous meal of Dover sole prepared by Sandra, during which the captain's stories raised my spirits considerably, Sandra left us, and we retired to the study.

Over the months, I had got to know the captain very well, and had been fascinated by all his tales. Yet somehow this day was different. He wasn't repeating himself, which would have been understandable for a man of his years. Rather, his passionate nature flamed with a new intensity that was both moving and disturbing. Then his thoughts became disjointed, as if the circuits of his brain were switching on and off. Throughout, I said nothing, simply observing him. Then he suddenly cried out, 'What on earth do people want to know about Mallory and Irvine? It makes no sense to me! What about Tasker and Boardman – they disappeared on Everest too! ... So did Mike Burke! ... People should make a fuss about them – their achievements are no less remarkable. I also don't know why the Russians want advice from me, about the state of the upper reaches of the East Rongbuk Glacier. It will have changed a great deal from the time I was up there ... '

His conversation then moved from the mountains to the miracle of Bernadette at Lourdes, and then to the First World War. After a period of silence, he said, 'Of course, we all hunted in those days. It was traditional to do so. Then one day in Sikkim I shot a deer. I remember it most vividly. I dismounted from my horse to inspect it. It was lying there … still alive … its eyes staring at me, as if to say, "Why have you shot me? This is my home, I would never have done you any harm" … I looked at the helpless, dying animal and cried like a baby. From that day on, I never shot another animal, not even a bird.'

For a while the captain cried, and after drying his eyes, remained perfectly still. During the pause I held his hands, finally breaking the silence.

'What is it, old boy? What's really on your mind?'

After a further pause, he gave me a forlorn look and asked weakly, 'You're not going to Everest, are you? It's not going to come off, is it?'

At that moment I almost let the project go. But the great man's questions spurred a stubbornness in me, and I responded positively.

'Absolute nonsense, Captain Noel! Nothing is going to stop me! By hook or by crook, I'll get there! If investors fail to come forward, I will go there through Explor-Asia. They can arrange for porters to get me to the head of the East Rongbuk Glacier, and from there I will make my way somehow up the North Col, to celebrate your fine achievement of getting up there in 1924 … I'll use my Video 8 camera, as I did on Kilimanjaro in 1988.'

'You'll need permission,' the captain interrupted.

'I had permission for 1988,' I replied. 'And paid for it. I'll ask for it to be transferred to spring 1990, to coincide with your hundredth birthday!'

Bold words, but I meant every one of them. The captain's face broke into a grin as he said, 'Well, Long John Silver, at least you won't have to darken your skin with walnut dye, like I did in 1913. It is strange how involved I have become in your film, and I am sure you have gathered from our conversations that I keep abreast of the times. I am well informed, Blessed, I assure you. Modern-day expeditions constantly seek my advice … I only wish I were younger, and then I could guide you up the East Rongbuk

Glacier. You must beware ... It is the Land of the Dead.'

As the ominous words sank in, he broke the silence again: 'You know, I am the last remaining British officer from the First World War. I was with the East Yorkshire Regiment, whose Commanding Officer is Her Majesty, The Queen Mother. That gracious lady honoured me with a letter the other day, congratulating me on this distinction ... '

I must confess that, unknown to the captain, I had written to her weeks before, highlighting his record, and hoping that it might be possible for him to meet her for tea. However, Her Majesty wrote and informed me that unfortunately this would not be possible, due to a full and demanding itinerary. The Queen Mother's letter to Captain Noel was of considerable length. It was informal, friendly and displayed a fine appreciation of the captain's achievements. He was thrilled by it, but I reminded myself of the old adage, 'No names, no pack drill'.

For the remaining daylight hours, we continued to swop stories with enjoyment and ease. Before I left we toasted Everest 1990 and when at last I was making my way to the door, I turned and held his hands firmly, then shook them vigorously.

'Goodnight, old boy,' I whispered. 'Thank you for a lovely day ... God bless ... Sleep tight.'

'Goodnight, friend Blessed,' he choked back.

After I closed the front door, I lingered for a while, then felt myself drawn to the study window. In the shadows I could see a pale face with glowing eyes, staring straight back at me. A huge hand waved.

It was to be the last time I ever saw Captain Noel alive.

Driving home, I whistled, hummed and sang, my joyful sounds punctuated from time to time by blasts of 'You bet your bottom dollar I'll get to Everest ... Screw 'em! ... Screw 'em! ... Screw 'em!' and 'I'll show the doubting bastards! ... Yes! ... John the Baptist!' My ravings would have done the wild prophet proud.

'We all need that bloody wildness sometimes in our poxy, crap-awful life.'

My brain was now on stalks, as if vibrating to the far reaches of the galaxy. People I drove past felt sure that they recognized Brian Blessed, only to dismiss the idea as a mirage as they saw the maniac in the car explode with insane laughter.

Suddenly I remembered a conversation that I had had with the actor Edward Hardwicke. He told a story about another fine actor, Colin Blakely, who with the rest of the cast once attended a note session in the theatre which was being held by a certain director, who was being rather destructive. The cast visibly winced as the director individually tore them apart, though every time he tried the same tactic with Colin, he received a firm, measured 'Bollocks'. The remembrance of this made my insane glee intensify, and now my imaginary dialogue with those I had encountered at so many meetings took on the style of Colin's curt response.

'Don't you think that you're too old for Everest, Mr Blessed?'
'Bollocks.'
'We think you need some love interest in your film ...'
'Bollocks.'
'I'm inclined to think that mountaineers are stupid, and need their heads examining ...'
'Bollocks.'
'The idea of wearing twenties clothing is absolutely silly.'
'Bollocks.'
'You're quite entertaining! ... A one-man show! ... You ought to film that and forget Everest ...'
'Bollocks.'
'Quite simply, Mr Blessed. We, as a committee, think you haven't got a hope in hell of getting there ...'
'Bollocks.'
'Trust us, Mr Blessed. We definitely have the money for this project. Now we only have to get down to the nitty gritty ...'
'Bollocks.'
'I suppose ... Ha, ha, ha ... You want to go to Everest ... Ha, ha, ha ... Because it's there! ... Ha, ha, ha, ha, ha!'
'Bollocks.'
My laughter now gave way to more songs and ditties, and I lilted away, 'I know where they should be ... Shovelling shale on the Isle of Capri ...'
Eventually I ran out of steam and put on a tape. The poignant sound of Sibelius's Fifth Symphony filled my senses with deep

contentment. I reflected on what that great actor George Sanders once said, which summed up my feelings perfectly: 'It's not the being let down that hurts ... It's the hope ... '

For the next few weeks my concentration was focused totally on arranging my tiny, solo expedition to Everest. Rowan Patterson, a tall, handsome, cheerful man who helped run the London-based Explor-Asia, set about this frightful task with humour and incredulity.

'It's going to cost about £14,000 minimum. It's also rather difficult to guarantee that what we organize here will be carried out there, in Tibet. It could prove to be impossible to get you to the foothills of the mountain. People can be held up for days at Friendship Bridge, on the border between Nepal and Tibet, and then be turned back. We would be very worried about you.

'Here, at Explor-Asia, we rather pride ourselves on our super-efficiency. It would certainly be stretched to the limits if you attempt this. We urge you to reconsider. Even if it miraculously worked out, to the extent of getting you some way up the East Rongbuk Glacier, we couldn't guarantee you having medical supervision. There would be every likelihood of having to nurse yourself. A daunting prospect, Brian; it simply doesn't bear thinking about.

'Just think: two weeks on that terrible glacier, in the company of four Sherpas who probably don't speak a word of English. The weather up there can be atrocious. You remember that a year or so ago people were snowed in right down to Base Camp, and in many cases had to be rescued ... You must seriously bear this in mind. Also, it is very doubtful that the Chinese will transfer the permission you had in 1988 to go to the North Col, to 1990. All in all, Brian, I would say that it's very doubtful that this can be arranged, but I'll do my best.'

I thanked him heartily, and prayed that he could pull it off. I must say that I liked Rowan and his team, and they were always courteous and kind to me. My main priority now was acquiring a good pair of high-altitude plastic boots, and the rest of the gear.

Over my years of climbing I had collected a great deal of equipment, but it was now rather out of date. The latest modern clothing is incredibly impressive, and there is a vast range to choose from. One of my favourite haunts is the YHA shop in Southampton Street, London. You can buy gear there at knock-down prices, and the staff are always very helpful, though on this occasion they were nonplussed to hear about my objective, all the time smiling and shaking their heads at my requests.

Captain Noel had promised to send me his concoction of honey. This, he said, would be in the form of jelly-coated bullets. These I could carry on me, popping one into my mouth whenever I needed a boost. I had written to Mr Ying Dao Shui, of the Chinese Mountaineering Association in Beijing, and was keeping my fingers crossed that he would allow me permission for a crack at the North Col. I'm afraid it was all in vain. The Chinese failed to respond to my many letters, and the gallant band at Explor-Asia felt in their hearts that it was not wise for me to persist with Tibet.

I sat bowed, but never beaten, by my koi pond in Bagshot, wondering what to do. Images of actors' faces floated in and out of my numbed brain: Anthony Calf, the actor in *My Family And Other Animals*, his face all covered in salt, saying, 'You know, you really must go to Everest...' Peter O'Toole, saying, 'You really have got a thing about that mountain, haven't you? You can't escape it ... You simply must go to it ...' Ken Branagh's worried face, creased up with tension about it, his voice concerned and warm, 'It looks a terrible place, Brian ... I'll be glad when it's all over, and you're safe home again. The thought of it worries me ... We all love you ...' Then the face of my teenage friend, Patrick Stewart, he of the new Starship Enterprise, 'Ah, Brian, my lad! I'm certain you'll go to Everest one day.'

Voices, too, from my childhood ... Calden Williams, Cedric Webster, Colin Picton, who gave me the news all those years ago that Eric Shipton had burst through the ice-fall to the Western Cym in 1951, opening the way to the south side of the mountain. The voices gave way to the vibrant image of a blue sky and sea in Cyprus, where, during the late 1970s, I filmed with the BBC the series *The Aphrodite Inheritance*, in which I played the Greek god, Dionysus. I remember the time when, swimming down deep in the sea to collect shells among rocks, my eye was drawn to a small piece of paper. Intrigued, I sped to the surface with it. It was the remains of a matchbox and it simply read, 'Everest Restaurant'. Zeus, yes. Aphrodite, yes. Dionysus, yes. But never in a million years, on Cyprus, the *Everest* Restaurant! Anyway, what the hell did it matter now? I simply hadn't a card left to play, yet I couldn't help feeling that somehow all would be well.

Back home, this conviction spurred me to start running again across Chobham Common, and I even made some ascents of the mighty Box Hill. Toad was himself again. Watch out for your laurels, Reinhold Messner!

During this strange time Ken Branagh offered me the part of the Duke of Exeter in the film of *Henry V*. Ken had performed a miracle in mounting the production. It was a magnificent achievement, providing a shot in the arm for the ailing British film industry. The fact that Ken had pulled off *Henry V* against all odds renewed my confidence and determination to succeed likewise with Everest. His newly realized dream gave fresh energy to my fading one.

The newspapers had been full of a certain gentleman named Stephen Evans, who had built himself a reputation in the financial world as a man to be trusted and respected. Furthermore, everyone appeared to like him enormously. He was in his early forties, tall and handsome, with bright, laughing eyes and a full head of hair. He was also very fit, choosing to run the odd marathon between business commitments. Stephen's open nature and kindly disposition inspired confidence wherever he went. He was to become the producer of Branagh's *Henry V*, and he had also proved most helpful when Ken had been forming his Renaissance Production Company. Branagh's great qualities were instantly recognized by Evans, and there was a natural affinity between them.

At this time I accompanied Stephen to numerous successful press launches of *Henry V*. As we were leaving one such occasion in Brighton, he drew me aside and whispered, 'I want to talk to you. Let me give you a lift back to Bagshot.'

In the car he told me, 'I've really enjoyed today. I like the way, Brian, that you let rip at these press launches, and give it all you've got. You don't spare yourself a minute. I appreciate that. You've the same energy as Ken!

'You know, I find the film world very exciting and satisfying, and certainly I've got my work cut out for a long time ahead promoting *Henry V* all over the world. Yet, you see, it's very hard to follow a film like this. My adrenalin's up, and I'm dead keen to get going with some other project ... '

My heart skipped a beat. Then Alf, Stephen's chauffeur, grinning like a Cheshire cat, interrupted, 'Aye, Taffy always likes to be involved with something. He likes to have his hands full.'

Taffy, apparently, is Stephen's nickname. Alf's remark set off several minutes of laughter, the humour becoming distinctly bawdy. Rather reminiscent of J.P., Stephen lit up a huge cigar and eased himself down in his seat, before introducing a rather more serious tone to the conversation.

'Brian,' he said, pausing dramatically. 'It would make me very happy if I could be part of your Everest film. I seriously would like to come in on the whole project. Can I meet J.P.? It sounds fascinating – could you tell me all about it?'

For a moment I felt like my legs had dropped off, and my arms. My stomach did a 180-degree turn, my teeth clattered about my toes, and I was so stunned I could not think of a word to say. But this condition did not last long.

'Stephen,' I said quietly. 'You have no idea what you have let yourself in for. How much time can you spare?'

He smiled broadly, replying, 'All the time in the world ... You hit me, Baby!'

One evening a few days later I sat in a comfortable chair in the warm atmosphere of J.P.'s old-world kitchen. Under explicit orders, my normally loud gob was firmly shut. My dazed eyes gazed on the two knights seated in front of me. In countenance noble, and in voice modulated, they nodded gracefully and agreeably, approving all before them.

Their concentration never falters as they move to an ineffable, uncomplicated union of minds. The black armour of Sir Galahad on my left, displaying signs of rust from the rains of the Kingdom of the Thunder Dragon, contrasted vividly with the white armour of Sir Taffy, still stained with the exploits of Agincourt. There is a moment's pause, a silence, a prayer possibly, and then the two titans embrace across the sacred space of the table. The accord is

57

celebrated with the ritualistic lighting of stout cigars. Now their eyes kindly turn to me, and two deep smiles light the way to my soul, as they announce: 'It is concluded: you are going to the Turquoise Mountain.'

The following morning, at home in Bagshot, I found myself imparting the news to my astonished mother-in-law. I related the whole story of J.P.'s meeting with Stephen and how splendidly they had got on.

'The wonderful Stephen will find half of the budget and the marvellous BBC will find the other!' I shouted joyously. 'Mind you, there is still a tremendous amount to be done, the whole expedition now has to be organized. A mammoth task!'

I had returned home in the early hours of the morning, and so had not had the opportunity to tell Hildegard. Now, at midday, she came through the door laden with groceries, and bearing on her face all the responsibilities of running a home. Certainly, her mind was on more important things than knights and dragons. First things first: I helped unload the rest of the week's shopping from the car.

When I told Hildegard that I was at last going to Everest, she smiled in that lovely way of hers, which developed into a chuckle, and said, 'Of course, you have been at this stage before, Brian, only for it to fall apart. Yet I must tell myself that this time, because it involves J.P. and Stephen Evans, it must be the real McCoy. Also, for the first time, I can recognize that you think it is, because you seem quite shaken.'

'I am,' I replied. 'I feel unsure and nervous. I keep seeing the face of the New Zealand climber, Peter Mulgrew, you know, Hildegard, the man that virtually blew up at 27,000 feet on Makalu, in 1968. He had cerebral oedema, or something. His face on the front of the book *No Place for Men* looked like something from Dante's *Inferno*.'

Hildegard's hand pressed mine firmly.

'You'll be fine,' she whispered. 'I have no doubts about that. You've kept fit all your life. You won't let anybody down. You'll be slow, but strong, just like you were on Kilimanjaro. J.P. will take good care of you – he's very experienced and will gather the finest people alongside you.

Me at the age of eleven, with my younger brother, Alan.

With my director, John-Paul Davidson (J.P.).

'If you had been with Mallory and Irvine, would you have wanted any better grave than the white snow of Everest?' Captain John Noel, at ninety-seven the last survivor of the 1924 expedition, was our link to Mallory.

'We go up to survive, to go to the limit between death and life.' Reinhold Messner gives me advice at his castle in the South Tyrol.

'This house isn't big enough for you and Mount Everest,' my wife, Hildegard, told me. Here we are at home in Bagshot with the canine branch of the family.

Our route from Bhutan across the Tibetan plateau to the North Face . . .

EVEREST

North Col

East Rongbuk Glacier

. . . and on up the East Rongbuk Glacier to the North Col and beyond.

The adventure begins: the 'Toy Train' leaves Siliguri for Darjeeling and, hours later, rounds a breathtaking corner during the happiest day's filming of my life.

The Kingdom of the Thunder Dragon: first steps into Bhutan and, below, our first night's camp. Note the girth.

'Darling Brian. How many times have you told me about that marvellous American climber, David Breashears, and how he would lead the climbing expedition? He's climbed Everest twice, hasn't he? Well then, for goodness sake, what are you worrying about? The best thing you can do is to put on your running shoes and head for them thar hills, with our eagerly awaiting tribe of dogs, and burn some shoe leather.'

I did exactly that, and repeated the exercise four times that day, until I was totally clapped out, and slept like a baby. A few days later I had a phone call that puzzled Hildegard.

'It was the insurance people from the BBC who are arranging the insurance for Everest. They just wanted a few details,' I explained.

Hildegard's eyes widened.

'Insurance people, indeed! I see, you really *are* going!'

As preparations for the expedition took wing, the Chorus of *Henry V* again came to mind:

> Now all the youth of England are on fire,
> And silken dalliance in the wardrobe lies;
> For now sits expectation in the air ...

The wardrobe was certainly progressing splendidly. For this, as usual, I was indebted to Adrian Rigelsford, who through his sister Nicola had arranged for me to attend a clothing exhibition at Olympia, our aim being to find a company who would provide us with the necessary materials for creating the style of the twenties.

A firm on the Isle of Man, Manx Handloom Weavers Ltd, under its director, Bob Jeavons, proved ideal and instantly became committed to the project. They sent me a variety of tweeds, and when I had selected my favourite, they dispatched the cloth post-haste to a renowned tailor in Leeds called Chris Dawes.

Adrian introduced me to a fascinating young lady named Pauline Plumb who enthusiastically demonstrated an impressive new material called Alpinex. Immediately, I gave it an enthusiastic thumbs up, and very soon several one-piece suits like babies' romper suits had been made up in adult sizes.

The plan was for me to wear the twenties clothing as much as I possibly could, and back it up with the most up-to-date gear, which was to be provided by that experienced company, Berghaus, whose managing director, David Udberg, and chairman, Gordon Davidson, bent over backwards to help me. The boots, which were to be tailor-made for me by an Italian expert called Luigi, proved a problem. Luigi is a stocky, normally cheerful man, but at the sight of my feet he despaired: 'Zees right one ees deeformed! What I do? Aye, aye, aye!'

A splendid young man named Stefan Lepowski, of Berghaus, was in charge of the whole kit and caboodle, and he constantly liaised with J.P. As the gear started to arrive and mount up, J.P.'s house started to look like a climbing shop.

Throughout all this, my mind blazed. Could I get fit enough? Would I break down? Would the thickening of my blood to the consistency of glue, up there at extreme altitude, at my age, give me a stroke?

Ah! Just pray, man! Pray! I thought. I'll give it my best shot, and that's that.

Hildegard spurred me on to new efforts, and up hill and down dale I ran, always wearing my sturdy hiking boots to strengthen my feet and ankles. Following Chris Bonington's advice, I varied the exercise by walking quickly across Chobham Common with my rucksack full of weights. Each day I generally ran between ten and fourteen miles, with the occasional marathon thrown in for good measure. Yet amazingly, my weight stayed around fifteen and a half stone, possibly because of my large bones. A local athlete advised me to try two-hundred-yard sprints punctuated by periods of walking. He maintained that I would get fitter, since jogging is only a step up from walking. Amusingly, at the time I thoroughly resented anything that interrupted my training. Of course, I still had to make a living, and this took up a great deal of my time.

For instance, a voice-over for a British Steel advertisement took me to the Saunders & Gordon recording studios in London's West End. In charge of the ad was a charming young man from British Steel named Menno Zigssen. As I looked up he softly began to sing:

Down from Old Mount Herman, on the small Toy Train,
After nine months mugging, back home again,
Teachers are so rosey, children are the same,

Everyone is happy, waiting for the train ...
Ghoom, Sonada, Kurseiong, are all left behind,
Though the journey's very long, I'm sure we do not mind,
When we reach Sealdah, hail it with a shout,
Pan Beeri cigarette, hop the bloomy out ...

'Good God!' I exclaimed. 'That song is about the "Toy Train" that travels backwards and forwards from Siliguri to Darjeeling in India.'

'Yes. You are right,' said Menno. 'And I travelled in my childhood many times to school in Darjeeling, and that is the traditional song of the "Toy Train" that we sang on our journey.'

'But this is a million to one,' I said. 'I mean, me being here with you, who went to school on this unique little train. It's absolutely amazing! You do realize I'm going to Everest in the footsteps of the twenties expeditions, and this is exactly the train they took!'

Menno laughed loudly at this, and begged me to try and get him on the expedition. I was completely nonplussed. This experience and the one in Cyprus, where I found the Everest Restaurant matchbox, made me feel like Pinocchio, with the mountain pulling the strings. Menno then said that he would help in any way he could, and would send on any addresses and phone numbers that might be of help. Such kindness!

The newspapers had now cottoned on to the expedition, and Stephen and the BBC decided that just before leaving we should hold a press conference. People who had read about it came up to me in the street, and shook my hand, wishing me all the best. A taxi-driver shouted, 'Good luck, Brian, me old love. I climbed Snowdon once!'

I was so impatient to start the adventure that I would find myself jumping up and down like a jumping bean, shouting: 'Hallelujah! Hallelujah! Eureka! Open up the Pearly Gates, and let the pilgrim in!'

If anyone had witnessed me running across Chobham Common with the dogs, they would have thought I was stark, staring mad, for now, on these jaunts, I would chatter and laugh to myself incessantly, occasionally breaking into a song, and jigging about like a jack-in-the-box. I would shout out my thanks to God, and the wind and sun and sky! Not forgetting every religion in the world, from Christianity to Buddhism to Islam, from Baha'i to Zoroastrianism, right through to the Sufis and Whirling Dervishes, and even the legendary Masters of Time and Space, the ancient Els, just in case they were still around. I was trembling with happiness and bliss. Aye! Bliss! Bliss! Bliss!

'God in heaven!' I roared. 'Thank you!'

On the hilltop overlooking the common, with model aircraft flying and buzzing around me, I lay on my back panting, my dogs nestled alongside me, licking my ears off. My energies subsided into a sublime stillness. With Surrey's gentle heath cushioning my body, I day-dreamed of Everest – the Turquoise Mountain – thousands of miles away. The snows would be heavy there now, yet soon the west wind would blow, and with the warming of the spring, with luck, we would scale its flanks.

Later, driving home, I fondly remembered all the people who had worked so hard to make it possible.

It was now February 1990, and I was back in Chiswick, walking down the pathway of Margaret and J.P.'s house to attend the first expedition meeting. The prospect of meeting David Breashears and the lads had made sleep almost impossible the night before.

David had ascended Mount Everest twice, and had made several other attempts at it. He filmed the Menlungtse climb for J.P. and is without doubt the finest climbing cameraman in the world. His feats at those great altitudes, carrying cameras and equipment, defy belief. When Bonington made his ascent of Everest in 1985, David followed him a few days later, guiding a gutsy character named Dick Bass to the summit. Bass, at fifty-five, became the oldest man to ascend the mountain. Now, at last, I was about to meet David. Before I could analyse his features, he enfolded me in his arms vigorously and lifted me off my feet with ease.

'I said he was a fit bugger, didn't I, Brian?' shouted J.P.

Quick handshakes were followed by brisk embraces. Then, as climbers do, we each examined the other's legs, biceps and deltoids. In an instant David had spirited himself atop a sturdy camera tripod, balancing his whole body on one hand. It was an impressive performance, and absolutely delighted me. His eyes were joyful, mad, intense and full of an unceasing zest for life. It was almost impossible to decipher their colour, as the passion in them bore the mystery of a prism. I liked him immensely.

He was slim and raw-boned, and his muscles were well defined, with no hint of fat. He was in his early thirties, black-haired and handsome. Debonair is probably the right description for him, for he was quite tall and had a slight look of Anthony Perkins about him.

Our profuse expression of delight at finally meeting set off peals of laughter from the onlookers. They were a merry band themselves: the all-important filming team. In this happy atmosphere, I eagerly took the hand of each of them.

'You realize,' I shouted, 'what we are attempting is stark, raving mad!'

'Well, it helps to be mad!' a voice bellowed through the din.

'I think you're all little boys who will never grow up!' put in Margaret. 'I must warn you all, John-Paul and Brian have been like this for weeks … They're both just a pair of Peter Pans!'

J.P., puffing happily on his cigar, introduced the crew.

'This is David Swan, cameraman … Julian Charrington, assistant cameraman … David Blackham, sound … And the sultry voice you know from the phone belongs to my assistant here, Sandi Scott.'

Their faces were open and friendly, and all expressed their enthusiasm for the expedition. Swan was tall, with a close-cropped beard, a thick head of greying hair and huge, popping eyes. His manner was reserved and gentlemanly, with a surprisingly broad, dashing smile that conveyed both deep humour and a tough nature. I found him rather quixotic.

Charrington was slightly shorter and stocky, and his face was sensitive and strong. His bearing, like Swan's, was rather aristocratic. His speech, likewise, was clear and without accent. Both men were perfect examples of the English gentleman. It was as if they were straight out of the twenties. They were also good friends, which was to prove a bonus during the trials ahead.

Blackham was also stocky. Kind and courteous, he was much more intense than the other two, with his piercing eyes and serious nature constantly probing David Breashears about the difficulties that lay ahead. His determination was reassuring, and he appeared to be quite an experienced climber.

Sandi Scott was a committed professional, with sandy hair as befits her name, and a pretty face.

These four were the nucleus of the team, with other people at the BBC, and in India and Nepal, to come into the picture later.

Buzzing with eagerness, I rushed out to my car and coaxed out of the back a large model of Everest that had been constructed for me by Studio Gallery in Cumbria. With J.P.'s help, we carried it down the path, just managing to avoid scraping off the final pyramid as we squeezed through the door.

David Breashears then outlined the expedition. We sat transfixed as he magicked us through the beauty of Nepal and the sweeping plains of Tibet, to the foothills of Everest itself, skilfully using the model to fill in every detail of the proposed ascent. When he had finished, we rose as one to thank him, for his professionalism and attention to detail were most impressive.

J.P., the BBC and I would film in England, Bhutan and India. When this had been completed, we would join Breashears and his team in Kathmandu and head for Friendship Bridge, which connects Nepal with Tibet, and proceed from there. J.P.'s and Breashears' tasks were totally beyond me; even attempting to understand the intricacies made me recoil in confusion. Borders, visas, passports, ponies, yaks, land-cruisers, lorries, planes, permits, treks, liaison officers, sirdars, cooks, Sherpas, porters, doctors, cameras, low- and high-altitude teams – even listing them makes me feel dizzy. But the two young leaders' keen, disciplined minds handled everything with ease. That year, 1990, there was to be a World Peace Expedition on Everest, bringing together Chinese, Soviet and American climbers. The brochure I received from the USA read:

THE VISION
The Peak: Qomolangma Eeng (Mount Everest) 8,848 metres, 29,028 feet.
The Route: North Col/North East Buttress.
Pioneered by George Mallory ('Because It's There') 1922 & 24.
Expedition Leader: Jim Whittaker, first American to climb Everest (May 1st, 1963). Leader of the first American ascent of K2 (1978).

The Team: Fifteen climbers: five each from the People's Republic of China, the Soviet Union and the United States.

The Goals: Place at least three climbers (one from each nation) together on the summit of the world's highest peak. Televise the accomplishment live by satellite to all three nations, with communication between the summit team and political leaders in China, the Soviet Union and the United States.

Demonstrate to the world that through international co-operation, commitment and team work — the Highest Goals on Earth can be reached: the Summit of Everest, Solutions to Global and Environmental Problems, World Peace.

Our goal is for the first team to make the peak on April 22nd, 1990. The 20th anniversary of Earth Day.

The million-dollar expedition certainly sounded impressive. To get on to the mountain, it was imperative that we be allowed to share the World Peace Climb's permit. Astonishingly, David Breashears achieved this, though it cost a considerable amount for the privilege. What was particularly fortunate was that the international team were attempting Mallory's route. This meant that we could use their doctors and oxygen. The BBC paid about $46,000 for the latter alone. The official meeting was now almost over, and J.P. waved aside suggestions that he should speak, and nodded to me to say a few words. My emotions got the better of me, and I was almost incoherent as my finger pointed to various spots on the mountain: 'Mallory did this ... Somervell ... up here, down there ... a hundred and fifty miles round the Kharta Valley to here, the Lhakpa La ... '

A handsome lady by the name of Audrey Salkeld joined us. She is well known for her wide knowledge of Himalayan literature and history. To have this delightful expert on our team was priceless, for what she doesn't know about Mallory isn't worth knowing. Self-effacing and graceful, she charmed us all.

Now we sauntered down the road for a celebratory lunch. Breashears and I lagged far behind, with arms round each other's shoulders, swopping ideas, fermenting with ambition, and firing on all cylinders. We were suddenly aware that the others had disappeared, and we didn't know where the restaurant was.

'This is rich!' I said. 'If we can't find our way to the restaurant, how are we going to find our way up the East Rongbuk Glacier!'

During the meal I pumped Audrey about her knowledge of Mallory, but most of the conversation around the table was about food. Breashears pulled out a large notebook and started to write down in great detail everybody's culinary preferences.

Later we returned to J.P.'s house, and tried out our first bit of filming. Audrey was the guinea pig, and I played the role of interviewer. After she had departed, and my tasks were also completed for the day, I sat back drowsy and contented in an armchair in the corner and watched the others, unnoticed.

At the far end of the room the camera team compared the merits of a French camera and the German Arriflex. Professionals at work are always good to watch. Their murmurings and appreciative nods about some mechanical feature or other appealed to my childlike curiosity. Breashears' face moved up and down the tripod at speed, and Swan did likewise, their motions fluid and almost poetic. Blackham, sporadically applying woolly-looking headphones to his ears, presented the perfect image of a yeti.

In rapt concentration, sitting at their feet, was Julian. I jerked out of my half sleep. He had a large black bag spread across his open legs, and his dexterous hands were feeling underneath at some protuberance that obviously gave him pleasure.

'I'm unloading the film magazine,' he whispered, smiling. 'The black bag is a darkroom – it keeps out the light … '

'If you say so,' I said. 'But it looks suspicious to me … '

At last, the ritual over, Julian gave a satisfied sigh and smiled contentedly.

Several days later I was in London at a party to celebrate the formation of Galahad Films, the company which was to partner the BBC in making the Everest film. Smiles abounded, champagne corks popped and handshakes broke out everywhere. Stephen Evans was full of energy, J.P. blew smoke rings with satisfaction, Tom Redfern and John Wilson, the other two directors of the company, were rightfully pleased.

Events were now overtaking me, and any spare time I had was taken up with radio and television interviews. But though I appeared relaxed on screen, the old fears had started to manifest themselves again. For the first time since my childhood, I experienced nightmares. Nor were these confined to my sleeping hours. During one attack I found myself roaring down the phone to my agent. He was kindness and light itself all through my tirade, speaking to me gently and trying patiently to calm my histrionics. Afterwards Hildegard took me for a walk and quietened me down.

Tony Anholt, a dear friend of mine, expressed his joy and also his apprehension. Phone calls to my mother and father in Yorkshire were terribly difficult. I think I could fool my mother into thinking that Everest was a large, friendly Ben Nevis, but not my father. My wonderful singing teacher Dorothy Kirkman, who had put so much painstaking work into my musical education, shared with her husband Gill a quiet dread of the mountain. These two friends offered kind reassurance and prayers.

A splendid esoteric society, under the guidance of a certain Lady Allen, arranged prayers and meditation for 30 April, as David Breashears had informed me that this would be roughly the time that we would be making our big push on the mountain. Many people abroad also offered up their prayers, which moved and surprised me.

My brother Alan and his wife Anne managed to put on a brave face, but they were visibly worried and would count the days till my return. It is true to say that none of my friends and family were happy about the trip. Their faces were always sad, and handshakes were held for an unnaturally long time, except of course for Hildegard, who, in her practical, matter-of-fact way, had no doubts that I would get there, put up a good show, finish the planned film and get home in one piece.

Rosalind seemed quiet and relaxed about it all. Whatever private fears she had, she kept to herself, all the time expressing a deep pride and giving me lots of kisses. My old dog, Jessie, knew. Her big, brown eyes never left my face. Throughout this period she followed me everywhere. Sitting at the wheel of the car, I would hear 'scratch, scratch, scratch' on the passenger door. It was no use – I had to take her everywhere with me.

The press conference, with me wearing my twenties clothes, was a complete success, the newspapers proving kind and encouraging.

67

Audrey Salkeld sent me the latest information and theories about Mallory, and wished me good luck. Geoff Arkless, who was unable to come with us, gave me great encouragement and advice. Letters and best wishes continued to flow in and the London taxi-drivers still waved and shouted enthusiastically.

But I've failed to mention one person. Until now I have been reluctant to write about Captain Noel's death. The dear fellow had died at ninety-nine years of age in Romney a few months earlier. I wrote an obituary in the *Independent*, and spoke on the telephone to his daughter Sandra the day after he passed away.

It seemed so cruel that he should go, just when we had at last mounted the expedition. He was so much a part of the whole dream. His enthusiasm and drive was so amazing that I had forgotten how old he was. Why, I even entertained wild thoughts of arranging, somehow, to transport him to Kathmandu, and when we were on Everest, have him fly over. Yet, sitting in my study, I distinctly felt that he was still alive, and embarking on new quests. His wise words came to mind.

'Honey ... Honey ... Take lots of honey ...'

'You must beware ... It is the Land of the Dead.'

'When I saw Everest for the first time, it was so big it filled the frame of my camera ... '

'Don't be intimidated ... Take it step by step.'

As his voice faded away, my eyes focused on the corner of the room. There stood the fur-lined boots that the good captain had used on Everest nearly seventy years ago.

We were now actually filming! Audrey Salkeld's interview had started the ball rolling, and my feet were firmly planted on the Yellow Brick Road as the BBC team whirred their camera into action. Hildegard, perfectly at ease with the camera, delightfully understated the domestic problems and dramas she had had to endure over the years. Rosalind nodded in agreement, and my mother-in-law, in her self-effacing manner, said nothing.

The filming outdoors was rustic and dog-orientated, with Peanut, our tiny white Jack Russell, suitably enthroned in the rucksack on my back. Round and round I ran with Peanut and the other dogs.

Our cottage sits just inside a beautiful, large estate that the owner, a delightful character named Major Spouse, has formed into a trust. His tender care has shaped it into a paradise: small lakes and islands abound, the banks flourish with all manner of wild flowers, giant rhubarb, azaleas, rhododendrons, maple trees and staggering Japanese acers. The waterways contain multitudes of pond life, including great crested and smooth newts, their smooth rhythm only slightly disturbed by the surface coots and wild ducks.

The weather was serene and the backdrop of spring blossom delighted the camerman, Nigel Meakin. Nigel was covering the English filming, while David Swan and company were making ready for abroad. J.P. was in control and in his element.

Up, up, up, past the Russell Hotel ...
Up, up, up, up, to the Heaviside Layer ...

It was strange to find myself again, after eight years, ascending the Heaviside Layer as Old Deuteronomy in *Cats*, at the New London Theatre. Cameron Mackintosh had very kindly agreed to let us shoot this last song of the show for the Everest film. The dramatic ascent on the smoking tyre would be related to our subject matter, but more importantly it showed me at work as an actor, in a show that I greatly loved. I was reminded by J.P. that it was important to show that I was an actor, and that this was the first time a Thespian had been allowed on Everest.

We finished at the theatre in the morning, and by way of contrast began shooting at the Royal Geographical Society in the afternoon. During a break in shooting, a man of medium build in his early forties, with greying beard and vibrant eyes, graciously stepped forward, informing me that he was leading a climb to celebrate the first British ascent of Everest in 1953. This would take place in 1993, forty years on.

'My name is Nick Mason,' he said. 'And I look forward to you being on the climb ... '

With that, he politely excused himself and said he would get in touch, after I had returned from Tibet. I was intrigued and totally flabbergasted by this. Quite apart from Mason's impressive style, after all these years of frustration I was now being offered a *second* expedition!

We were certainly ringing the changes on the filming, for the following day I found myself face to face with the redoubtable Lord Hunt, the famous leader of the historic first ascent of Everest in 1953. As I sat with him in his private chambers in the House of Lords, you would never have thought that my still countenance hid such a blazing mind. I was thrilled out of my skull to meet the graceful man, for his inspired and courageous leadership of that legendary first ascent had moved the world, serving as a mighty clarion call to all lovers of adventure. I found myself remembering what Sir Edmund Hillary had said, after he and Tenzing Norgay had made that momentous climb: 'Wouldn't Mallory have been pleased?'

In the never-ending saga of 'Did Mallory and Irvine climb it?', I always find these words the mark of a fine gentleman with a generous spirit. In the short time available Lord Hunt conveyed to us all that here was a man whose love of spirit and adventure transcended all. To quote his own words: 'There is no height ... no depth ... that the spirit of man, guided by a higher spirit, cannot attain ... '

As I was about to leave, he added, 'It would be quite pointless to get up mountains if there wasn't an element of danger that you might fall off! ... That is the challenge, that is the adventure of the thing!'

The delights of the day were not over. After leaving the House of Lords, I had but a short journey to make to St James's Park. There, to greet me for the piece of filming, was the tall, trim figure of Chris Bonington.

'What's this – a slimmer Blessed?' he laughed.

My drop in weight from sixteen stone to fifteen and a half duly impressed him.

'You've still got plenty of girth! You'll be able to live off it on the mountain!' he added.

Invaluable advice flowed cheerfully from Chris as the camera whirred.

'When I am climbing at great altitude I set myself a target, like ten paces, then I rest and do the same again ... Don't be concerned about your age. On the K2 disaster, for instance, it was the two fifty-year-olds who got down and survived ... You'll find you're not as fast as the younger chaps, but nevertheless, you may find you have more staying power and stamina ... '

That same month, March 1990, I found myself aboard a flight for Milan. Destination: South Tyrol, to meet Reinhold Messner. J.P. had arranged it all; my Sir Galahad was forging ahead at such a pace I hardly had time to draw breath. Bonington had said that, without a doubt, the greatest climber in the world was Messner, and he was perhaps the greatest climber of all time.

Messner was the first man to have climbed all fourteen 8,000-metre (26,250 feet) peaks in the world. He, and another great climber, Peter Habeler, defied all the doom-ridden predictions of the experts, and in 1978 made the first ascent of Everest by the South Col route, without oxygen. If that wasn't enough, Messner climbed the mountain again in 1980, once more without oxygen and this time on his own.

He followed Mallory's route for a while, then veered across the North Face a little lower than Norton and Somervell's line, finally entering the great couloir and heading up from there. This feat is so extraordinary that it has not yet been fully evaluated.

Messner's solo ascent of Everest, and of the equally forbidding Nanga Parbat, required guts and fortitude of the highest order. He had to cope with terrible physical and mental strain. The loneliness must have been like that of Christ's forty days and nights in the wilderness. My admiration for Messner is shared by millions, and now I was going to meet him.

In true knightly fashion, this heroic Siegfried of the mountains lived in a castle, near Merano in the Italian Tyrol. I was going to ask the Master for his advice on how to cope with Everest. Suddenly I felt shy and utterly ridiculous. Me, of all people, meeting such a man. What had I let myself in for? Also, by the sound of it, he wasn't too enthusiastic, for he had only just come back from an epic trek across Antarctica to the South Pole. He was certainly in no mood to talk to a greenhorn like me. He would give me a few minutes, he had said on the phone.

As we drove up to the castle I was beginning to have second thoughts. Higher and higher we went, the grand vista of the mountains all around us. The door was shut and firmly locked, and the forbidding castle, with its Tibetan prayer flag flying in the breeze, echoed to the barking of guard dogs.

J.P. decided, with Sandi alongside him, to look for a side door. I stayed behind, sitting on a rock. Minutes passed by uneventfully, for we were early. Then, gently and smoothly, a car arrived with a solitary figure inside. The door opened and the embodiment of all that was heroic emerged.

The body was long and finely muscled, and the long, tousled brown hair flowed into the full, light-brown beard. The face, striking and noble, at a glance revealed a map of all the trials of this modern adventurer. The experienced, piercing eyes, surrounded by delicate crow's feet and set above high cheek bones, rapidly surveyed our alien car, at the same time taking in the camera crew, who stood transfixed.

Unnoticed and half-hidden, I appeared suddenly alongside Messner and introduced myself. Our eyes met and all was fine. I roared to J.P. that Reinhold had arrived, telling him to make haste. The climber smiled broadly, saying, 'Your voice and personality is perfect for the villain in a film I am going to make in South America ... Pleased to meet you all. Please, let me show you around.'

His manner was calm and gentle as he led us through the portals of the castle. He roared with laughter as we beheld a huge, ten-foot model of a yeti-cum-demon, which guarded the entrance to the courtyard. Here, among trees that he informed us were planted in 1924, the year Mallory died, were his Tibetan mastiffs, which recognized us as friends and licked us accordingly.

Inside, we were privileged to see Messner's private collection of Himalayan rugs, Tibetan *thangkas* (wall hangings), rare masks, pictures of quality, and objects and oriental antiques depicting various deities of the East. The massive wooden beams in the vast room had been carved expertly to match the contents therein. It was a graceful feast for the senses, and one felt instantly the mystery and depth of the collector who had brought this art together.

Reinhold rustled up some delicious coffee in his rather rustic kitchen. Time stood still as we gazed from his windows on the valley below.

'I am fortunate, Brian, to have these mountains so close ... That high one there, I run up and down each day for training ... '

'You do what!' I gasped. It looked about 8,000 feet, and steep.

The time limit Reinhold had originally set for the interview was forgotten as we got on famously. Much to my pride and joy, we even had a little scramble on the rocks together outside.

Fortunately I had read all of his books, and he was visibly surprised when I mentioned some small detail that he had long forgotten. Anyone who imagines that Messner might have suffered brain damage from his two oxygenless ascents of Everest needs his own head examined.

Reinhold's English flows delightfully, without his, for one moment, losing the thread of what he is talking about. It's as if his brain were a house with all the lights on. If he wishes to turn one light off, he does so, diverting its power to some other area. Alert, artistic, imaginative, philosophical and kind, he displays the gifts of a profound visionary.

We had been talking for so long that the sun was beginning to set, and we were in danger of running out of film. I was fully aware of the magic of the encounter as our two silhouettes formed a union of silence. Then quietly he whispered, 'When you are at the base of Everest, the last step is dependent on the first, and the first step is dependent on the last. You are right to be frightened and have nightmares. I was frightened too when I was going there. This teaches you to show respect for the mountain. If you hallucinate, this is healthy also. Because if you are alone, the brain is creating something tangible for you, to help to sustain you so that you will not be alone.

'For instance, up there, my rucksack became my companion. It is a rule with me, that when I arrive at a mountain, if it smells bad, I turn back. If, for any reason, you suspect that something is wrong that day, obey that instinct and come down ... There is always another day.

'On Everest, you must go slowly from the Tibetan plains, at maybe 15,000 feet, to Base Camp at 17,000 feet. There, you stay ten days maybe. See how you feel. Listen to David Breashears, he is an excellent climber. From there, I recommend you go to 19,000 feet, stay a night and come down to Base Camp again. After a further period of rest, try for Camp III at 21,500 feet. Then after a night's rest, go for the North Col, 23,150 feet. Afterwards, return all the way back to Base Camp again. Then stay there for eight days of rest and food. Then, after this ... go for it!'

Back home in Bagshot, I imparted the excitement of the meeting to Hildegard. She showed keen interest, yet her resigned face said it all: I was now close to going.

I phoned my parents, telling them I would send a message to them via the John Dunn Show on Radio Two. A few days later, this done, I returned home, scarcely knowing what time of day it was. As I sat by my koi pond, with my old dog Jessie licking my bare feet, the inside of my head felt like a vacuum.

That evening I checked my bags that I had packed weeks before. Adrian Rigelsford was staying with us to help me on my way. Late at night we walked with the dogs through Major Spouse's estate, two flat-footed compañeros, me ahead as always, the Mole immediately behind, in perfect unison. The dogs were happy chasing foxes, and Adrian was happy talking about yetis.

I slept fleetingly that night. Day dawned, and it was time to get ready. It was 21 March 1990. There I was at last, kitted out with the twenties gear that Adrian had acquired for me: Homburg, pith helmet, pipe, tobacco, white scarf, and period torch and rucksack. He was a real trouper.

My walking boots were from the army stores, and David Breas-hears had provided high-quality umbrellas for all the members of the expedition. My tweed jacket and plus-fours fitted perfectly, and I rang Manx Handloom Weavers to thank them. All in all, I resembled General Bruce, rather than Mallory.

'Oh, Brian! You look like the perfect gentleman! I shan't have a minute's peace till you get back!' my mother-in-law said tearfully.

I kissed her, and all the animals, and Hildegard, Rosalind and Adrian accompanied me to Heathrow. In the car, Hildegard started to chuckle, and then laughed out loud.

'You really are going! After all this time! I never remotely thought it would happen. It's hard to conceive that you'll be on Everest in a few weeks' time!'

We all laughed. It was absolutely ridiculous!

At the airport I got into a mild panic.

'Where's J.P.? ... Where is he, eh? ... Can you see him?'

This was quite silly, because I was a very experienced traveller, but I felt as if I'd never flown before. Also, J.P. had been looking after me as if I were a little baby. Hildegard smiled and reassured me that we were very early, and not to worry. Of course, she and the others were right: there was plenty of time. An hour later, all three of them produced a smiling J.P. from the swelling crowds.

'Oh, we're very early ... Plenty of time,' said my Sir Galahad. 'I've been here for ages with the camera crew, getting all our equipment through. All in order, everything's fine.'

J.P.'s manner amused Hildegard no end.

'I hear Margaret's gone ahead to India, to arrange the filming schedule there. She seems quite a lady!' she said.

J.P. smiled.

'Well, it does help having one's wife as the assistant producer. I'm just glad that I could borrow her from *Newsnight*. She's much in demand.'

'Also,' I added, 'it means I won't be able to swear as much.'

'Just as well,' popped in Hildegard. 'A certain amount of purity won't go amiss.'

Our banter came to an abrupt end as J.P. suggested we go through to the departure lounge, as he had lots of telephone calls to make. The farewells were short and poignant, and my loving threesome were no longer there.

'Got your passport, General?' J.P. asked.

The General Bruce tag was already sticking.

J.P. headed for the phones, shouting, 'Bob Harrison, the film operation manager, has been fantastic! Without him it all would have been impossible!'

Phone calls concluded, we both relaxed with a coffee, boyish grins on our faces. Everything else was a blur, until I found myself sitting alongside J.P. in the plane. We just couldn't stop giggling.

Julian Charrington, the assistant cameraman, sat across the aisle, directly in front of the film screen. He appeared totally clapped out, but his sleepy face managed a friendly smile before he put his eye shades on to keep out the light and promptly fell asleep.

For me, planes are always exciting. I love the manoeuvring into position, and the final, dramatic take-off. Today it was even more exciting than usual, for it marked the start of our journey to Everest.

Julian was not asleep after all, and he shook our hands with a hearty, 'Good luck to you both on this auspicious occasion!'

'Good luck to you too, Julian!' we echoed back, and at once the two Davids, Swan and Blackham, with wide, flashing smiles, were proffering their hands too. Amid much hugging and backslapping, we were gently instructed to return to our seats and strap ourselves in.

Almost immediately, the engine throttled, the plane moved forward and we were off.

4

The Kingdom of the
Thunder Dragon

My head was swimming. India! The land of tropical jungles, sandy plains, hidden mystical valleys, vast rivers, ancient temples, mild-mannered elephants, tigers, exotic birds and butterfies, the Taj Mahal, Rudyard Kipling, holy men and, of course, the towering mountains of the Himalayas. What prospects, what adventures!

But even the wonders of India would have to wait. Within an hour or so of landing in Delhi, we would be heading for Paro, in Bhutan, the hidden Kingdom of the Thunder Dragon. I had never been to the Far East before, and the prospect of visiting this small, mysterious country totally intrigued me. J.P., too, was thrilled to be visiting once again this magical land and its Buddhist Emperor.

My brain buzzed with J.P.'s stories, and Joe Gargery's words from Dickens's *Great Expectations* popped into my head: 'Oh, what larks, eh, Pip? ... What larks!'

In fact, the acting side in both of us came out. I was surprised to hear that J.P. had studied drama in Bristol, like myself, and had done a great deal of acting, particularly in Europe. Finally, his decision to be a film director won out over all his other ambitions. We passed the hours swopping stories about the theatre. We were a couple of kids in Seventh Heaven.

When we landed at Delhi at eight the following morning, every-thing appeared vacant and empty. The large marble walls and floors of the airport were being brushed by a solitary Indian, who stopped dead in his tracks when he spotted my twenties outfit.

Even in so barren an environment, there was no mistaking the rich aroma of India. My nose followed a straight course to the transit lounge, and the smell of Indian tea and coffee.

'Look! ... Look!' said a familiar female voice. 'It's Brian ... Hello, Brian! ... Over here!'

Lo and behold, there was Margaret, her pretty face and blonde hair catching the morning light, and alongside her a pretty, slim young Indian lady by the name of Shenni Italia, from the expedition's Delhi office. Shenni was to stay in Delhi to arrange our filming there.

There they were, calm, totally organized and with tickets in hand for our journey to Darjeeling, and then Dharamsala, where the Dalai Lama was to give us an audience.

'You do look very English, Brian,' they cooed. 'Terribly British Raj, what! ... Oh, I say!'

After a coffee, my impatience to see India propelled me somewhat out of bounds, but before fastidious officials ordered me back I managed to see distant trees and waterways seductively beckoning in the distance.

'Come on, Brian,' chided Margaret. 'You'll have plenty of time for India, after Bhutan. We need your muscles for help, loading the camera gear.'

I hadn't realized until then how much actors take for granted. Usually, when filming abroad, we arrive at the hotel in good time and await the call to appear on the set. Here, working on a documentary, it was entirely different: we were all expected to muck in. This I found refreshing, and great fun.

How delighted it was to see the little jet that would carry us to Paro. Our departure time would be 11.20, arriving in Bhutan at 13.55. It was almost like having our own, private, executive plane. Apparently this was the only one in the entire fleet of Bhutan's Druk Air. Also, it was reassuring to learn that here was a kingdom, in this hi-tech world, that was still comparatively unknown, for no European had ever set foot in the eastern part of Bhutan.

The flight was fabulous, and reminded me of the film of Ronald Colman on board his plane, heading for the 'Lost Horizon'. Everything felt intimate and near, as we thrilled to the sight of beautiful wooded valleys and impressive mountains. If you've ever experienced the Big Dipper at a funfair, this is exactly what it felt like as we came in to land at Paro. The tiny plane banked and wove its way through the labyrinth of valleys, finally straightening up and heading for the runway, where it abruptly plunged down, making the heart skip a beat.

'Best flight I've ever known!' I shouted.

David Swan smiled boyishly, and Julian and David Blackham applauded as if at a concert.

Of course, J.P. had been to Paro before, and his description of the country matched the way we felt. The peace was something I had never experienced in any other country before. All the noise of the twentieth century evaporated from my mind, as pop, pop, pop, my ears cleared. The tales of farmers, in the quiet of the night, hearing the sound of the earth spinning on its axis, seemed more than possible here. We could also feel something else alive in the atmosphere, that even transcended the calm; it was a feeling of happiness.

It was patently obvious, when we met the customs men in the tiny hut that served as an airport, that their natures dissolved the artificial aura that surrounds us, opening up feelings of innocence and trust. My appearance created great merriment, and they found it incredible that I was eventually going to Everest. They giggled and laughed, and when, by an effort of will, some semblance of order was achieved, they kindly hoped I would get to Base Camp.

Once through customs, we began to take in the breathtaking scenery. What earth-shattering Titan conceived the mighty building, Paro Dzong, which dominates the far end of the valley? Beyond, far, far away, the mighty mountains soared. Deeper in that range, hidden from view, was the mighty, sacred Chomolhari, at 24,029 feet.

But now it was all hands on deck, as we loaded up the much-used Landrovers and headed for the hotel. Round and round the winding roads we went, with windows open, taking in the pure air. The roadsides, green fields and farms contained masses of flowers; primulas, orchises, fritillaries, anemones and myriad ranunculi danced and dazzled our senses. The midday sun poured its welcome on us, lighting up the snow-capped mountains that overlooked the luxurious valley, with its pretty, terraced rice fields.

'My, oh my!' I said, gripping J.P.'s shoulders, and giving Margaret a kiss. 'Thank you for making this possible.'

Then we arrived at the Mothithang Hotel, which was so massive and impressively Bhutanese that one felt that the King himself must live there.

Bhutan, I understand, allows only 2,500 tourists in a year, thus protecting itself from the dubious influences of the West. The small tourist industry is mainly based on trekking expeditions, and so you can appreciate the country's beauty only by bold endeavour. It is a rugged land, and to get around it a certain standard of fitness is called for.

It was early in the season, and therefore not economical to heat the hotel. So, at 7,000 feet, it was quite chilly, although this was more than compensated for by the warmth and kindness of the staff. Gentle bows and smiles greeted our humble requests, as the Bhutanese, with their captivating almond eyes, moved all heaven and Bhutan to make our stay memorable. Their delightful amusement at my twenties garb ensured ceaseless laughter throughout the majestic building.

Each of us was given a spacious wooden cabin outside, a kind of Bhutanese Swiss chalet. The cold did penetrate, but we all had marvellous thermal gear, so it didn't pose any problems. I adored my Alpinex baby suit, and with my twenties gear over it I was as warm as toast. In bed it kept any damp out. This reassuring garment, plus a small electric heater and atmospheric candles placed around the room, put me in a state of nirvana.

We all congregated that evening in the large dining room upstairs in the hotel. The food was gorgeously hot and hit the spot: rampantly hot chillies and curried beef. There was a great local beer too, as thumping as Barnsley bitter, called Mohan Meakin. We were confronted with a sweet dilemma, for three of our party were called David. David Breashears, of course, was in Kathmandu, organizing the full Everest expedition. In his absence J.P. had elected to call him 'Daphne' – not quite the name I would have suggested for such a butch guy. David Blackham became 'Blackie', and David Swan, 'Swanee', after the river.

'Thank God you don't have to select a name for me!' laughed Julian Charrington, who is affectionately known simply as 'Jules'.

His jolly outburst was immediately seized on by me.

'Excuse me, Julian, for being personal, but some little bird whispered to me that the ladies find you rather irresistible. In fact, and I'm sure it's a gross exaggeration, some people say that you'd shag anything that moves!'

Everybody exploded with laughter, but Julian, who is such a lovely chap, took it all in his stride, maintaining in a gentlemanly manner that this was not the case, and that his sexual exploits in no way departed from the norm. It was this definition of the 'norm' that was hard to pin down, and more laughter broke out when I recommended that we split the difference and call him the 'Shagger'. Julian has a rather aristocratic bearing, and with great reluctance, permitting himself only the smallest of smiles, conceded. 'Oh! ... If you must!'

Margaret, grinning from ear to ear, loved it all. If she had thought that J.P. and myself were Peter Pans, then she was certainly Tinkerbell, with her tinkling laugh. But she was very much in charge with J.P. and constantly kept all of us in order, particularly me. Therefore she was known as 'Boss Cat', but this was to change when we got to Darjeeling.

J.P. was forever dealing with chitties, and so I named him the 'Chitty Yeti'. All, in unison, dubbed me 'Big Yeti', and, to sound like T. S. Eliot, 'the naming of names' was completed.

During our merriment, a small, slim, strong Bhutanese named Kimsun, our guide for the trek to Chomolhari, introduced himself. His almond-shaped eyes and refined cheek bones quivered with sensitivity and fun. Like the hotel staff, he found me hilarious. I felt at liberty to touch his person, and prodded his stomach with my finger, tickling him no end, at the same time asking where he kept the yetis.

'No yetis, sir,' he giggled.

'I don't believe that!' I insisted, tickling him more. 'Not even one, teeny-weeny one?'

'There is no yeti, sir ... Only, maybe you!'

'Me?' I roared. 'You think I am yeti? After expedition I think I maybe eat you!'

Kimsun now giggled uncontrollably.

'Anything to please, sir! ... Just do not tickle any more.'

Late that evening, in the pitch dark of my cabin, I lit my candles. Outside several gentle, large, labrador-like dogs hovered around.

They belonged to the hotel and were very friendly, making me think of my dogs at home, so I fed them lots of my biscuits and chocolate.

The next day was a semi-rest day, as J.P. and Margaret still had a great deal to organize, what with telexes to London and complicated phone calls to India and Nepal. As we were completely in the wilderness, trying to get through to other countries could be frustrating.

Margaret and J.P. worked together beautifully as a team. Periodically, like the Indian love call, Margaret's voice would echo round the building or the surrounding countryside.

'John-Paul? ... John-Paul? ... Where are you?'

'Here, Mags,' J.P.'s practical-sounding voice would drift back. 'By the phone at reception.'

We were at 7,000 feet, and J.P. very wisely instructed us to take it easy. Blackie, Swanee and Jules welcomed the pause, as they had a great deal of equipment to check. I took the opportunity to descend the valley and explore the hills, always keen to use any chance to exercise. Near the end of the afternoon, I came back and went on a little way higher than the hotel. Even at 7,000 feet, you could certainly feel the altitude.

It was a rather cloudy day, and quite cold; mists were beginning to sweep down from the mountains. Lammergeyers (large vultures) and eagles soaring majestically on the warmer air currents became ghostly spectres as they finally disappeared out of sight. My mind, too, soared down that valley beyond the colossal Paro Dzong: on, on, racing past the distant peaks to far-away Chomolhari, and then not resting there but speeding 200 miles further to Everest itself. Amazingly, we were that close to the mountain.

My eyes returned again to my immediate surroundings. What a blissful land! I thought. How beautiful this planet Earth is.

At dinner that night J.P. announced that we would start our filming the next day. Our objective was a leisurely ascent up the valley to 10,000 feet, to the Takstang Monastery. We were all quietly delighted about the news, and eagerly looked forward to it. The purpose of the whole Bhutan visit and the Chomolhari trek was to film, as closely as possible, where Mallory and his companions went in 1921. The line across country that we would be following would be parallel with his route, and only a few miles from it.

During coffee in the lounge, Blackie was a little concerned that we were not practising any climbing techniques. We all shrugged our shoulders, murmuring that David Breashears would put us through our paces when we were near Everest. Blackie remained unconvinced and urged us to consider some practice abseiling from the hotel roof. There was a long silence, broken by me.

'Bloody hell, Blackie. If I got up there, with my weight, I'd go straight through the bloody roof. Anyway, I can't stand heights!'

The following morning we meandered gently up the opposite side of the valley towards the monastery. A light breeze blew away our early morning sleepiness, and the sun shone brightly in a clear sky. We took our time, filming at our leisure. Several little paths that had clearly been used over the centuries led upwards towards the purple haze of the mountains.

Kimsun was our faithful guide, methodically organizing his porters and grinning infectiously if I threatened to tickle him. There are times when walking in the countryside, when the air is so deliciously intoxicating that the cells of the brain hum with rare delight. This was happening now, as I took in the panorama of smiling, happy ladies in their brightly coloured dresses.

'Tashidelek, tashidelek! How are you?' They greeted me, smiling and nodding all the while.

All around us spread picturesque terraced rice fields and almond trees. What a Garden of Eden! Trees, breezes, blossoms, fields, rocks, clear streams, mountains and hundreds and hundreds of white prayer flags, set on poles between five and ten feet high, that fluttered like clouds of cabbage white butterflies everywhere. Prayers in praise of Buddha vibrated from these flags; cascading down the hillsides, they sent their tremulous offerings throughout the world for the good of mankind.

Our hearts opened like the flowers around us, and received the blessings of the sacred one. Swanee smiled handsomely, Blackie's eyes lost some of their intensity, Jules sighed contentedly, and J.P. and Margaret held hands in childlike harmony. As for me, I had Kimsun.

'Tell me, O unbeliever in yetis, about the monastery above us,' I beseeched him.

Kimsun's face instantly became serious as he explained: 'That's Taktsang. It means Tiger's Den. In the eighth century, Guru Rinpoche, the Second Buddha, mounted on a flying tiger, landed here, to bring Buddhism to Bhutan. It's a very holy place. Pilgrims come from all over the country to worship here.'

Our guide's melodious voice harmonized perfectly with the surroundings, as we gained height appreciably, stopping occasionally to film a white *chorten,* a dome built to keep demons underground, with its multi-coloured prayer wheels turning in the gentle flow of a flashing stream.

I'm sure that we all at times get so fed up with bureaucracy and the whole lousy rat race that we yearn deeply for the peace and solitude of some kind of retreat. Taktsang Monastery, of all the places I have seen, embodies perfectly that dream. There it nestles, at 10,000 feet, perched securely in the mountainside. There are no discernible pathways, so what a colossal effort must have been required to carry up the materials to build such an impressive structure. What a labour of love!

Two hours later we managed to get a little above the monastery and view it more closely. The walls were white, with light-brown windows, and the two-tier roof was a subtle red. A riot of flowered creepers embraced the walls, and as we entered the tiny courtyard we spied a further building beyond, beneath a huge overhanging rock.

This was the climax of filming for the day. Here, in my pith helmet and tweeds, I attempted to light my pipe, but my efforts proved useless, as I don't smoke. J.P. gently took the pipe and lit it for me. The camera rolled and I puffed away as if I'd smoked all my life. Then J.P. quietly said cut, and after the necessary checks by the crew, we sat down, content to have experienced a blissful day. A little later a perfumed breeze wafted up the faintest sound of worshippers chanting, as we drank tea and ate biscuits in a wooden building 200 feet lower.

As if anticipating my fantasies of a lost horizon, J.P. stood before me with a small Buddhist bell from the monastery. It consisted of two round pieces of metal, connected by a cord, which he energetically clashed together with a broad grin. We all smiled as the delightful sound went on and on and on, evoking an age-old memory dear to all our souls.

The next day, with droves of ponies and their colourful min-
ders, we set off on the first real stage of our trek. This was my very
first Himalayan expedition, and I was so excited that I raced
around like a Chinese firecracker, not forgetting, of course, to
tickle and hinder the much preoccupied Kimsun.

The weather was great, and even the majestic ruins of the
Drugyel Dzong appeared to be grinning. With my tweeds and
umbrella, I was the incarnation of every British explorer you could
think of, from Scott of the Antarctic, Shackleton, Shipton, Noel,
Kellas, to Speke, Sir Richard Burton and all the rest. Yes, I was all
of them, but particularly Professor Challenger, from Sir Arthur
Conan Doyle's novel *The Lost World*.

'We might meet carnivorous monsters, eh, Kimsun?'

'What, sir?'

'Man-eating yetis!' I roared.

'No, sir … No, sir,' Kimsun giggled. 'No yetis, only you!'

The laughter grew louder as I gave J.P. a great smacking kiss on
the cheeks. The Bhutanese loved this. Swanee and Jules broke into
the occasional smile, but they were far more concerned about the
camera and equipment, rapidly making last-minute checks that
everything was there.

If I was Professor Challenger, then Blackie looked like Messner,
Bonington and Berghaus rolled into one. The previous day, I had
noticed that he appeared to be dressed for a winter ascent of Zero
Gully on Ben Nevis. Now, in his high climbing boots and high-
altitude gear, plus ice axe, he looked ready for an assault on the
Eiger's North Face. Like the Scouts, he felt that one must be
prepared. Though the weather would be chilly on this first part of
the trek, there was no indication that we would encounter severe
conditions. Still, Blackie was as happy as a sandboy and ready for
the off. When he, Swanee and Jules were in position, J.P. shouted
'Action!', and we were off! Destination: Chomolhari, the White
Goddess, the Glass Mountain, that Mallory so passionately
wanted to have a crack at. Chomolhari was the mighty watch-
tower that showed the way to Everest. How tantalizingly close we
now were to the great mountain.

We had eight hours of walking in front of us. Besides running
roughly parallel to Mallory's reconnaissance route, this trek was

ideal for getting us fit and acclimatized. I was careful not to put too much weight in my rucksack, loading most of my gear on the ponies' backs. It was a simple and sensible precaution, for if I pulled a muscle, it would jeopardize the whole film, which would hardly please the BBC and the investors. I also needed sometimes to sprint ahead, or dash down a ravine, as J.P. discovered another shot. Never did a man have so much fun.

The rhododendrons had not yet opened on the trail, but there were masses of small flowers everywhere. The weather fluctuated between blazing sunshine one minute and sudden downpours of rain the next, and even occasional snow. Maybe Blackie was right about the weather after all; it certainly had all the vigour and vibrancy of spring.

Margaret was going very well, and working hard. She appeared very fit to me, as did J.P. The camera boys were carrying quite a lot of heavy gear, which was tough going. J.P. advised that they should take their time but get used to carrying it all right from the beginning, as they would be called upon to hump quite heavy gear on Everest. I would say that they were carrying forty pounds or more. Margaret and J.P. were also each humping this considerable weight. And yet everyone appeared to be performing splendidly, and it was a cheerful ascent. The climb to the monastery had taken us to 10,000 feet, but now we were at about 11,000 feet, and feeling it. Our first night was to be spent at an army camp at almost 12,000 feet.

Sometimes we would stop filming for half an hour or so, and get on with the task of covering some distance, otherwise we would fall so far behind that darkness would be upon us. My pace was slow but sure, and inside I felt that I was doing well, even though everybody seemed to be faster than me.

Now and again I would round a corner and be startled as Jules appeared from nowhere and staggered across my path like a drunkard, colliding with me. Immediately, he was courtesy itself and would apologize sweetly. Swanee, all the while, gritted his teeth and drove on. He possessed a graceful rhythm that was quite beautiful to watch, whereas Jules tended to power on with his head down. Despite Jules's concentrated efforts, he was still able to chat constantly with Swanee.

Margaret walked nice and upright, and I was looking forward to seeing her on Everest. Would she become more like the Hunchback of Notre Dame, as she had on Kilimanjaro? J.P. bounced up and down the pathway like a yo-yo; a hard man, it seemed to me, to live with uphill. Blackie worried me — he was very fit and had done quite a bit of climbing, but I thought he was going much too fast with that weight. He would rest for a while, then suddenly shoot past us at great speed. Towards evening, when we were close to our camp, he pulled up abruptly. It appeared that something was seriously wrong with his leg.

Walking slowly alongside him, I helped Blackie into the camp. His knee didn't look too good at all; it was badly swollen. J.P. looked none too happy about it, for if the injury prevented Blackie from going on, we would be minus our sound recordist, which would mean that Margaret and also probably J.P., on top of their other responsibilities, would have to do it.

For the moment, rest was the only hope for the poor fellow. He was given some painkillers, and his knee was swathed in bandages and tape. With a bit of luck, the swelling would subside, and we would soon enjoy again his kindly disposition and Messner-inspired outfit. He gave us all a gutsy wave, and we quickly recovered our good spirits.

'We'd have been on our guard anyway,' I whispered to Kimsun. 'For we're getting deeper into yeti territory ... '

'No, no! Please, sir!' giggled Kimsun. 'There is no yeti ... Only you, and Bhutan Mist, our very own whisky.'

I'm not much of a drinker, but I knocked back a glass toasting Kimsun and his merry men, and all red female yetis with big tits. After another glass, I understood why it was called mist. This was the stuff all right. What service we were getting! Bhutan Mist plus a roaring fire, tents, sleeping bags with hot-water bottles, tables and chairs, delightful company, mouth-watering food cooking away perfectly in the pots, and a starry night that seemed to reveal the secrets of a dancing galaxy. The whisky came in glassfuls, as the Milky Way drew ever closer, finally resting on Margaret and J.P.'s heads. I loved them! I loved the world! We laughed and kissed and ate to our hearts' content.

The biggest appetite was Swanee's, with Jules not far behind. In manner profound and dignified, they ever so graciously asked for more, like Oliver Twist, and then set about stuffing their faces.

We were all jovial and out of our minds. Even Blackie, from the open flap of his tent, displayed a happy red face, visibly enjoying the effects of the mist. I burst into song, in a Scots accent.

We're off to the camp in the country. Hurray! Hurray!
We're off to the camp in the country. Hurray!
Irish stew for dinner, apple pie for tea,
Roly Poly down yer belly,
Hip, hip, hip, hip, Hurray!

The night enclosed us with its soothing velvet darkness, and from every tent came tiny 'Good nights' from a happy team of trekkers. I ended the evening by shouting out, from the warmth of my sleeping bag, 'Kimsun, are you sure there are no yetis?'

'No, no, no, sir! Only you!'

The following morning I was woken by a rattle, rattle, rattle, zip, zip, zip. The flap of my tent was open, and a grinning porter with a hot bowl of water presented himself.

'Good morning, sir ... Breakfast ready soon.'

Washed and refreshed, I made my way over to the food. There was quite a selection: delicious fresh bread and marmalade, porridge and eggs and wonderful tea, too! We all felt totally at home and completely spoilt. J.P. was endeavouring to find ways of grinding a tin of coffee beans from his Fortnum and Mason hamper. It was that famous store that had supplied luxurious hampers for the Everest expeditions of the twenties. Showing great initiative, J.P. had persuaded them to renew the tradition with us.

In the midst of this scrumptious breakfast, Blackie made his appearance, looking positively lousy. The knee showed no signs of improvement, and he was obviously in pain. Naturally he was also terribly disappointed that he would have to return to London. Despite this, he immediately set about teaching Margaret and J.P. all the complexities of the sound machine. It was obvious that Margaret and J.P.'s BBC training and knowledge of all aspects of technical equipment was sound, yet they had barely half an hour to understand the subtleties of the new stereo mikes and the DAT recorder. Eventually, they appeared to get the hang of it, and once the ponies were loaded it was time to depart.

Accompanied by a porter, and with a good supply of painkillers and bandages, Blackie hobbled miserably out of sight, his dream of Everest in ruins. As we were soon to find out, it was to be 'one of those days'. Happy with life and breezy of foot, I walked nonchalantly up the pathway a hundred yards towards the first shot of the day. The trees and rhododendrons started to thin out, and I found myself in a sunny clearing. To my right, I could discern the camera crew and J.P., who had assumed the role of director and sound man.

It was a perfect day, and here in the valley, I could see for miles. The huge grey-blue mountains stretched for mile upon mile, *ad infinitum*. It was heavenly!

Displaying all the finesse of the true English gentleman, I had just moved smoothly past the camera towards my next objective, when J.P. said quietly, 'Hold it, hold it, Brian ... '

Swanee grimaced slightly and fiddled with the camera.

'Something sparked!' added Jules.

Smoke started to pour out of the base of the camera. Of course, my knowledge of acting would blow the minds of alien civilizations beyond the far reaches of our galaxy. And my amazingly profound philosophy of life is deeper than the Mariana Trench in the Sea of Japan. But I know nothing about cameras. There, in sunny Bhutan, in the middle of nowhere, the cream of German camera technology, the Arriflex, had clapped out. Even to attempt to explain what had happened would pickle my brain. I'm sure the very thought of it would have forced Fritz Lang's robot in *Metropolis* to unscrew her arse with boredom!

There we were, ready to blaze our way to the beckoning Godlike experiences of extreme altitude, to follow in the footsteps of our heroes, and some Düsseldorf dickhead had apparently put the wrong wires together.

I cannot tell you how frustrated we all were. Our two other Arriflex cameras were in Kathmandu with David Breashears, awaiting the Everest expedition. J.P. managed to catch the limping Blackie, who was waiting for a pony to take him down. The spare circuit board that we needed had been left behind, at the Mothithang Hotel. When Blackie got there, he could locate it and a runner — rather reminiscent for me of the old days — would bring it up to us. It was going to take three days for the runner to reach us, as we had to keep to our schedule and keep going up. We felt that any part of the trek we had not filmed could be done on the way down.

Poor Swanee, contorted with frustration, eyed the mouth-watering shots before him. But we all agreed that there was nothing to do but accept it, and use the time available to walk easily and acclimatize.

Most directors would have been out of their tree, but J.P., my Sir Galahad, was made of calmer, sterner stuff. On receiving all this bad news, he simply emitted a teeny-weeny squeak of disappointment – an example to every ranting fifteen-stone yeti.

We were soon a merry band again, for J.P., in his infinite wisdom, had brought a large Sony Super Video 8 camera with him, and he filmed me freely at every opportunity. On explicit orders from on high, that is, from Alan Yentob, BBC2's Programme Controller, I was always to watch my p's and q's on camera. 'No Swearing' was the order of the day. If I felt tempted, I should say the word 'Yentob', and then good taste would be assured.

This did not strictly apply to J.P.'s camera work. One shot would be for real, and on the other we could say what the hell we liked. This made for a mixed bag of footage. To pursue my dedication to Mallory and his companions has been my life's ambition, yet I couldn't resist, in this relaxed atmosphere, having some fun at their expense. I am quite sure they would have approved, most certainly General Bruce, nicknamed 'Bruiser' by his friends, for he was renowned for his colourful expletives. My frightful stories of the rampant, raging sexual habits of the members of the twenties expeditions and their doings with all manner of yetis, delighted my enthusiastic cameraman.

That evening, at Camp II, at about 12,500 feet, the yeti theme took wing, what with the Bhutan Mist and Mohan Meakin beer, combined with the goodies from the Fortnum's hamper. A good time was had by all.

The fire burned merrily, and we all, from East and West alike, enjoyed its lively flames and periodic firework displays. Outside this small, civilized circle of fire, friends and tents, the forest loomed large and forbidding. Snow was now falling quite heavily, the flakes melting the instant they hit the fire, creating a constant, sinister hissing sound that sparked off tales of the Abominable Snowman.

Jigme, large and cheerful, was in charge of supervising the whole expedition. In the film world he is known as the 'Bhutan Fixer'. We had heard, and he confirmed it, that a certain lady from Bhumtang, in the far eastern part of the country, had been living with a yeti for two years. Apparently she had been very happy with our furry friend. The relationship ended when she was discovered by a crowd of villagers, drinking water from a river, accompanied by the yeti. The villagers made a great commotion and frightened the creature, who immediately ran for the shelter of the woods. Thus the lady was rescued, but she was none too happy about it.

For the first few days she was uncommunicative, but then she began to speak in monosyllables and broken sentences. Eventually her normal speech returned. So famous did she become that the King of Bhutan demanded to see her.

Now the King is a Buddhist, and an evolved man. His dedication to truth is absolute, and he is much loved and totally trusted by his people. All the empty words and platitudes that fall trippingly from the lips of our Western political leaders are totally alien to him. His sole objective for his people is happiness.

To return to the story, the good lady was questioned intimately by the King, with a doctor in attendance. She explained she had been walking from one village to another, and had been abducted by the yeti. He was about six and a half feet tall and covered in black hair, except for his face. He was tremendously strong, and this was confirmed when with ease he carried her in his arms for mile upon mile. The skin on his face was dark, and his nose flat. His eyes were bright blue. The forehead was dome-shaped, with full, strong hair above it.

The jaw, she maintained, was pronounced. He spoke no language as such, but emitted a wide variety of sounds. His arms were long and powerfully muscled. His legs were normal in length and he walked upright. She said he was a hairy man, and *not* an ape. He insisted on moving each day from one location to the next, and they frequently lived in caves. The woman said that they lived on roots and berries, and that he was not a flesh eater. As for sex, she explained that he used the missionary position, and on occasion did it doggy fashion. Above all, she said, he had always been protective and gentle.

On completing the story, Jigme said he felt that it was completely true. More stories were offered up by all and sundry, and it all ended in the usual codswallop and laughter. For the umpteenth time, my finger prodded into Kimsun's tummy, as I asked him if the yeti existed. Just as he was about to give me the usual answer, one of the porters stepped forward, with mind and face set and deadly serious. He was a large man, and looked like Lon Chaney on a bad night. Reluctantly, and with great courage, he growled out with a voice full of iron filings,

'There is a yak yeti ... '

'A what?' I gently asked.

'A yak yeti,' he repeated. 'It attacks and eats yaks, and has plenty red hair on its head.'

On hearing this, Kimsun fell off his log, holding his stomach. He seemed in danger of a heart attack, as his normally high-pitched laughter ascended even higher into the realms of the banshee. He rolled all over the place, quite incapable of controlling himself. The Lon Chaney character found this not at all amusing. He was mortified, rooted to the spot. Immediately, I stood up and pulled him forward, desperately trying not to join in with Kimsun's laughter, which was undeniably infectious.

'He must be a big yeti to kill a yak!' I said.

'Oh, yes,' replied the serious gentleman. 'He has big teeth, which he bites yak with ... He big as two yaks ... He much strong and crush yak's head.'

By now it seemed that most of the porters were in a state of hysterical collapse, as they desperately hugged one another, in the hope that their partner might relieve the pain that the continuous laughter gave them. But I was not about to lose my new-found star. I questioned him further, and his answers continued to cause the heaving mass of porters more unbearable glee. If this was not enough, another shadowy figure stepped forward, as pissed as a newt.

'There is a horse yeti, too,' he said unsteadily.

Kimsun, lying on his back, looked like a frog with its four legs sticking stiffly up in the air, as if he had rigor mortis. The only way you knew he was alive was by the tiny tummy, which convulsed in and out as the air forced a sound from his vocal chords like an expired parrot.

The rest of the porters, who had not reached this stage, simply bent over double or rolled on the floor from side to side. In his prostrate position Kimsun, in paralytic supplication, desperately entreated me to stop. I at once did so, though I was unable to resist periodically starting it all up again. J.P. had been videoing most of this throughout the evening, joining in the lovely nonsense at any opportunity.

From that day on we both regarded everybody and everything as some form of yeti. It was becoming an impressive list. Swanee, as befitted his appetite, had become the 'Stuff Your Face Yeti', and now we had the 'Yak Yeti' and the equally impressive 'Horse Yeti'. The disease was spreading, as J.P. and I would discuss the merits of the 'Lesser Spotted Yeti', the 'Polka Dot Yeti', the 'Mouse' and 'Carrot' Yeti, and the most dreaded yeti of all, the terrifying 'Radish Yeti'. All of this fun at least helped to keep our minds off the fact that we had no film camera.

The following morning, after completing my ablutions and breakfasting, I was raring to go. But first a reluctant word about our bodily functions. Why on earth has nature afflicted us in this way? I once asked a sweet young Buddhist monk what he most looked forward to as he approached nirvana.

'To not have to go to the toilet!' was his answer.

I found the whole subject mortifying, but Swanee appeared even more embarrassed about it. He avoided the official latrine like the plague. Shading my eyes from the early morning sun, I would vaguely recognize his figure disappearing on some far horizon, searching, as befits the 'Stuff Your Face Yeti', for some private spot.

At this height I found eating meat rather difficult, and the only food that really appealed to me was porridge and fruit. Margaret watched me like a hawk, nagging me until I drank the right amount of water. She was absolutely right — it was vitally important not to become dehydrated. Therefore, by the time we were ready to leave for Camp III, I had drunk about a litre of water.

Jules mentioned that he had a bit of a headache, which was to be expected at this height. He was strong and in good shape, and an aspirin worked wonders for his complaint. Apart from poor old Blackie's misfortune, we were a fit, happy bunch.

This day, I wanted to see if my months of running had paid off, and I set off at a good pace, the intrepid explorer once again. It was a day of days — a lovely breeze, fleeting clouds and a yellow road leading to heavenly heights. What extraordinary travellers had covered this journey over the centuries, for this was a greatly used trade route by which the Bhutanese exchanged their goods with the people of Tibet. I found myself among these ascending, happy caravans, also nodding a good morning to those ones coming down. It was all one continuous flowing movement, reminding me of a line from the poet James Elroy Flecker:

'We take the golden road to Samarkand!'

It made me quietly invent a dialogue in my head.

'What brings you here, oh Master of the Caravan?'

Thus replied the Master:

'We have coffee, sugar, salt and goods from Oxfam, from the far-away sea shore; Mohan Meakin beer and Bhutan Mist that free the shackles of the imprisoned mind. Our minds are set, our bodies light, with gifts of love and labour and height, from there to Tibet and soul's delight, for we take the golden road to Samarkand ... '

After the continuous chatter of the night before, it was refreshing to turn off and feel the silence and peace everywhere. Sometimes I would find myself alongside J.P. and Margaret, or one of the lads, and we instinctively kept silent. Rushing ahead like a true show-off, I found myself alone again along the twisting trail. On my left, unbelievably, Everest was about a hundred and fifty miles away.

I longed to see it. Patience, Brian! I said to myself, pushing the thought to the back of my mind. My blood pounded, and all my thoughts started to recede as the silence deepened. Snow flurries danced all around me. Now, for the first time in my life, I was entering the abode of snow and ice – the mighty Himalayas. Two more days, and I would see the giant mountain, Chomolhari, that had captivated Mallory so.

I arrived at Camp III breathless, but happy with my overall fitness. Margaret arrived immediately after me. She appeared very fit and strong, and I felt that she would do very well on Everest. There was a confidence about her that was very impressive.

Kimsun, as usual, had already erected the entire camp. It was a great delight to open your tent and find the mattress and sleeping bag, and all your personal effects, painstakingly laid out. And then to be given a bowl of hot water for your face and tired feet was a real treat. Afterwards the customary mug of tea was kindly placed in your hand. Has Heaven more to offer? My eyes locked on to Kimsun's as I whispered my gratitude.

'You are welcome, sir,' he smiled back. 'I think maybe, sir, you are good trekker and go higher than Base Camp on Everest.'

We were now at 13,000 feet. This camp had the luxury of a stone hut, with gaps in the roof to let out the smoke of the fire. But the industrious architect who designed this must have been slightly under the influence of the delights of Mohan Meakin. The smoke whirled around the hut, blinding us confused yetis. But it would take a lot more to dampen the spirits of this happy band of souls. The Fortnum's hamper continued to reveal surprises. A gourmet's delight, brimful of delicacies. It was, I should add, under the complete control of J.P., the Chitty Yeti. With twinkling eyes and fingers as busy as Chopin's, he alone selected the goodies for the evening. All manner of delectable treats were fleetingly seen, only to disappear to our chorus of moans, as he decided to save them for another day. I had been told before the expedition that our main topic of conversation would be food, and with the Chitty Yeti's careful stewardship of the hamper, I could see why.

Our destination the following day was Camp IV, Chomolhari Base Camp. Everywhere snow! Snow that glistened like a trillion prisms, as the early morning sun subtly pierced the giant nimbus clouds with its dazzling rays.

Kimsun had been sent down that corridor of snow to pick up from the runner the replacement circuit board that would galvanize our camera into life. Our fingers were crossed for him as we waited.

Shaking with joy, I embraced J.P., pouring out my feelings. I admit it would have been easier on everybody's ears if I could have assumed the air of a mature man. It was simply that I had been dreaming of this for most of my life, and the reality kept hitting me. This sublime feeling would bubble up without warning, and I immediately became a child again. J.P. understood perfectly, for he was in a similar state.

It was late in the morning, and we would soon have to break camp if we were to reach Chomolhari by nightfall. Then suddenly, moving at speed, the heroic Kimsun appeared. Even for an acclimatized man of the mountains, he blew hard and his face was tightly drawn with the effort.

Immediately, Jules and Swanee set to work to apply the piece of equipment to the camera. At the end of their effort, J.P. let out a tiny squeak ... It was the wrong circuit board. Still, the lads had somehow managed to manipulate it into position, which meant that the camera would work, but at half speed. Overcoming his disappointment, J.P. said that if I moved as slowly as was humanly possible during filming, they might possibly get away with it. With my weight, to move in slow motion would, in certain situations, not be easy. Still, I comforted myself with Wayne Sleep's encouraging words when I was in *Cats* with him:

'Oh, darling! You're such a lovely mover!'

We were in business again, and I was burning with energy and life. The upward path was clear, and the golden orb kissed it with its rays.

'Wham, bam, alakazam! Wonderful you went by!' I sang to a bemused nun.

Round corners, up hidden gullies, we pounded and filmed, sweat pouring freely. We were in our element.

'This is what life is!' I roared. 'This is to be free and not give a toss for all the constraints of bureaucracy ... Open up those pearly gates. California, here I come!'

Then, as we rounded a corner, our hearts and heads hammered at the sight before us. This damn pen is useless! I need my voice to impart the emotions of that vision before us, for it transcended all that humanity has achieved. Mankind wonderfully creates pieces of art that must bring a deep, happy, contented smile to the face of the Creator. How many times has he smiled at such efforts as the cathedral at Chartres, the Acropolis and the ceilings of the Sistine Chapel. When Michelangelo completed his statue of Moses, he shouted to it, 'Now speak!'

Now the vision in front of us *was* speaking. We bowed instinctively in its presence. None but the good Lord had conceived and formed this sacred mount, whose beauty and symmetry spoke of the limitless evolution that lies ahead of mankind.

All was still. The mountain shimmered in the golden evening light, the cobalt-blue sky was almost totally hidden by the colossus of snow. Vast ridges, stretching for miles, pointed the way to its distant summit. The fantastic shapes of its awesome precipices and titanic ice walls throbbed almost surrealistically, like frozen symbols of the mighty energy of the universe.

The fluted ribs of ice connected majestically with the mighty glaciers that reached out powerfully towards us, giving life to the valleys below. For this was Chomolhari, the Lily White Goddess, the Glass Mountain. Amid that silence, here in the Buddhist Kingdom of Bhutan, Kimsun and the porters quietly chanted, '*Om Mani Padme Hum*' ('Hail! Jewel in the Lotus Flower').

That evening we watched the sun disappear from the sky, and Chomolhari turn from gold to dark red, to iridescent blue and finally black. We dined quietly at 14,500 feet, and retired to our tents.

My appetite was poor the following morning because of the altitude, and a little porridge was all I could manage. Margaret's pretty eyes showed her disapproval of my scant breakfast, though when it came to my quota of liquid I obeyed her like the good soldier I was.

The morning's filming was leisurely and static, for J.P. felt that the most important thing was to film me in rapt contemplation studying Chomolhari. After a further hour or so he kindly let me take off on my own. Slowly and carefully I made my way to the terminal moraine at the base of the main glacier. As I approached this spot, I skirted alongside the glacier, climbing the firm rocks with ease. After about a hundred yards I manoeuvred myself on to a solid stretch of ice, and stopped. The height was about 15,000 feet, and I was totally thrilled to think that I was actually on the great mountain.

Where I was standing was perfectly safe, and everyone knew exactly where I was. The view I had was astonishing: the whole of the East Face hovered above me, resembling a giant amphitheatre that swept grandiosely for miles in all directions.

The stillness of the previous evening persisted. There were no clouds, not even a suggestion of mist, and the only sky I could see was directly over my head. My senses were wide awake to any eventuality, and the constant hammering of my heart confirmed the growing dread that was pervading my being. Yet despite all these feelings, I was determined to stay until the mood passed.

It may seem strange that I should have felt this way, after the spirituality of the night before, but I am now relaying my impressions as a green mountaineer. From my viewpoint, I could not detect any possible route to the top. It looked deadly dangerous and avalanche-prone from any direction. Indeed the authorities had forbidden any attempt to scale it, as several expeditions had suffered fatalities.

The flutings of the blue ice above me looked unstable, as did the giant white buttresses and the shining, castle-like snow structures, which appeared to be held together tenuously by underpinning green ice ribs. The silence was broken by the moaning and groaning of the entire gargantuan face, as millions of tons of pressure bore down on the suffering lower ice fields.

Sharp, cracking sounds cut through the thin air, playing havoc with my incredulous senses. My eyes were well protected by strong sunglasses, but even so I could detect the intense brightness of the reflected sunlight. It was a sinister, savage place. To scale its flanks would require climbing of the finest order, and prayers and offerings to boot.

Mallory, in 1921, viewing it from the other side and from a fair distance, stated that he would have liked to have had a shot at it. When he inspected it later at close quarters, his feelings about it proved to have been not dissimilar to mine.

'Kampa Dzong. 5th June, 1921 ... It is no use pretending that mountains are all beautiful ... Chomolhari (about 24,000 feet) rising abruptly out of the plain to more than 9,000 feet above us, was certainly a very tremendous sight, astounding and magnificent. But in broad daylight, however much one may be interested by its prodigious cliffs, one is not charmed ... One remains cold and rather horrified.'

There are times when nature can strip you bare, and render you defenceless and impotent. She is capable of inflicting the most savage and nightmarish loneliness on the over-confident, who do not pay the correct courtesies. I retreated slowly and carefully back to Base Camp. There I sat down, quietly chastised.

The ever-watchful J.P. placed a mug of tea in my hand, and I related my feelings to him. In the afternoon we walked for a few miles, following a bubbling stream that came from that other great mountain, Jitsu Drake, which had been climbed for the first time by the amazing British climber, Doug Scott. Stupendous peaks everywhere! We really were in the land of the giants. Would my heart and mind ever catch up and grasp that it was all real?

We entered a small house, and J.P. introduced me to an old friend of his, a monk who looked as old as the landscape. The crew filmed me being blessed by him. In that shaded room with ancient artefacts around me, the ceremony was simple and strangely moving. Any fear remaining from my experience on Chomolhari was suddenly removed, as the soothing eyes and vibrating chant of the little old man chased the demons away.

We had now achieved our objective of reaching Camp IV. The camera was performing adequately for our needs, and the acclimatization programme had gone perfectly. It had been a fine team effort. Kimsun and his porters had worked hard to make the trek a success. J.P. and Margaret had shared Blackie's duties between them, and like Jules and Swanee, had carried up heavy rucksacks. Over the past three years I had got to know J.P. very well. When we shared that mug of tea at Base Camp, with Chomolhari in the background, I felt particularly close to him.

Now it was time to descend, for the sun was quite low in the sky. We felt exhilarated and went down laughing and competing all the way. As the oxygen thickened, our lungs and legs responded accordingly. Margaret was moving like a ferret, but I was determined to keep in front of her. She was too fast for me, though.

Two days later, below Camp I, I jogged enthusiastically and

managed to get some distance ahead. It was all great fun, and our fitness and confidence grew all the time. J.P. found a stalwart pony for me to ride for a film sequence depicting Mallory in 1921. Mounted on my faithful steed, I sang as we wound and trundled our way along the hillsides.

There's a long, long trail awinding, into the land of my dreams,
Where the nightingale is singing, and the white moon beams ...

Late at night, on the third day, Kimsun, who had gone ahead, greeted us as we completed our descent. Within minutes we were on board the bus waiting at Drugyel Dzong, and soon back at the Mothithang Hotel, soaking in hot baths.

The next day was horrendous. Blackie had been sent back to London. His leg had deteriorated, for apparently on the descent he had taken a bit of a tumble which had opened up the wound on the swelling and started an infection, and this meant a replacement recordist would need to be sent out. Then we heard on the BBC World Service News that the BBC British Expedition to Everest was in jeopardy. They announced that we should, on no account, try to cross the border into India from Bhutan, as we would be arrested and put in jail and our gear and equipment confiscated. This news was confirmed by telexes from London.

The situation was ridiculous. It meant we could fly into India – we had permission for that – but we couldn't walk there. This was ruining a sweet, simple plan! Having completed the Bhutan filming, we had been looking forward to a short car journey to the border, and then to walk and take trains to Siliguri. There we intended to film the little 'Toy Train' that went to Darjeeling, following in the footsteps of Mallory. What was so difficult about that?

The Indian authorities had no objection to our filming in Darjeeling. Did they think I was the reincarnation of Captain Noel, leading a division of soldiers from the East Yorkshire Regiment, armed to the teeth with gattling guns? Or maybe they thought J.P. was a latterday Genghis Khan, bearing down on them with the full power of his mighty Golden Horde.

'Sweet God in Heaven!' I roared. 'Protect us from the banal world of bureaucracy. You know, J.P., all bureaucrats should be dispatched to the far reaches of an unmanifested universe and shagged sideways by a cosmic Tyrannosaurus rex!'

After a while I simmered down.

'After all, we are only a tiny bunch of yetis, trying to fulfil a simple quest!' I said.

Little did we know that a young man called Graham Hoyland, the replacement sound recordist, was at this moment also gnashing his teeth in frustration. His hire car had broken down, and he was in danger of missing his flight from Heathrow. The lad was in agony, for he was, amazingly, the great-nephew of Howard Somervell, who climbed with Mallory on the 1922 and 1924 expeditions.

Of course, by now, our farcical situation had stimulated our good humour, and we were in high spirits again. Our gallant leader informed us that we would have to go to the capital of Bhutan to meet the Sikh consul of the Indian Embassy, for we needed to get visas without delay. We arrived late on a Saturday night in colourful Thimphu.

The consul was tall and graceful, and wore a smart, light-beige suit and matching turban. He appreciated our predicament, and was kind and sensitive to our needs. I was on my best behaviour, discussing with him films and cricket, with a smattering of Mallory thrown in. He was most impressed, and found my twenties clothing intriguing. All in all he proved to be a terrific fellow. My manners would have impressed Alan Yentob no end, and the rest of the team held their breath in prayer, in case I transgressed by swearing.

As in my quiet baritone I waxed lyrical about India's fast bowler, Kapil Dev, I suddenly found my stomach heaving with pain, for I had the trots. In mid sentence I vanished from the room, leaving behind a confused consul. J.P. and the others dutifully took up the conversation where I left off, but this was not an easy task, as the toilet was next door and the walls were paper thin.

I was in a terrible state, for, apart from the awful noise I was making, I was also in agony. Never have I known such pain! But the greatest agony of all was my mortification. I said earlier how much I loathe toilets and all that takes place there; the whole thing makes me terribly shy. Now, in the civilized atmosphere of the Indian Embassy, I was exploding like Vesuvius. In my frightful state, I prayed to the great God of the Khazi to give me some respite, and after ten minutes the tremors ceased. I washed and refreshed myself and rejoined the consul as if nothing had happened.

I managed a few minutes' further conversation about the mysteries of India, and, in particular, the Shankachyari, the spiritual leader of the Northern Territory, when I was hit midships again. Walking bow-legged, cross-eyed and contorted, I moved like a pregnant duck towards the toilets, barely attaining my prime objective. There was no God of the Khazi after all!

This performance was repeated many times, much to the suppressed mirth of my companions. By this time the consul was only too glad to grant our request, and bid us farewell.

We could now fly out to Calcutta, hundreds of miles away, then fly back to Bagdogra, then bus it to Siliguri, and then take the 'Toy Train' to Darjeeling, and then back to Calcutta once again, before finally going on to Kathmandu and Everest. Confusion about this tortuous itinerary was as nothing compared with our relief that we were on our way.

Days later we stepped off the plane at Dumdum airport, in Calcutta, to be greeted by Graham Hoyland. Our replacement sound man had gone through fire and brimstone to get to us, and his ecstatic face showed it all. I liked him on sight. He was tall, boyish and handsome. He knew a great deal about Mallory, but never, for one moment, shoved it down my throat. He was a tremendous addition to the team, lending a hand immediately to any task, for he was a true jack of all trades. His cheerful personality was appreciated by all, and he was hard-working. To cap it all, he was an experienced mountaineer, having reached 23,000 feet on Himal Chuli in 1989.

We had not anticipated being in Calcutta, but having been forced here by a border dispute we decided to make use of the opportunity and film it. After days of living in tents, we found ourselves entering the Grand Hotel, in the middle of Chowringhee. What a contrast to the beetling streets outside. Calcutta is a fascinating, absorbing place, bursting with people and traffic. Can there be so many souls on this planet? I thought.

Hundreds of old British cars of all makes chugged loudly round the streets. Ancient buses clanged along, stuffed to the gills, reminding me of the Keystone Cops films as they perilously rounded corners, with people hanging on by their fingernails.

I joined this throbbing mass of humanity with Jules and Swanee, having to fight for space to film. Thousands of beggars, maimed horribly, held up their hands in supplication. Every square yard was full of something new and intriguing. There were roadside stalls serving delicious sweet, milky tea from shining, long, metal tea pots. Mouth-watering goodies were cooking at every turn.

J.P. and I took a rickshaw, and an energetic, smiling driver pulled us along with ease. Hundreds of people thronged around us, cheering enthusiastically and laughing at my antiquated clothing. I was the epitome of the British Raj, and it delighted them. There was certainly no animosity.

Every avenue and side street seemed to be inhabited by water buffaloes, which ambled across the main roads, lazily avoiding the trams. The city was simply alive with eating, drinking, bumping and jostling people and animals.

Our rickshaw stopped, and I found myself being stared at by hundreds of faces, immobile and unsmiling. The large, dark eyes looked left and right nervously, for as night approached the city was in terror of the 'Stone Man', a murderer who had already claimed the lives of eighteen people. His victims were mainly crippled beggars, and his method of killing was gruesome, for he smashed their skulls with a stone which he left behind as a memento.

The Grand Hotel was resplendent and white, removing all images of a nut with a stone. Opulent in style, it hosted only the very best. Every nook and cranny was a tribute to the bygone British Raj. Our unloading and stacking of several tons of equipment in a side room was viewed with suspicious curiosity. In the middle of our doing this, a white cadillac cruised in and paused outside the reception. A very important Indian in a white suit glided out of the front seat, tossing his keys to the doorman and not even sparing him a glance. The exterior gates of the hotel were entwined by the writhing arms and hands of destitute beggars. What a world of contrasts!

I felt slightly sad at being in Calcutta, hundreds of miles from

Everest, when we had been so near in Bhutan. This luxury didn't suit me at all. Give me back my tent and lighted candles, I thought. Our sombre mood was made worse by some appalling news. Shenni, our pretty Indian fixer, informed J.P. that a revolution was under way in Kathmandu, the capital of Nepal.

Now Kathmandu is reknowned for its smiling people, peace and love and musical temples, while Nepal is a land of light and luxuriant rice fields that stretch to the distant Himalayas. It seemed impossible to believe. Nevertheless, all flights had been cancelled and a total curfew was in force in the capital.

This was quite dreadful! Our dream of going to Everest now looked hopeless, for all our equipment for the expedition was in Kathmandu. The whole project was absolutely impossible without David Breashears and his team, and their activities would be limited because of the curfew. During dinner that night, we were a depressed bunch of yetis, yet we were a stubborn, pugnacious lot, and it would take a lot more than this to stop us.

It was a great pity to have missed out on our planned audience with the Dalai Lama. Having to make this great detour had lost us the prearranged meeting, for His Holiness was now in meditation. In 1920, after an epic trek, Sir Charles Bell, the political officer for Tibetan affairs, managed to obtain permission from the Thirteenth Dalai Lama to attempt to climb Everest. We had wished to repeat and film this ceremony. However, J.P. felt that we could possibly do it later.

All along, I had felt very deeply that we had to approach the mountain with prayers, flowers and humility. I was happy to hear from Shenni that His Holiness had sent a message to say that he would pray for us. This is the message sent by the Thirteenth Dalai Lama in 1920, to the Indian and British governments:

'Be it known to Officers and Headmen of Phari Jong, Khampa, Tin-Ki and Shekar, that a party of Sahibs will come to the sacred Mountain, Chomolungma ... You shall render all help and safeguard them ... We have requested the Sahibs to keep the Laws of the Country when they visit Chomolungma, and not to kill Birds and Animals, as the People will feel sorry for this ... His Holiness, The Dalai Lama, is now on friendly terms with the Government of India ...'

We Sahibs of 1990 travelled by plane to Bagdogora, and bus thereafter, finally arriving at busy Siliguri to board the little 'Toy Train' to Darjeeling, maintaining all the time our determination to follow in Mallory's footsteps.

The small town of Siliguri is totally captivating, for it has the same energy as Calcutta but none of its traffic. The dusty streets ring to the sound of hundreds of tri-shaws, which have three wheels the size of an ordinary bicycle, and a carriage attached to the back to carry up to three people. How quiet and clean it would be if these were used in the country lanes of Britain.

The shops constantly seduced J.P. and me, reminding me of those I knew in Yorkshire as a small boy during the war. There was a cobbler's shop, a little grocery shop and an old-fashioned barber's shop: the influence of the British Raj was everywhere to be seen. I eagerly bought my father a packet of filter-tipped Gold Flake cigarettes. It must have been sitting there for years.

Eventually we tore ourselves away from the shops and dimly lit tea rooms, as it was time to see the legendary 'Toy Train'. I would say that my age at that moment was six. Memories came to mind of my dad putting the finishing touches to my train set, with its circular line running round the table and chairs of the sitting room. Now, right in front of me, was a slightly larger version. It was a proper beauty with a compact green body and lots of steam and smoke. The whistle was really loud and piercing.

I wanted to get on board there and then, but there were forms to fill in, and J.P. and I entered a tiny room, where Margaret and Shenni were making arrangements with the station master. A moment later we were off. J.P., Margaret and the crew would follow alongside in a large van, filming.

Shenni was with me on the train, filling my hands with lots of goodies for the day's journey. Steam poured out everywhere, and the pistons worked nineteen to the dozen, pumping out their energetic song along the line. Songs burst from me, too, as Menno Ziggsen's words danced in my mind:

Ghoom, Sonada, Kurseiong, are all left behind,
Though the journey's very long, I'm sure we do not mind ...

'You're right!' I laughed. 'This journey can go on for ever!' It would take the best part of a day, anyway, for it was fifty miles from Siliguri to Darjeeling, an ascent of 8,000 feet.

The train would frequently stop for a well-earned drink of water. Once replenished, it would take a deep breath, suck up the heat from its well-stoked furnace, and power on again cheerfully. Up and up we went, turning and twisting, and shunting backwards and forwards. A dozen times, it made a figure of eight, and zigzags and loops too. The engine even passed the tail of the train, and the driver talked to the passengers in the end coach.

We were now passing the Terai, whose jungles were still the home of the tiger.

'Can you get up on the roof?' shouted J.P. from the van, which either kept alongside us or raced ahead for some spiffing shot.

'Yes, of course I can!' I shouted back, and in a flash I was up on top, with a concerned Shenni shouting warnings from the window and an official following me like a demented Gunga Din.

'Please, sir! ... No, sir! ... You must be careful, sir!'

I calmed him with a confident smile, and cooed at the spectacular scenery around me: great plunging cliffs and deep green valleys.

'Can you *stand* on the roof, Brian?' roared J.P. 'Look over here ... That's great! Now we're coming aboard for close-ups.'

There I was, standing just like Mallory when Captain Noel filmed him in 1924. You could run right round the moon, and it wouldn't be as good as this!

When the train briefly stopped, the crew joined me on the roof, breathless and jolly. I made a big effort to be serious, but it was all in vain. Giggling and grinning, I hummed 'Pasadena', immersed in my childhood. Yet if I was six, the crew were barely six and a half, with Margaret, Swanee, Jules and Graham by turn erupting in giggles.

'Down, please! ... Down!' shouted my Indian minder, as a low bridge presented itself. My face was blacker by the minute, as the smoke from the funnel enveloped me.

We were growing impatient now to see the promised vision of mighty Kanchenjunga, at the end of our journey. But, instead, we were greeted by a dark-grey sky and wet mist. After the colourful panorama of our trip, we witnessed weather that was much more suited to Manchester. Our heroic train, whistling with pride, its smoke and steam mingling with the mist around us, came to a pulsating stop. You couldn't help but be moved by its performance.

For the last twenty minutes I had been up front with the two drivers, helping to shovel coal into the furnace. Now I patted the 'Toy Train', thanking it and the drivers for making this part of the dream come true.

Contentedly, we made our way through the dark, damp streets of Darjeeling, towards the inviting warmth of the famous Windermere Hotel. Everywhere soft lights lit the way, and each house displayed happy families and hot dinners. As we mounted the hill, I peered hopefully through the mist in the direction of Kanchenjunga, but the pea-soup mist jealously hid the giant, refusing me even a glimpse of its outline.

My overactive mind yearned for x-ray eyes that could penetrate even further afield, to Everest itself, a hundred miles away. They told me that it could be seen from the city, shy and retiring, like a small dot, lost in the massive Himalayas inbetween.

When, O Lord! I thought. When shall I see it?

The delightful Windermere Hotel swept away all such thoughts. To Margaret and Shenni went the laurels for making it possible for us to stay at such a gorgeous residence. It was built in the colonial style, with white bricks and green corrugated roofs topped with graceful, white chimney pots.

There was a large, meandering veranda, filled with tables and pretty, coloured shades overlooking a dense green valley. Connected to the hotel were numerous bungalow-type buildings, where we stayed. The hotel had been built during the twenties, mainly for visiting tea planters and special guests.

The owner was Mrs Luff, a sweet, gracious Sikkimese, who, as luck would have it, was at the parties thrown for the expeditions of the twenties. Surprisingly, it was not Mallory who had stayed in her memory, but the redoubtable General Bruce, the expedition leader. Though she was only a child at the time, she found him a most impressive character. The general, it seems, was adored by everybody, from the Everest Committee and Alpine Club in London, right through the ranks of the army, to the expedition members themselves. He was a great bull of a man whose feats of strength were legendary, and his favourite trick at these parties was to lie flat, with his head and feet bridging two tables. Try as they might, the strongest of men could not bend his spine.

Luxuriating in a hot bath, I was agreeably surprised when a young Sikkimese lad entered the room, and made me a good old-fashioned fire. J.P. entered, smiling as always, with a fat cigar in his chops. How *did* he make those smoke rings?

'Come on, lazybones! Time for chomping!' he laughed.

The next day we set off for the famous Tiger Hill at two in the morning, there to witness, with multitudes of others, the glorious sunrise slowly firing the giant Himalayas, and at last revealing the colossus, Kanchenjunga.

Graham, with eyes popping and face lit up with expectancy, nodded that his apparatus was working, and Swanee and Jules, with experienced calm, also gave the thumbs up that all stations were on red alert. J.P. held Margaret's hand tightly, and puffed deeply on his Burma cheroot.

'Any minute now! ... Wait for it! ... '

The huge crowd was already breaking out into muffled orgiastic screams. Several had even fainted. The magic moment arrived. A flicker of light shot across the sky, and the crowd groaned with ecstacy. Then ... Nothing! ... Nothing at all!

It was like the end of time. Over the next two hours, the dark, misty, depressing dawn dragged itself forward like a drunken slug. The camera whirred into action. I peered into the mist, imitating the delivery of a television commentator reporting a match in murky Manchester. We all laughed and returned to the town. I was beginning to wonder whether there was some devious demon of the snows who was preventing me seeing Everest. Nonsense! The mountain loved me.

In the afternoon we went back in time by visiting the Planters' Club, where Mallory and his companions stayed. It was a strange and disturbing experience, full of ghosts and nostalgia. The building was delapidated, and the rooms cold and empty, with the odd broken-down billiard table. As I walked on the veranda I could almost hear those Everesteers talking and laughing, and the tunes of a bygone era danced through my mind.

During all of this J.P. and his team unobtrusively filmed me. It is strange when you've had a dream for so many years and then you start to live it. You frequently wonder if it's real.

Mallory, Bruce, Norton, Somervell, Irvine and the other fine gentlemen of those first expeditions had all been so alive to me. I had sweated blood over their deeds! Reading for the umpteenth time the last chapter of Robertson's 1924 book about the fatal expedition, I had hoped that Mallory and Irvine would make it to the top and come back safe. God knows, I'm sure Mallory's son, John, must have had this feeling. Now, for the first time, I realized they were dead.

Where is their laughter now? Their wit, love, comradeship and deeds — where are they? They can't have disappeared, for they were such mighty characters. The Planters' Club, so decayed and empty, with its faded yellow walls and dark-green wood, offered no explanation, and left me deeply confused.

'Come on, Brian.' It was the wise J.P. who broke my reverie. 'Let's film somebody who is alive!'

Sherpa Tenzing's nephew, Gombu, had been to the summit of Everest twice, once on the expedition with Jim Whittaker, the first American to climb the mountain, in 1963. Gombu proved to be a cheerful character. Short and stocky, and in his late forties, he offered me lots of advice, the most important being, 'Go slowly'. He also told us how the first Sherpas who went with Mallory were convinced that the British wanted to climb Everest to milk the 'White Lion' that lives on the summit, and, by drinking its milk, obtain the knowledge of life.

Gombu was in charge of a climbing school in Darjeeling, where he trained Sherpas, and he cordially invited us to see it, and his climbing museum. Our visit proved fascinating, for the famous Sherpa Tenzing Norgay's ashes lay there, and people came from far and wide to pay their respects. It was sad saying goodbye to Gombu, who is a delightful man, and whose last words to me were: 'Be careful, Blessed, Everest is very hard. Second time I go, I am very tired when I was coming down. My legs and back ache, I was worried I don't get down ... Remember, you have to get down ... '

That evening we all congregated in my room around a big fire for which we had to pay a hundred-rupee supplement. I was writing out a letter of Mallory's to his wife Ruth. This was to be one of the conventions in the film for revealing his thoughts. Watching the film, you would listen to his thoughts, then mine.

My hero's name reverberated in my head as I delivered his first letter. Mallory ... Mallory ... Mallory ...

Dearest Girl
I think of you often and with ever so much love, and wish for your company ... Would there were some way of bringing you nearer ... I think the nearness depends very much on the state of one's imagination ... I know you must have been feeling lonely some evenings ... I often want you with me in my arms and to kiss you ... Here it's a great holiday time and you not with me! ... But we'll have a wonderful holiday when I get back ... My love to the children, ever your loving George.

5

The Turquoise Mountain

It was goodbye to Darjeeling. We had seen it in a mist. I intend to return some day to that magical town, and on Tiger Hill see the sun rise on a clear day.

Now we found ourselves back in Calcutta, at the Grand Hotel. Fingers were firmly crossed in the hope that the revolution in Kathmandu was over. But the news was as bad as ever. There was still a twenty-three hour curfew in the Nepalese capital. All the planes were grounded, and it was impossible to get there from India. After the troubles with the Indian border, to be thwarted by a revolution! It was all too much!

I found myself swimming madly up and down the pool of the hotel in manic frustration, like a lion in a zoo. The hotel was loathsome and posh and utterly boring. In my room, I switched on my TV, and the trite *Dallas* spurted into life. A variation on the theme was achieved by a push of the button, giving me *Daisy Does Dallas*.

Bloody hell! I thought. Has everybody worked so hard finally to arrive at *Daisy*?

On one occasion we all sat despondent downstairs, outside the reception, pondering what the hell to do.

'Couldn't we use the Indian Air Force?' I suggested. 'And parachute in? And meet David Breashears at Base Camp, or something?'

J.P. laughed.

'The air is so thin that we'd probably plummet straight down! No, Brian. Using planes and parachutes is out of the question. All our expedition gear is in Kathmandu, so is David. That's the big problem ... If, by some miracle, we could get into Tibet, David, at the moment, couldn't join us.'

J.P. then outlined the rather desperate alternatives. We could fly back to London, then on to Hong Kong, then on to Chengdu, then to Lhasa, and finally endure a three-day truck ride to Everest Base Camp. He even considered going back to Bhutan and doing the Chomolhari trek again, crossing over into Tibet from there.

It was astonishing to think that we had been barely a hundred miles from Everest, and we might have to go back through London, 5,000 miles away, to have any chance of getting near it again! Poor Shenni and Margaret were running around like blue-arsed flies. Their efforts were fabulous, phoning Indian Airlines, Kathmandu and London. Were we giving up? ... Not on your life! We were a gutsy outfit, and the courage and enterprise of everyone would surely have impressed General Bruce.

Suddenly the Tannoy burst into life and J.P. was called to reception. It appeared that Indian Airlines had decided to fly into Kathmandu that evening, in order to pick up the hundreds of tourists who were stranded there. J.P. decided that we should go for it. Anything to get to Kathmandu — at least there was a chance we could join up with David Breashears. As J.P. said, 'At worst, we could camp out on the tarmac of the airport.'

For we had plenty of tents and equipment. We rapidly loaded our tons of gear, and headed for Dumdum airport. Frantically clawing our way through customs and insane crowds, we man-anged to get the equipment on to the plane, and finally we sat down in the aircraft, pouring with sweat and relief. Would you believe it, the plane wouldn't start!

Apparently the dashboard was the problem. It was a mass of disconnected wires, and demented technicians pressed this and that to no good effect. It was left to the crew to save the day, a single screwdriver doing the trick.

The journey was short and swift, and soon we were descending towards Kathmandu.

It was getting late, and it was a weird, even sinister experience approaching a city where there were no lights on. As we taxied in, the sky was dark and forbidding, and it was raining heavily. There were no buses to take us to the terminal, and we made a mad dash to avoid getting soaked. Inside, it was all eerie and empty. Where were the multitudes of trekkers and Sherpas?

There was only one solitary figure manning the customs desk, but I was in Seventh Heaven! Kathmandu! If I'd had tin legs, wooden arms and a turnip for a skull, I'd still not have let anything put me off my quest to get to the mountain.

Where was David Breashears? That's what I wanted to know. Shenni, phoning ahead, had managed to get through to Mark Tully, the BBC correspondent in Nepal, who, in turn, had been trying to locate David. Mark had succeeded.

My eyes burned with hope, as I ignored the gun-toting soldiers and recent arrivals, and searched high and low for our climbing leader.

'Brian! ... Brian! ... Brian!'

Turning, I saw a slim man with a slim face, and eyes flashing like an eternal prism, beckoning to me. It was Sir Gawain himself, David Breashears. The relief on his face reflected my own. Never had I been so relieved to see another human being. David had almost given up hope of our ever getting in, but when he heard the plane coming in to land he had jumped on a bicycle and, avoiding the roadblocks and patrolling soldiers, arrived at the airport.

'You wonderful, gorgeous man!' I roared, and we embraced passionately.

Despite the curfew and the heavy military presence everywhere, there was a great feeling of hope.

'You must all do as I tell you,' David said. 'It's very dangerous here – guns are going off everywhere. You mustn't step out of line for a moment.'

With charm and initiative, David had persuaded the airport authorities to give him a couple of rooms, where he had miraculously stacked most of the expedition gear. Now, moving at the speed of light, he found more space in these rooms for the tons of equipment we had brought. Up and down the huge stacks he moved, lifting this object and placing that. The humidity was stifling. His industry and painstaking care and attention to every detail reflected a professional, dedicated mind.

When customs were satisfied that our passports and visas were in order, our minds focused on how to get to where we were to stay, the Tibet Guest House, for we found ourselves outside the airport without transport. We were informed by an official that there might be a bus, but if not, we would have to stay at the airport. Then, rule Britannia!, a dusty, much-used Landrover turned up, and the Defence Attaché and Commander British Forces Nepal, Colonel Michael Allen, leaned out.

'Anyone here British?'

Our eager arms hit the air like schoolchildren.

Packed in like sardines, we were delighted at our good fortune. The BBC Everest Expedition owes a debt of gratitude to this fine ambassador and his gallant assistant. Their behaviour in the midst of such danger was admirable, for there were soldiers everywhere who appeared nervous and trigger-happy, and so it was vitally important that the assistant kept the beam of his torch focused on the small Union Jack that fluttered bravely on the bonnet of the Landrover.

We were flagged down constantly, and guns flashed menacingly. Totally unperturbed, the colonel, with a strong, calm voice, said, 'British Embassy, with British citizens.'

After a quick examination of our documents, suspicious soldiers nodded us on. This happened a dozen times and each time the tension grew. The empty streets were dark and ghostly, the only life being our lone vehicle. Grinding slowly to a halt, we found ourselves outside the Thamel district, a sensitive area where many of the revolutionaries were situated. Now we were in trouble.

I was seated at the front by the open window, and I looked directly down the barrel of a sub-machine-gun. Soldiers were everywhere and lights flashed in our faces. The soldier holding the gun to my face looked no older than fifteen. He appeared extremely nervous, and could have blown my head off at any minute. For the first time, I realized now dangerous a dream could be. The diplomacy of the ambassador nevertheless saw us safely into the Thamel district, although he had to turn back.

At last the full team were together at the Tibet Guest House, a delightful place, rather like an Oriental bed-and-breakfast hotel in Blackpool. A sumptuous feast had been prepared by Veronique Choa, David's girlfriend, a beautiful, young, dark-haired American, with high cheek bones and Oriental features. David was justifiably proud of her, and she greeted me warmly with a great hug.

'Allow me to introduce myself,' said a giant of a man, towering over us all. 'My name is Jeff Long, and I will be your climbing minder.'

Not only was Jeff tall, about six foot six, but he was massively muscled. Yet the most striking quality about him was his gentleness, for he spoke in a quiet, well-modulated voice.

All through the night you could hear distant gunfire. The portents were not good. But my analysis of the situation couldn't have been further from the truth, for when I awoke in the morning I discovered that what had sounded like gunfire, had been celebration fireworks. The king had agreed to democracy! The staff of the guest house beamed with happiness.

'It's true, Mr Blessed!' they shouted. 'We have democracy!'

'Does that mean we can go?' I asked breathlessly. It was J.P. who answered, 'Yes, Big Yeti. We can! Tomorrow, we'll be in Tibet!'

'It's a miracle!' I kept shouting. 'Thank God! It's a bloody miracle!'

Immediately, J.P., Swanee and Jules unpacked the camera gear to film the momentous event. Graham Hoyland had to go off to the Chinese Embassy, to see if he could get a visa, which he hadn't had time to get in London. Failure to obtain one would have meant the end of the journey for him, so we kept our fingers crossed. He was such a lovable and vital part of the team.

Veronique rushed into town with her tiny Sherpa cook, Krisna, to get fresh supplies, and David Breashears and Jeff sped off to arrange lorries and land-cruisers to carry the tons of equipment. It was all gorgeously frantic. On to the streets we went, running and dancing with everybody we came across. The noise was absolutely deafening.

'This is Wongchu,' shouted J.P. 'He, with Jeff, will get you up the mountain. He's lovely, isn't he?'

'He is indeed!' I roared back.

The Sherpa's face beamed with happiness, and he laughed and nodded vigorously. His smile was as wide as the River Indus, and lit up his refined Nepalese cheek bones. Every time I asked him a question, he appeared to misunderstand totally and his face went blank. Then, suddenly, words poured forth: 'Me, go sir. For food, much things. No finish tourist American. Yes, please ... Not today ... Maybe yak and yeti ... Go hotel ... Get money. Annapurna trek ... Yes, then maybe go with food and dollars!'

I gave him a big hug, and shouted over the din, 'You do what you want, Sunshine. As long as you're alongside me on Everest!'

Everywhere the crowds filled the previously empty streets, singing and dancing. Good-naturedly, they poured sacred red dust all over me. The red powder was flung far and wide, causing wild applause and merriment. It was simple to brush off, but there were times when I looked like a pillar-box.

The atmosphere reminded me very much of the song of the Munchkins in *The Wizard of Oz*, celebrating the death of the Wicked Witch.

Later, as I showered, I reflected that it had been a wonderful day. More good news followed the next morning: Graham had obtained his visa and would be with us. What a relief!

The large truck was packed with three and a half tons of equipment. Breashears begged everyone to be careful of the eggs.

'Brian!' he shouted. 'When we get to Base Camp, I'm going to make you the most delicious omelette you've ever tasted!'

Accordingly, Krisna, all five foot three of him, was placed on top of the heap of gear to safeguard the precious eggs.

J.P., Margaret, me and the camera crew were in a sturdy land-cruiser, while David, Veronique, Jeff and the Sherpas, Chuldim, Nawang and Phuli, went in the lorry. We were at last heading for Friendship Bridge, and Tibet. Honking and hooting, we made our way through the amazing Nepalese countryside. We passed the mysterious splendours of ancient Bhaktapur, drove along glorious tree-lined roads that lead the way to the great mountains. The euphoria of new-found democracy had penetrated the whole countryside, and villagers waved and cheered excitedly as we passed. The haze of early morning started to clear, revealing the intricate patterns of the extensive rice fields, where beautiful women in vibrant dresses of green, blue, red and yellow toiled away rhythmically.

Having climbed gradually, we stopped for breakfast at a

beautiful wooden hillside restaurant. The disappointment of Tiger Hill evaporated from my mind as I marvelled at a two-hundred-degree panorama of Himalayan peaks. Somehow it was all beyond emotion. Any show of passion would have felt disrespectful here. In hallowed whispers, Breashears, Jeff and J.P. pointed out the mountains: Himal Chuli, Ganesh, Shisha Pangma, Dorje Lhakpa, Gaurishankar and Menlungtse, where they had been with Chris Bonington.

'Where is Everest?' I pleaded.

'You can't see it from here. It's way, way over there, deep, deep inside the interior. You'll see it in a few days,' I was told. I sat back in the chair, my senses drunk and overfed.

Soon we were back on the road. Down, down we now went, into the luxuriant valleys. This spectacular, rough-hewn domain was carved out by the devastating power of the water from the mountains, forming the beginnings of the Indus and the Ganges. On reaching Friendship Bridge, as much as we were eager to get across and into Tibet, we felt sad to leave Nepal. The miracle of the day of democracy, and the kindness of the staff of the guest house, and indeed of people everywhere, had melted our hearts. We knew that we were now in for an entirely different experience.

The Chinese border guards on the bridge, with their sub-machine-guns, looked none too friendly. Breashears had instructed us to do exactly as the Chinese told us. If it took hours, or even days, we must patiently nod and do as we were told, or the whole expedition could be in jeopardy.

Tentatively, we moved across the bridge, and the Chinese guards made us unload all our equipment. In this we were greatly helped by the scores of children who lived nearby. Supervised with authority and humour by Breashears and Jeff, they joyfully accomplished the task. The lorry and the land-cruiser now turned round and went back to Nepal; our vehicles henceforth would be rented from the Chinese authorities.

I was astonished at the amount of equipment and food as it lay at the roadside — it looked like a miniature Everest in itself. What massive effort and skilful organization had gone into this expedition. Until that moment, I hadn't fully realized the scale of it all. It was deeply reassuring to be in such professional company.

'Watch the eggs!' Breashears kept shouting. 'Come on, Veronique. Up the hill to Xangmu to organize the lorries.'

He and Veronique were both tremendously fit, and instead of taking the long, winding road to the village, they took a short, very steep route up the hillside, an ascent of 600 yards or so.

We could imagine the wheeling and dealing they would have to put up with when they arrived there. After an hour, to our roars of triumph, they arrived with a large lorry and a driver, and we loaded up. Breashears worked like a man possessed. He, his close friend Jeff and Veronique made for a most impressive team. There was no doubt at all that the Chinese knew and trusted Breashears; his industry and tenacity impressed them enormously. The whole rigmarole of customs, passports and visas took about two hours. But as Breashears pointed out, we were lucky, for they can keep you hanging around for days.

The Chinese questioned me closely about my copy of Robertson's book on Mallory, and when they were satisfied that it had nothing in it that could harm the state, they gave it the official stamp of approval. We were about to head for the hotel, just up the road, when they queried my passport. The problem was that it was new, whereas they had my old passport number on their records, which had been sent some months before. The new information had not yet arrived. Surely to God! I thought, the whole project couldn't now fall down over such a triviality?

The officials frowned. Breashears and J.P., with the help of Wongchu, exhausted their diplomacy in a bid to save the day. I instinctively did what I always do in such situations, and showed the Sherpas and the soldiers a few judo holds. They particularly liked a throw called Kata Garuma, which is simply a technique of lifting someone off his feet. Some of the Chinese wanted to try it out on me, and when they failed, their comrades fell about laughing. The top official holding my passport was completely taken with it all, and laughed the loudest. He returned the passport, admonishing me with a shake of the head for being a naughty boy.

In the meantime, Jules had attempted to lift me, and slightly strained his back as he, too, failed. Breashears now stepped forward to much applause, and hoisted me up easily. Jeff the giant looked on impassively, giving the impression that the task was not worthy of his attention. Another high-ranking Chinese official stepped forward and tried, and I felt it prudent not to resist. His success was cheered enthusiastically by the soldiers, and we were allowed to pass on to the huge, depressing Xangu Hotel.

This was supposed to be a high-class hotel, and it cost a fortune to stay there, J.P. told me. Our rooms were damp and cold, and the pathetic electrical fittings hung loosely from the walls. It was quite impossible to get a decent wash, and the water was stale and discoloured.

The evening meal, in a large hall, was frugal and plain, yet reasonably nourishing. We were thrilled to be through the border and on our way. Our thoughts were for the morrow and filming, and seeing Tibet. We retired to bed feeling that, at last, the gods were smiling on us.

But the following day there were further problems, for the Chinese bureaucrats insisted that we unload most of the equipment from the lorry. This was tiresome, as they had inspected every item the night before. With the patience of Jove, Breashears, with the help of Jeff and our Sherpas, emptied the lorry, all the time keeping an eye on the eggs.

At last the officials were satisfied, and we were on our way into the heart of mysterious Tibet. The plan was that David and his team would go ahead to Shekar Dzong while we filmed our journey to there. It was all unbearably exciting for me. Were they really going to set up Base Camp on Everest? I wondered if I was dreaming again in my back garden in Bagshot. But as we set up our first shot, looking across a great gorge with a huge waterfall powering down the cliff, I saw their lorry disappear, and realized that it was actually happening.

Our two land-cruisers were very comfortable, and easily took all the filming gear. The towering cliffs overlooking the rough road we were motoring on were stunning and intimidating. The road had been washed away four years previously. We could understand why, for time and again we found ourselves travelling under a gigantic rocky overhang with thousands of tons of water thundering over it into the deep valley below. As much as one at first resents a road in such a wild place, one has to admit that the Chinese and Tibetans have done an amazing job in constructing it.

Round and round we followed its intricate, winding course, stopping here and there to film the astonishing scenery. From the start of our journey, from Xangmu at 4,500 feet, we had now risen to 8,000 feet, from which height the immensity of the spectacular gorge was revealed to us.

The land-cruiser now audibly strained as it pushed onward and upward. Margaret and Graham were just behind us all the way, in the second cruiser. With speed and expertise, they set up the sound equipment, and were always ready for action as the admirable Jules and Swanee rolled the camera.

Thank God we were going slowly, owing to our constant stops for filming. These ensured that we frequently walked half a mile or so as we simulated Mallory's journey, which aided acclimatization perfectly. We were now feeling the full benefit of our Chomolhari trek, where everyone except Graham had been to 14,000 feet or more. Even so, Graham was bearing up very well.

From the Tibetan border you can get to Everest Base Camp in three days by land-cruiser. Compare this to the 1922 expedition, when Mallory and his companions set out from Darjeeling on 26 March, not arriving at Base Camp until 4 May! Their round trek of about three hundred miles was a mixture of pony-riding and walking. Their gradual acclimatization was generally first-rate, but they were subjected to the cold, dust-infested westerly wind of Tibet, often described as an old wind with an old anger. It bunged up their noses and irritated their throats, causing all kinds of respiratory troubles.

As we left the awesome splendour of the rocky cliffs and ravines below, we found ourselves on the Tibetan Plateau at 10,000 feet. After being hemmed in by the previous massive structures, it was a complete surprise to find our gaze being carried for hundreds of miles over a multi-coloured desert. For once, the expected 'Old Wind' was still. We drove on for a few miles, and then stopped and filmed, and viewed this rare land.

On entering the crater rim of Kibo on Kilimanjaro in 1988, I had been intrigued by the varied colours of sand and rock; it looked rather like the pictures of Mars. Now I found myself standing in a vast, sandy plain with gentle mountains all around me, that for all the world looked Martian in character.

Such stillness and harmony. The thin air allowed our eyes to see the full depth of the rich cobalt blue of the sky. The striking colour highlighted the soft pinks and beiges of the smooth hills as they rolled on and on to the distant azure and deep purple of the floating heights of the Himalayas. Taking in the kisses of the laughing sun was the mighty presence of the great mountain, Shishapangma. In the far distance a herd of yaks was being urged on by a woolly-hatted herdsman.

We were now at 16,500 feet, and our thickening blood and increased heart rate pulsated as one with the heavenly kingdom around us. We filmed, and stopped, and were still again. Our eyes widened to take in more, and our awareness of the divine in each other was self-evident. A hymn of praise came from the lips of all.

Captain Noel felt that despite its charm, Tibet is unquestionably the most frightful and desolate country in the world.

'No other land,' he explained, 'can be so harsh and forbidding as that table-land, raised 15,000 feet, where stone and ice and mountain seem to conspire against all life.'

The people live in the most extreme poverty and discomfort, yet, Captain Noel maintained, they are contented and happy.

'Mallory found the country rather unfriendly and far, though,' he added. 'But in the evening light,' Mallory himself wrote, 'this country can be beautiful, snow mountains and all: the harshness becomes subdued; shadows soften the hillsides; there's a blending of lines and folds until the last light, so that one came to bless the absolute bareness, feeling that here is pure beauty of form, a kind of ultimate harmony.'

We had lost all sense of time, and the all-powerful sun was losing its strength, as it moved quickly to its resting place in the west.

Everest was close now, so tantalizingly close! We all sensed it, but so far, amazingly, we had seen nothing of it. In that almost surrealistic golden afternoon light, and the equally haunting silence, we felt we were in a strange dreamscape. All these years I had waited, from my earliest days. Could it be possible after so long that I was actually going to see Everest? Maybe I had imagined it all. I do not exaggerate. Such is the power of the mind!

Our vehicle purred along effortlessly, as if it were travelling on velvet. The setting sun painted the hills with its enchanting rays, and the resulting subtle pastel shades of red and pink deepened, heralding the appearance of the 'Goddess Mother of the Earth'.

It was reminiscent of that mystical, hushed moment in *Moby Dick*, when Captain Ahab whispers, 'He is near! ... He is very near!'

Then, in a mighty voice as the white whale appears, 'He rises! ... '

How do I describe that moment? I wasn't ready for it. How could I be? One moment we were driving round a corner, and the next we were hit by a vision that for starkness, grandeur and majesty dwarfed the imagination!

My legs went, my arms went, my head throbbed and thumped. I simply couldn't control myself. The land-cruiser stopped, and I tumbled out.

'Everest! ... It's Everest! ... God in heaven! J.P., look at it! Never, never, did I ever think it would look like this! ... It's so big! It's just ... I don't ... '

I was having a hell of a struggle with my emotions.

'Look at its size, J.P.! And it's so steep! It's so massive ... Mallory's there ... '

The thought of Mallory being there hit me between the eyes like a laser. I couldn't get over the simple fact that Mallory *was* there. My words sounded like the ravings of a man who was discharging energy like a supernova.

'Mallory's there ... Yes! Yes! Yes, Mallory's there! ... Look at it, J.P. ... It's so big! It looks like the end of the world, don't you think? ... Eh? ... Eh? ... There's nothing beyond it!'

I turned on poor J.P., who was having his own ten-dimensional experience, and poured out my soul to him.

Words and passions, dancing and leaping became fused in an incoherent celebration of the life force that emanated from that colossal, beatific symbol of all that is inspirational in nature.

'You have made this happen, J.P.!' I cried, holding him close. 'This wonderful moment and this great adventure has all been brought about by you! Your expertise, your drive in the face of terrible opposition! ... I know what you've faced. Because of you, we are all here, sharing in this miracle. My dear fellow! ... Thank you, sugar pie, for making it possible!'

We embraced long and hard, and J.P., somehow, throughout it

Tiger's Den, Taktsang Monastery, the sacred site where Guru Rinpoche landed on the back of a flying tiger to bring Buddhism to Bhutan.

At Paro Dzong, watching the dancing girls rehearse a Buddhist ceremony.

Chomolhari Base Camp at 14,500 feet, at the border with Tibet. This was Mallory's favourite mountain *en route* for Everest.

Blessings from His Holiness the Fourteenth Dalai Lama in Dharamsala. We go to Everest with flowers and prayers.

Shekar Dzong, Tibet: the rocky 'White Glass Fort'. This monastery was almost entirely destroyed by the Chinese.

On the Tibetan plateau between Shekar and Tingri at 15,000 feet. 'Here,' said Mallory, 'is a beauty of form, a kind of ultimate harmony.'

The Rongbuk Monastery – the highest in the world, at 16,400 feet – guards the approach to Everest, below.

Opposite: Everest, or Chomolungma – Goddess Mother of the Earth – from Base Camp, at 17,000 feet.

The *puja* at Base Camp conducted by the lama from the Rongbuk Monastery.

Chinese, Soviet and American members of the Peace Climb discuss tactics at their Base Camp.

all, had been instructing Swanee and Jules to film it. Poor lads, they and Graham were having a tricky time filming, as I repeatedly squashed them with excitement. For Graham, it was particularly poignant, as he was actually following in the footsteps of his great uncle, for Howard Somervell in 1924 reached 28,000 feet without oxygen.

Graham had fond memories of the great Everesteer, referring to him as 'Uncle Hunch'. Margaret remained still, her face radiating happiness. She, more than anyone, knew how much effort and sacrifice J.P. had put into mounting the expedition. We missed Jeff, David, Veronique and the Sherpas, who were ahead of us. Our celebrations would have been perfect had they been there.

My emotions swelled up inside me again, and burst out in a constant stream of joyous reverence. I leave it to J.P. to describe it best: 'I knew the experience would be intense, so I had prepared Swanee to turn over [film] if it looked interesting. Brian gazed on the goddess and wept, we hugged each other and danced in the glowing light, and as always, his words and reactions were from the heart: "It [Brian had yet to address the mountain as 'She', though he would do so later] looks so beautiful ... I can see the North Col ... I can see the Hornbein Couloir ... I can see the top, I can see where we're going ... I think that's where Mallory is ... I just can't believe I'm here, it's a dream come true ... It's just so beautiful, it's not ugly. I thought it would be horrible, ugly, frightening, but it looks so beckoning from here ... The whole mountain's glowing, it looks so golden ... She feels like a friend. I can't wait to get up there, just look at those colours! Thank you, J.P., for bringing me here. This miracle wouldn't have taken place if it hadn't been for you, it's a privilege to be here!"

'And I felt, like Brian, that it was a miracle that we'd actually made it this far. It was the most joyous moment of filming that I'd experienced, tempered only by the lack of film. In the excitement, Jules had forgotten to load another magazine. While he went into the "black bag" to reload, Brian and I sat and gazed as the light rapidly left the valley, till only the top of Everest, 14,000 feet higher, was bathed in the golden light. It was a kind of epiphany. Brian became quiet, as he sometimes does, and philosophic: "Since I was a child, it's been in my mind, and it's got bigger and bigger and bigger. It looks massive, it looks huge, it looks golden. It looks as if it's got soul. For the first time in my life, I feel I'm near God, that's what it feels like; I believe in God ... It's wonderful, it makes me believe."

'And then the camera was ready again, but the moment had passed, and we got back in the truck and sped through the darkening night towards Shekar.'

As J.P. so rightly said, we did not film all of this, and the words were recorded on the DAT machine. The wonders of the day were not over, for as the sun was on the point of disappearing, Everest and the surrounding mountains turned a deep burgundy red. We showed no emotion, exhausted by the wonder of it all! We had stopped the car to have one final look, when a land-cruiser approached, coming from Shekar. Out jumped a cheerful young blonde American lady, who was part of the World Peace Expedition.

'Are you the BBC expedition?' she asked.

We all nodded happily as she went on to say, 'Welcome to the Peace Expedition! ... The climbers have done wonderfully, in spite of the appalling weather conditions. They've had many setbacks, yet they've managed to ascend the North Col and establish Camp IV ... Good luck with your filming!'

With a friendly wave, she had gone, and our eyes returned to the mountain. Mallory's words came to mind: 'The wind is blowing ... The sand, and all the landscape to leeward is like a wriggling nightmare of watered silk ... There, by some miracle, is a spring of water, and to the south is Everest, absolutely clear and glorious ... '

Now, as darkness enfolded us, we approached historic Shekar, where we would spend three days filming and acclimatizing, before finally moving into Base Camp. When we arrived, it was completely dark, and torches were in use everywhere. We were shown to our rooms by a stern-faced Tibetan matron in her sixties, who seemed put out that we had arived so late in the evening. We were only interested in sleep. I quickly put on my Alpinex gear to keep out the intense cold, made myself comfortable with a bar of chocolate, and soon fell asleep.

The following morning was cold and bright, and I left my grey, cell-like room and crossed the passage to peer out of the window. There, catching the first rays of the sun, were the majestic ruins of Shekar Dzong, rising to a height of over 15,000 feet. The Dzongpens, or Lords of Tibet, in the early days of the century, described it as the 'White Glass Fort' of Shekar Dzong, and within its protective walls was the 'Shining Crystal Monastery'. They referred also to the 'Rocky Valley Monastery'. This is the Rongbuk Monastery, which would be our next port of call after Shekar.

Tragically, it seems that the Chinese Cultural Revolution all but destroyed the Tibetan monastic tradition. Our memorable journey of the day before had many disquieting aspects. The monasteries that had been built over two thousand years before had been ransacked and destroyed by the Chinese, and their walls and *mani* stones had been used for building roads. Countless monasteries were subjected to this treatment throughout the length and breadth of Tibet.

What desecration of a harmonious and sacred way of life! To reduce the once proud fort of Shekar Dzong, with its luminously beautiful white terraced buildings, which carefully followed the long, winding, rocky ridge to almost touch the sky, must have needed an appalling cretinous energy. Because of the fort's considerable altitude, its destruction was carried out by tanks, mortar bombs and MIG fighter planes, which together pounded at its fortifications for days on end.

Two thousand monks prayed and meditated in a special room on the summit, as the dogs of war snarled and tore away the very fabric of their way of life. And yet the skeletal remains possess a dignity that survives it all. The monks have returned, albeit but a few, and the slow process of renovation has begun.

To return to my own activities, breakfast beckoned, and I made my way down to the cold, charmless passage that led to a bleak outside courtyard. The hotel proudly proclaimed that its standards were equal to those of a four-star hotel. J.P. added ruefully that only its prices were. I'll leave the description of the food to him: 'On the wall was a certificate, awarding the hotel a Chinese Michelin Star, but what was in the bowls that were unceremoniously plonked down on the table, once tasted, could only be described as like compost. Only Swanee, skinny as a goat, seemed able to put it into his stomach ... Perhaps he had been a plant in a previous life. The rest of us retched and cursed. We were, after all, paying $150 a night for the experience. Krisna was soon busy unpacking our stores, precious eggs were delivered to the cookhouse, and Krisna was seen teaching the cooks how to crack one.

'Margaret fainted leaving the latrines, and bonked her head on the hard concrete floor. The loudspeakers droned all night. It would be great to get to Base Camp, and have the big, green Bulgarian mess tent set up. Shekar was to be endured. In the morning we loafed around, short of breath and frequently making for the latrines, and even that was a struggle.'

Towards evening we went out to the plains to film the sunset. Once again I was Mallory as I spoke his words: 'The country is so bare that it reminds me of a crumpled Egyptian desert, the strangeness and wonder are hugely increased by the entire south of the valley being filled with this great mass of mountain. There is a monastery at Shekar, which means "shining glass". The head lama, the Dzongpen, is an extremely cunning old person, and a first-class trader. The crowd that gathered round us were incredibly dirty, washing appears to be almost entirely unknown. A noble Tibetan once boasted that during his lifetime, he had two baths: one at birth, and the other on the day of his marriage!

'Apart from this rather penetrating drawback, the Tibetans are a most likeable people; cheery, contented, good-natured and hard working, truthful and scrupulously honest. The lamas proved as attractive as their simpler countrymen; kindly, courteous and appreciative of little attentions. They were always ready to lend a hand. These few of my last impressions would be incomplete without a mention of Tibetan music.

'It is doubtless beautiful to the Tibetan ear, but to the Western ear, it is elementary in the extreme, and in point of view of extreme ugliness of sound, competes with the jarring, clashing squeaks, bangs and hoots of the jazz bands that were so fashionable at home, at the time of our departure for India.'

The following afternoon was to be spent filming me ascending the 'White Glass Fort', as had many members of the twenties expeditions. This was a thrilling prospect, and would bring the entire filming team into play. With a mild breeze, the weather fine and the scenery so breathtaking, everyone felt confident that the day's shoot would prove very special.

Starting from the base, at 14,000 feet, I began to climb slowly. It was a lovely feeling to be moving upwards at this height, and I welcomed the opportunity to keep myself in good condition. When I left England I was about sixteen stone, but I was now about fourteen and a half and losing weight by the day.

Mallory, when approaching Everest, frequently compared his condition with that of the other climbers, proudly writing to his wife that he felt strong and full of energy, and that he had not the least doubt that he would remain so.

Gradually gaining height, I was asked to pause while Swanee and Jules set up the camera. It was great fun, and gave me a chance to observe everyone. To a soul, they all appeared happy and well, though there was a significant difference in fitness between the BBC team, including myself, and what you might call the 'High-altitude Squad' of David, Jeff, Veronique and Wongchu. To my calculating eye they looked in a different class, and in all my mountain experience I have never seen anyone as fit as David Breashears. Jeff's tremendous strength was obvious, and he looked the perfect anchor man.

David had designated Jeff personally responsible for my safety; in other words, my 'minder'. He would go high, as he had been up to 26,000 feet on Makalu. Wongchu was lithe and cat-like, and was an acknowledged 'tiger climber'. He, too, would go high. David had painstakingly taught Veronique a great deal about climbing, and her efforts to keep up with him on previous expeditions had resulted in her present fine condition. She was also learning from David the complex art of filming.

It was most refreshing to have two couples with us who were so in love, and Margaret was just as impressive as her female counterpart. I felt she was slightly fitter than the rest of the BBC team, and her work rate and attention to detail were second to none.

Swanee, Jules and Graham thrived on work and their professionalism was a joy to watch. J.P. appeared not to be troubled by anything, and continued to bounce and lollop around like a human yo-yo. Here and there he jumped, examining some terrain, looking in the camera and admonishing me for pinching his chocolate.

As I approached a steep section David made me stop, and Jeff tested the ground first, before I was allowed to go on. This simple action was repeated many times, as I continued to ascend. Wearing my beige shirt, plus-fours and pith helmet, I also had with me my period umbrella and rucksack.

David and Jeff periodically instructed me to slow down.

'Don't try and impress us, Big Yeti!' smiled David. 'You've got a long way to go yet, before you reach the mountain ... '

His words were heeded by all, and Swanee and Jules breathed deeply as their faces tightened at the thought of Everest. Before this expedition they had not been higher than 10,000 feet. The day before, we had reached 16,500 feet by land-cruiser, and they were delighted. Now they were actually climbing towards 15,000 feet under their own steam.

Swanee was determined to do some ambitious shot from some distance away, and this entailed crossing a wide gully and going up a steep hill opposite. J.P. gave the nod, and the climbers guided them over the tricky terrain.

A stiff breeze was now blowing, making work difficult. The shot was completed, and we continued up. Time had passed quickly, and the sun was getting low in the sky. The whole climb had a feeling of reverence and we were like pilgrims fulfilling our quest. The fragile rocks on the steep sections required delicate handling, for we had no desire to add to the destruction the fort had already suffered. To use J.P.'s words: 'We continued up the steep path that leads to the meditation room. A dog was climbing the almost vertical hillside, parallel with us, curious. Probably a reincarnated lama; they are often said to return in the next life as dogs, if they have misbehaved. For that reason, there are always lots of dogs hanging round the monasteries.

'I took Swanee ahead, as again I wanted to record Brian's first reaction to the scene. David had prepared me by saying, for him, it was the most magical place in all Tibet ... I knew it must be something special.'

David was quite right, for when I pulled myself through the

broken wall into the roofless meditation room, I was totally stunned and speechless.

Marghanita Laski, the writer and philosopher, once said that
there are moments in life when we have a peak experience that
provides a starting point for deeper development. This was exactly
what was happening to me.

All thoughts of filming faded, and I concentrated on the higher
energies around me. The craggy walls bore witness to the shells
that had hit them, and the gaping holes revealed the town and
patterned fields far, far below. The scarcity of air was the more
noticeable because the constant icy wind took our breath away.
The ruined room bewitched the senses with its hallowed offerings.
Zip, zip, zip – the wind peppered the hundreds of coloured prayer
flags. Its wild energy kissed every vestige of those fluttering butterflies, and carried their message of devotion from that roofless
room on the roof of the world to mankind and the heavens
beyond.

It was remarkable that the Tibetans had climbed here, and
placed so many bunches of prayer flags. The vortex of wind and
energy stimulated constant laughter in me, which was shared by
all.

'This is the White Glass Fort!' I kept repeating. 'I can't believe
I'm here ... I read about this when I was a child ... This is where
they all came ... General Bruce, Mallory, Captain Noel ... They
were greeted by the Dzongpen way down there ... They were given
sweetmeats, flowers and gifts ... And celebratory dances were
performed in front of them ... This is actually it, the fabled White
Glass Fort, the most beautiful and sacred part of Tibet ... '

God, it was wonderful! The wind blew in celebration, and I
remained mute and as still as a rock. I broke the silence by looking
at J.P. and sadly observing, 'Oh, I wish Captain Noel were still
alive! ... He would have loved to have seen this on film.'

J.P. nodded in agreement. He recalls: 'To finish that sequence, I
wanted Brian to stand on the crumbling old walls of the Dzong
and look out. David was to run down the mountain and up
another, to get a spectacular shot from afar; I can think of no
other cameraman who would volunteer for such a shot, but he did,
and it's one of my favourites in the whole film. Brian, meanwhile

was being persuaded to climb up the wall. Jeff, Jules, Swanee and myself all held on to parts of his anatomy. He was most unhappy, which was understandable as there was a sheer thousand-foot drop. I did worry, though, as we finished the shot, that Everest might prove a little more precarious than the monastery wall.'

What amazed me was that David, Jeff and Veronique, after such a gruelling day, went off ahead of us, with Krisna, Wongchu and the Sherpas, to set up Base Camp. We stayed another day, to film in the fields. There I watched a farmer with his two yaks plough a barley field in circles. This is done to push the devil to the corner and freeze him out of the field. Digging is always done by two people, with one wooden spade. One pushes the spade slowly by the handle, and the other draws it by a rope. At 15,000 feet manual labour is a strain on the heart.

The following day we made our way to Tingri, to take some shots before moving on to Everest Base Camp. We were hit by an awe-inspiring sight: Everest loomed up, forbidding and gigantic, with her immense brothers and sisters in attendance. There, along-side her, was Changtse, the north peak, and mighty Makalu, and glittering white Cho-oyu. Giants and more giants stretching out endlessly.

Clouds from below occasionally obscured the view, and for the first time I cast my eyes on Everest's famous 'streamer'. The powerful west wind tears at its summit, carrying tiny ice crystals in a stream stretching for miles. Climbers dread this, for its signifies that conditions are severe for summit attempts. We were drawn to it like a magnet as we moved slowly over the plains, at about 15,500 feet.

We were now within thirty miles of the mountain. For the first time I could understand why Everest had been named by the ancients the 'Turquoise Mountain'. In that early-morning sunlight there was no division between mountain and sky. Everest appeared to be floating in the heavens, its rocks dark turquoise and the great snow fields a shade lighter. We stared long and hard, transfixed. Mallory's words on first seeing it were: 'Suddenly, our eyes caught a glint of snow through the clouds; and gradually, very gradually, in the course of two hours or so, visions of great mountainsides and glaciers and ridges, now here, now there, forms invisible for the most part to the naked eye, or indistinguishable from the clouds themselves, appeared through the floating rifts, and had meaning for us ... One whole, clear meaning, pieced from these fragments. For we had seen a whole mountain range, little by little, the lesser to the greater, until, incredibly higher in the sky than imagination had dared to dream, the top of Everest itself appeared.'

J.P. thought it was a good idea at this point to have me ride a yak, as Captain Noel did in 1922. The driver covers the beast's eyes, while the rider mounts from behind. If the yak sees you, then you're in trouble; mine did, and tossed me off with disdain. Try as we might, he wouldn't tolerate me, and it seemed a good time to move closer to the mountain.

The land-cruisers now proved their worth, as they bounced and bumped their way south, towards Base Camp. We found ourselves deep in the Rongbuk Valley, with soaring peaks all around us, for a while quite unable to see Everest.

I was aching with excitement! Soon I would be there, yet, really, all my life I had been there on the mountain. I realized I'd been climbing it for years. Now the final act was approaching! I thought of all those marvellous people who'd helped get me there, from Geoff Arkless and Nick Shearman, right through to Stephen Evans. Would you believe it? Evans was coming on a trek to Base Camp, and higher. Our executive producer was making that kind of effort!

The land-cruisers were having a hell of a job coping with the boulder-strewn road. We all felt a bit battered, and disembarked for a while to walk part of the way and film.

I rounded a corner ahead of the others, and found myself looking at a huge, broken *chorten*, and a few low-lying white and red buildings with old green roofs. I blinked and stared at it all, like a baby waking in its cot. Certainly my brain was working slowly, as if in a slow-motion dream, for I was looking at possibly the most breathtaking sight on earth.

I was standing 16,400 feet above sea level, and in front of me was the highest monastery in the world: the legendary Rongbuk Monastery. The valley, more than a mile wide, ran directly ahead for nearly twenty miles. At its far end, filling the valley with its gargantuan North Face of granite and snow, was Everest. Behind the seemingly monolithic structure of the monastery, Nature's genius had completed the picture with a hall of grandeur that led to the mountain.

'Look, it's the Rongbuk Monastery!' I whispered to my friends.

We all sank to our knees and remained motionless. The sky was clear and the day windless. To think that Captain Noel, in 1913 after three previous attempts, got to within forty miles of Everest. It had been rumoured for centuries that the monastery existed, though many thought it was simply a myth. Captain Noel knew otherwise, and finally saw it in 1922. Now I was seeing it at last in 1990.

Quietly, I thanked Chomolungma, the Mother Goddess of the Earth, for giving us such lovely weather and allowing us into her domain, but how was I ever going to get up that terrifying mountain? I was well enough at 16,000 feet, but what would I be like higher up? Indeed, could I get higher? What if I failed miserably at the East Rongbuk Glacier, at 20,000 feet.

Then there would be no film, and I wouldn't be able to tell Mallory's story. The BBC and Stephen Evans's sponsors would lose all their money, and I would let all those people down who had helped me. Silly thoughts, I know! But I wasn't a young man any more.

Could I possibly get up the North Col at 23,000 feet, as Captain Noel had done? If I could, this would be enough to complete the film. Would I survive the 'death zone' above 22,000 feet?

If? If? If? It was all 'ifs'. The dream had finally become a reality, and I was here. I felt as if I was at the centre of the world. J.P. said action, and I walked slowly to the monastery.

Occasionally, in that pristine, rarefied air, I heard birds singing. This delighted me, for it confirmed that this was indeed Chamalung, 'The Sanctuary for Birds'.

As I walked to the monastery, their song increased and made me remember that birds were considered by the Tibetans to be the reincarnated spirits of former human lives. Apart from the birds, there was not a soul in sight. The monastery was silent, but we knew the monks were there, and probably meditating. We would return later to receive the lama's blessing, and film the ceremony.

J.P. and the camera crew felt that we should take full advantage of the good weather, and film some more. We moved a hundred yards further up, working enjoyably and steadily. It was at this point that Graham Hoyland's name began to change. Because of his status as Somervell's great-nephew, we had always addressed him with that title. Over the weeks, as we bumbled about filming, it varied between Somervell's sister, mother or even grandfather. But now, his infernal DAT sound equipment was forever breaking down, and just when I was about to say something inspired, against a particularly good background, he would announce that it wasn't working. In mock horror, I would rage at him, 'That bloody awful shag DAT machine! ... Blow the bloody thing up!

So 'Shag DAT' became Graham's nickname for a while. Poor Graham also had a bit of a fright when earlier J.P. had questioned whether he should be retained for higher up the mountain, or possibly returned to the BBC in Bristol, since J.P. now had plenty of people to handle the sound. In reply, Graham said he would do anything to stay on the expedition.

'You can even call me "Dogbollock", if you like.'

Therefore, he received his official nickname, 'Dogbollock', and was kept on the team. I must say that the name suited him, as his boyish handsomeness was decreasing daily as the sun, and short-wave ultraviolet rays played havoc with his face and nose. We deeply valued his contribution to the project, and it was to prove priceless later. J.P. was simply doing his job as producer, and was delighted to find any excuse to keep the enterprising man on. Thankfully, there above the monastery, the sound worked splendidly and we continued filming.

The closer we moved towards Everest, the larger it seemed. I looked into the camera, and said, 'It looks absolutely terrifying – any idea of an easy snow slope is ridiculous. Captain Noel warned me. He said it filled the entire frame of his camera, but he told me not to be intimidated and to take it step by step ... and eat lots of honey!'

After completing this sequence we boarded our land-cruiser, driven by a patient, smiling Chinese named Chan, and fifteen minutes later arrived at Base Camp, at 17,000 feet. J.P. takes up the story: 'The first day was spent organizing, for there was much to do, since a good base camp is essential for the smooth running of both the climb and the filming. Our Sherpas, under the ever-smiling eyes of our sirdar, Wongchu, busied themselves erecting the big green mess tent which would be the focus of life for the next six weeks.

'Krisna unpacked his precious eggs, proudly showing that not a single one had been broken. David, Veronique and Jeff were demons of activity, laying out the stores, sorting through the climbing gear and helping Chuldim, Nawang and Phuli organize the camp. Most importantly, a toilet had to be dug.

'Base Camp has had a lot of expeditions over the past ten years, and they have all left their mark. It is not a pretty sight: broken bottles, tin cans and gas canisters litter the valley. Luckily, the wind and sun quickly dehydrate the turds, but there is a lot of toilet paper flapping around. We didn't want to add to the mess.

'A pit was dug, not an easy task at that altitude with the shale and rock frozen solid, but after an hour of shift work we had a decent-sized hole about four feet deep. The positioning was glorious: squatting over the hole, nimbly balanced on an overhanging rock, you could look on to the highest mountain on earth. As long as you didn't fall in, it was the best khazi Everest had ever seen. The erection of a flag system to warn others when it was occupied was the final touch that marked our expedition as one of class.

'And class it was: the Fortnum and Mason hampers were soon unpacked; champagne, port, Stilton, biscuits, smoked salmon and a variety of pâtés and hams were laid out, but it was then that a major catastrophe took place. While the unsuspecting Krisna's back was turned, a cunning dog snatched a huge leg of ham and bounded off, chewing and guzzling it as he went. Krisna turned to see the precious ham disappear over the hill and leapt after it, cursing in Nepali, Sherpa and I know not what canine tongue. The dog stopped, dropped its treasure and under a hail of rocks, scurried away.

'The leg had lost a huge chunk of flesh. Krisna was bereft and profoundly worried because this was a serious loss. On the "Yeti Expedition", when Krisna had served us so well, our yak herders managed to stealth away with an entire yak-load of forty kilos of salami, ham and cheese. It had been a bitter blow to the expedition;

we never got it back and, as a result, the quality of food degenerated as the expedition progressed. Krisna knows better than anyone that an expedition climbs on its stomach, and the stomach at altitude is a capricious thing: food is invariably unappetizing and the body seems uninteresting in chomping, yet chomp one must.

'Weight loss is inevitable, and it is not unusual to lose twenty to thirty pounds, so the more appetizing the food, the better the chance of keeping fit. David was well aware of the need for high-quality nosh, and he and Veronique had put together a gourmet's supply of meals. Add to this the treats from the hampers, and we had the best food of any expedition.

'Even the International Peace Climb, whose camp resembled a superstore, came to us and were impressed, "You Brits do it in style!" they would say as they quaffed a glass of port, popped a smoked oyster and looked longingly at our pile of fresh eggs. We could have had anything for a dozen eggs, such is the attraction of fresh food to the oxygen-starved palate.

'So, the loss of the ham was bad news. Krisna went fearfully to tell Veronique of the loss, for she was now the food boss and a highly efficient one at that. An arched eyebrow was all the reprimand he needed. That dog was dead if it dared to show its muzzle in our camp again. Krisna looked ill that night; in fact he became ill, so ill that in the end we had to call the American doctor over from the Peace Climb.

'Dr Kurt was worried. Krisna had a fever, cramps and his heart was beating like a captured bird's. Oxygen and injections were administered, and we were fearful for his life, for such is the speed of sickness at this altitude that a simple malady can be fatal; the body's defences are at their weakest. We wanted no chances to be taken, and it was a good week before little Krisna was up and at the cooker again. I blame the dog.

'Meanwhile, the Peace Climb members ventured over from their camp, a half-hour further up the valley. It was the first time I had met them, although we had telephoned and faxed copiously in the weeks leading up to our departure from England. Warren Thompson, the deputy leader, and now in charge, as Jim Whittaker had returned temporarily to Kathmandu with a blood clot in his leg, was the first to introduce himself. Extremely pleasant and helpful, he gave us every assistance we needed.

'Their expedition was huge compared with ours: sixty people in all. They had satellite communications, a supply of food to last the year, and the best climbing gear available. We had agreed to share the use of their fixed ropes, oxygen and medical personnel, so we were like part of their team, though quite separate. Without them, our ascent of the mountain would be impossible. They had already been at Base Camp for over a month and were well established on the mountain.

'Like Mallory, and most big Himalayan expeditions, they were laying siege to the mountain. A series of camps was being set up, and stocked with food and oxygen, and so far the team had made good progress, despite extremely fierce winds and biting cold.

'It was still early in the season, 15 April, Easter Sunday, but they hoped to put men on the summit on Earth Day, a mere week away. It seemed unlikely, as they had only just established Camp V at 26,000 feet, and needed to make two more before they would be within reach of the summit. The weather would determine everything.

'No matter how organized or how brilliant your team may be, in the end it is Everest that decides when you can climb; you cannot fight her severe moods. You just wait them out and hope that a window of clear weather finds you well prepared and ready for the final push. Mallory and Irvine, like so many after them, were beaten by the weather, and Mallory was fully aware of the power of the goddess: "A mountaineer must have good fortune, and the greatest good fortune is some constant kindness in Mount Everest itself, for we must remember the highest of mountains has a severity so awful and fatal, that the wisest of men do well to think and tremble, even on the threshold of their endeavour."

'Brian fully understood that in the end it was Everest that would decide how high he went. He was convinced that if we came with prayers and flowers the mountain would be kind to us ... But would he be proved right?'

The following morning I immediately homed in on Krisna, who was quietly sitting in his warm tent drinking tea. He was lucky to be alive: he looked pale and drawn and totally bemused. He was alive, that was all that mattered. We had to thank Dr Kurt for that. The injections and a good supply of oxygen had saved the day, but it had been a near thing. Poor Krisna, he was such a sweet, cheerful little fellow.

David Breashears had been a tower of strength, racing up to the Peace Climb's Base Camp, 500 feet above us, to find the doctor. He, Jeff and Veronique conveyed vividly their total commitment to safeguarding everyone on the expedition. Hour in, hour out until dawn, they did everything in their power to help Krisna, giving him love and encouragement and wiping his feverish head, and making sure that the correct flow of oxygen was getting to him. Only in the early hours, when they were satisfied that the crisis was over, did they get some sleep. At breakfast, they too looked drawn and washed out. No wonder, when you think that this had happened right after their massive effort to build Base Camp, and what a marvellous place it was.

It was the envy of all the other expeditions. David's big old Bulgarian tent was roomy and warm, easily accommodating our food stores, as well as providing kitchen space and a large dining area that easily housed the long line of tables and chairs. It had a cheerful, warm atmosphere, and we felt totally at home in it.

After the initial elation of arriving at Base Camp, the Krisna crisis had brought us down to earth with a bump. David was confident that Krisna would soon be helping in the kitchen, and advised us to be cheerful and take it easy. As we had just reached 17,000 feet, this was good advice. We all felt the altitude, and Jules was suffering from a headache and Swanee had a bad cough, so we relaxed on our sleeping bags, only stirring into life for coffee, tea and lunch.

Krisna's illness had been a shock to us all, and this feeling was not helped when we learned from the visiting Dr Kurt that the World Peace Climb Leader, 'Big' Jim Whittaker, who was sixty, was now suspected to have thrombosis in his leg, and was still in Kathmandu. As if that wasn't enough, a powerful woman climber on the same expedition had also been taken down to Kathmandu, and flown to America with clots in her lungs. Also, one of the super-fit Soviet climbers was suffering from suspected pulmonary oedema, which simply means the lungs fill up with liquid. If not treated quickly, the afflicted person becomes unconscious, rapidly deteriorates and dies. The only answer is to get him down to the safety of lower altitudes, and during the descent administer certain drugs and apply oxygen. But it is the lower altitude that is the key to recovery.

This is difficult on the northern Tibetan side of the mountain, as the Tibetan plain goes on for over a hundred miles at 14,000 feet or so. The Soviet climber, a sweet young man named Velodin Victor, was making a slow recovery, but it was extremely unlikely that he could now go high. In Krisna's case, when he was almost dying, Dr Kurt felt it would have been senseless to move him anywhere, as he would not have survived.

In the afternoon sun I sat in my Alpinex baby suit and gazed at Everest and its white streamer. The Peace Climb had managed to fix ropes up the North Col, but had suffered hell. One Soviet climber described how the dreadful west wind had cut through their modern clothing and chilled them to the bone. The wind was so strong that it had lifted him on the fixed rope, thirty feet into the air, terrifying him.

So far, the few American and Soviet climbers I had seen from the Peace Climb looked spaced out with tiredness. I had not yet seen the Chinese contingent. They all appeared a fine bunch of young men, and Warren Thompson, the deputy leader, was friendly and helpful. But it was disquieting to hear them all coughing so badly, and there can be no doubt that if the White Goddess is in one of her black moods, even the finest climbing expertise and ultra-modern clothing are powerless against her.

These climbers had been there for weeks, and had taken a pounding. But fitness they had in abundance, for the Peace Climb had been together on and off since June 1989, climbing Mount Rainier in Washington State, USA, and Mount Elbrus, in the Soviet Caucasus, the following September − all in preparation for the mighty Everest.

It was thrilling news to hear too that the great Everesteer, Peter Habeler, was on the mountain, attempting the Hornbein Couloir via the West Ridge route. In 1978 Habeler and Messner had reached the summit by the South Col route without oxygen. The amazing images taken by Messner from the summit, of Habeler making those final steps, is the most moving piece of film I have ever seen. I simply kept my fingers crossed in the hope that I might meet Habeler.

It was rumoured that he too was having a frightful time on the mountain, and that he might have contracted pneumonia. This growing catalogue of illness weighed on my mind. From where I was sitting, I could see clearly that Everest's North Face was in the grip of a hurricane-like storm, with winds from the jet stream scouring its ramparts. At this moment I became aware of David and Jeff by my side. They gently pressed a huge mug of decontaminated water in my hand, saying, 'Drink, Big Yeti.'

I drank deeply and laughed heartily, but my false cheerfulness failed to convince either of them, and I lapsed into silence. For a long while they watched the mountain and me. Finally, David said, 'Brian ... You have nothing to fear but your fear ... You will be fine on the mountain. Don't be concerned about the bad weather and cold. From now on it will get warmer, and there will be periods of good weather, in which we will coordinate, hopefully, our ascents of the higher camps ... We are here for several weeks, which gives us plenty of time for gradual acclimatization. Do everything slowly and be patient, and above all, don't do anything foolish! ... You seem, to Jeff and myself, to be in fine condition, though you must eat more.'

'I can't stand spicy food. My preference is for plain stuff, like porridge and eggs,' I replied.

David smiled at this.

'All right, Big Yeti. Tonight I'll cook you the finest omelette you've ever tasted, but don't forget: drink all the time, even if you have to spend the day peeing!'

And with that he was gone. Jeff popped a lump of chocolate in my mouth, and said kindly, 'Brian, we think you're a swell guy, and we're very proud to be on this expedition.'

I voiced my reservations about it all, and related my misgivings about subjecting people like Krisna to the hazards of altitude because of my selfish obsession. Jeff silenced me.

'No, Brian. That is all meaningless ... Krisna is here because he wants to be here. He's an experienced cook and has been on many expeditions. We're all devoted to this expedition and its objectives. Making this film in this unique way is exactly what we believe in. Of all the places on earth, this is where we want to be; for that we are grateful. We're all aware of the pressure you're under, and are here to help. If you don't take another step, the fact that you've turned up is enough. Now in a few days David and I are going to teach you some extra climbing techniques. In the meantime, enjoy the scenery.'

Jeff strolled off.

What kindness! He and David were marvellous blokes. Cheered up and rejuvenated, I walked upwards for a hundred yards to look at the mountain again. More of Mallory's words came to mind: 'At the end of the valley, and above the glacier, Everest rises not so much as a peak, as a prodigious mass. There is no complication for the eye. The highest of the world's great mountains, it seems, has to make but a single gesture of magnificence to be Lord of all, vast in unchallenged and isolated supremacy. To the discerning eye, other mountains are visible. Giants between 23,000 and 26,000 feet high. Not one of their slender heads even reaches their chief's shoulders; beside Everest, they escape notice, such is the pre-eminence of the greatest!'

Looking at those words, I am forced to say, as they say in the theatre, 'Follow that.'

I then took a newly formed path that led to the Base Camp of the Peace Climb. Several yards short of it, I stopped, feeling out of place. A mixture of languages rent the air, and climbers of many nationalities, in garish, vibrant colours, milled about everywhere. Nice people, I thought, but I'm not ready for this yet. Looking at my twenties clothes, I turned and headed for David's tent. But I was stopped in my tracks by a Chinese gentleman, who addressed me in pidgin English. His manner was quite repellant, or, as a Danish friend of mine at drama school used to put it, 'most undelicious'.

The diminutive Chinaman possessed a most irritating voice. Throughout my travels in Asia, the people of that marvellous continent had found my appearance wonderfully funny, their humour being always solidly based on kindness and fun. Not so with this gentleman. He viewed me with deep suspicion, and his patronizing manner had a charmless, cruel edge to it. His derisory laughter at my clothes sounded like a rattlesnake with a cactus up its arse.

'What are you, Mr Lordship?' he sneered. 'Oh, yes! ... I see ... You is Mallory! ... Ha, ha, ha, ha! ... You tink you go on Everest? Ha, ha, ha, ha! ... You big, fat Engliss gentleman, who will not go higher than Base Camp! ... How? ... You dooo fat, Meester Mallory! ... Maybe you pay more money to me? ... I introduce myself. I am Mr Ping, liaison officer in charge from the Chinese Mountaineering Association.'

As I looked at him the words came to mind of Achilles in Shakespeare's *Troilus And Cressida*, as he examines Hector: 'Tell me, you heavens, in which part of his body shall I destroy him? ... Whether there, or there, or there or there?'

Of course, I did nothing of the kind, but smiled courteously and introduced myself. Then I realized that this was the same Mr Ping to whom two years previously I had sent £1,300 for permission to climb the North Col.

So! I thought. You are the four-eyed pillock who didn't return my money!

Again, I smiled and touched my hat, as he whined and sneered. I left him as I found him − Lord of All. Never did an Englishman conduct himself so impeccably.

Returning to our camp, I spied David Breashears sitting on a rock on top of the hill that overlooked the tents. He was in a blue anorak and grimacing with half a smile in the cold breeze.

'Join me, Big Yeti!' he called.

As I mounted the hill I found that J.P., Margaret and the rest were clambering up to watch the sun set on Everest. It is interesting how the winds intensify, even after only ascending a hundred feet. David and I found ourselves hugging each other for warmth. He gripped me hard, with tears from the cold smarting his cheeks.

Three-quarters of Chomolungma was in darkness, with the final pyramid scarlet red in the evening sun. Once that life-giver leaves the sky, the Rongbuk Valley's temperature rapidly plummets way below freezing point, forcing the best of constitutions to scurry for cover and warmth. This moment was fast approaching.

'I think that I'll retire, gentlemen,' said Swanee, in his polished, quixotic way.

'Yes,' added Julian, in his graceful, stiff-upper-lip manner. 'I think I'll join you.'

Dogbollock remained steadfast, with his red nose getting bigger by the minute. Margaret and J.P. had gone beyond hugging, and in their intense efforts to get warm gave the impression of a 'Two-headed Bird Yeti', perched and frozen eternally in time. Margaret finally broke the image by saying that she couldn't feel her bottom. J.P. popped a piece of chocolate in her mouth that he had stolen from the Fortnum's hamper, and holding on to his beloved's hand, he sped down the hill without a word.

'What about some chocolate for me?' I shouted.

'No, Big Yeti!' he shouted back. 'You must use your own … '

'We're here at last,' said David to me, interrupting the banter.

He then slapped me on the back in celebration. Graham laughed, and his red Comic Relief nose quivered. Below, in the distance, the Peace Climb's tents lit one by one and shone incandescently against the dark blue of the approaching night.

David gripped me, saying, 'We're going to have a tremendous time! … Don't worry, we'll all carry you up the mountain. I'll arrange a pulley system to winch you up the final pyramid, and have all the Russian, American and Chinese climbers waiting at the summit. Then they can form a human pyramid, and you can climb up and stand on the head, and be the highest, sexiest and biggest yeti to have climbed Everest! … What do you think?'

'That suits me fine, David … Just fine!' I replied.

Our frozen eyes watched the last light on the mountain fade, and her black outline stood out against the star-studded sky. As we approached the warmth of our tent, we popped our heads into the nearby tent of Krisna. Though still deathly pale, he was much improved. He held a hot mug of soup and managed a faint smile.

'You keep still and sleep for the next few days, Krisna,' David said.

'No!' replied the Sherpa. 'I come work tomorrow … '

'You come back, Krisna, when doctor say so!' said David firmly.

As we were walking away, David muttered to me, 'It's a tricky business, altitude sickness, Brian … People can appear to be getting better, and suddenly have a relapse.'

Dr Kurt had been most attentive to Krisna. This, added to his duties with the Peace Climb, kept him more than busy. The international team were licking their wounds, and welcomed the opportunity for a respite from the harsh conditions up high.

Veronique was doing a great job supervising and helping with the cooking, and David kept his promise and made me the most delicious omelette full of cheese and herbs. The lamps burned brightly, and Sherpas, climbers and BBC staff ate happily, as kettles boiled and pans simmered in the kitchen area behind.

The large canvas tent had been bought years ago by David for a modest sum, and he felt that this was possibly its last season. This made us sad, as it was wonderfully cosy and snug. It was interesting that during the day, the flaps of the plastic windows were open, but once the sun went down, they were closed immediately as the temperature fell many degrees below zero.

This was our second night at 17,000 feet. So far, so good. After dinner we all wished each other a friendly goodnight, and made our way to our tents. It was that particular journey of forty yards that you had to brace yourself for. Coming out of the warmth of the dining tent into the freezing night air was a nightmare.

I felt my eyeballs go stiff with cold and shock, and the rest of my body followed suit. With our head-mounted torches flashing, we dashed like maniacs for cover. Of course, you also had to steel yourself to having a pee before retiring, and this was particularly abhorrent. Groans came from all sides, and suffering voices rang out, 'What are we doing in this bloody awful place?'

This task completed, I always found my fingers tingling with cold as I opened the reluctant zip of my fly sheet. I then tackled the circular zip of the inner tent, having become by now a heap of shivering jelly. With the outer and inner flaps zipped up again, you are still freezing and continue speaking and singing breathlessly as you adjust your sleeping bag and lantern. The worst moment comes when you struggle to get your coat and boots off. Now the manic singing really increases in intensity.

The overhead twenties lamp, given to me by Adrian Rigelsford back in England, rocks back and forth as I get into my Alpinex baby suit. Bump, bump, bump it goes in response to the exertions of activity at 17,000 feet. I dive into the huge sleeping bag, zip it up and put a bonnet on my head.

The interior of the tent is covered with white ice, and a strong wind blows down the valley from the sleeping black goddess, shaking its foundations. Well done, Jeff, I think, for he has secured the guy-lines and edges of the tent with large rocks that hold firm. I reach out and switch off the lamp, snuggle deeper into my cocoon and sleep like a caterpillar.

For the next few days, the routine was very much the same. You simply had to take it easy and acclimatize. For instance, if anyone was foolish enough, at these altitudes, to rush ahead and attempt to climb the mountain, he would quickly collapse and die.

The adaptation of the body to low atmospheric pressure has interested physiologists for many years. It was discovered that with increasing altitude there is an increase in the number and concentration of the red cells of the blood that contain oxygen. Quite simply, this increase in red cells compensates for the lack of oxygen at altitude. The higher you get, the more red cells you produce. However, this process has to be given time.

One of the problems is that as you get very high, say to 21,000 feet, the blood thickens considerably and there is a real danger of thrombosis and strokes. There seem to be no safety guidelines, for the performance by an individual one year can be totally different the next.

A great many climbers find that they cannot go any higher than, say, 21,000 feet; this would seem to be their ceiling, and try as they might, they cannot push it any further. Then there are some people who find that 15,000 feet, or even lower, is their maximum. Whatever height they reach, they are delighted with their accomplishment. Wanting to go high but surviving is a fundamental part of the spirit of mountaineering.

Many experts feel that despite extensive research, problems of altitude are still not totally understood. However, it is generally agreed that you deteriorate rapidly above 22,500 feet, which is why it is called the 'death zone'.

The higher you get, particularly without oxygen, the greater danger you are in. At these great heights the brain, starved of its customary sea-level oxygen, does not operate efficiently. In many cases the climber is not aware of the seriousness of his condition, and needs his companions to point it out.

Therefore we would ascend gradually, and, during acclimatization, tolerable headaches were permitted, but no more. If they became serious, or there was continuous nausea or vomiting, we should immediately come down. My real concern was cerebral haemorrhage; the thought of that made me wince.

One afternoon, Swanee and Jules filmed me painting a picture of Everest, in the guise of Somervell. Veronique was the real artist, for I simply brushed over her artwork. It was pleasing to film this, as Somervell's paintings, in the twenties books, are fascinating.

Though the day was clear, you could see that Everest was beset by demon winds as its streamer poured out powerfully from the summit. After an hour or so of filming, J.P. called it a day, and I wandered slowly up the valley. After all the emotion of seeing the great mountain days before, I started to view it in a different light. Mallory's words express it perfectly: 'Everest has become something more than a fantastic vision ... The problem of its great ridges and glaciers began to take shape, and to haunt the mind, presenting itself at odd moments and leading to definite plans.'

My plans were about to get me into trouble, for my impatience was beginning to show. Feeling fit and raring to go, I headed for the Peace Camp at 17,000 feet, but veered off when I was near it and walked half a mile further on to the start of the central Rongbuk Glacier.

The terminal moraine was about a hundred feet high, and I made my way along its base to my immediate left, where I had observed the Soviets exiting from a gully the day before. After twenty minutes, I found the entrance and carried on. The cliffs on my left were light brown, and looked like sandstone. To my right was the boulder-strewn lip of the glacier. The natural stone-filled path presented no problems, and I went on my merry way.

After a couple of hundred yards, I moved on to the rim of the glacier, again on an obvious, natural path, and continued my ramble. Though Everest was storm-bound, the weather where I walked was fine and still. The mountain drew me on and on. After about a mile, I decided to stop.

There I was, alone on the central Rongbuk Glacier. This was where Mallory explored with Bullock in 1921 on their reconnaissance, the first people on earth to do so. The glacier took my breath away. It went on and on for miles, with what looked like thousands of white and green fins of ice, varying in size from five to a hundred feet in height. They looked like sharks and dolphins frozen in a white sea by the power of Chomolungma herself.

From a distance of twelve miles, I could clearly see the Hornbein Couloir and West Ridge, and the beauty of the Lingtren Peaks. It was amazingly still; the glaciers made no sound. Only by straining my ears could I hear the distant moan of the streamer, high on Everest.

I'd better go, I thought, as the weather could change and I had no knowledge of this kind of terrain. Slowly and carefully I left that hallowed and hushed landscape, and made my way back. When I passed the Peace Camp, I saw a lone figure standing still, close to our Base Camp. Some distance behind was another figure. It was David and Jeff.

I went straight to David, who said not a word, but walked silently alongside me. On meeting Jeff, the same thing happened, and I found myself walking in between them. As we entered the camp, J.P. waved me over. He was talking to Warren Thompson of the Peace Climb.

Warren was, as usual, warm and outgoing, and advising J.P. on handling Mr Ping. Bursting with my experience on the glacier, I unfolded the story of my little trek to them. My emotional, colourful tale was received in stony silence. I could see that J.P. loved it, but he was obviously sworn to silence.

'I thought I could trust you, Brian.'

It was David's voice, coming from right behind me. I turned to face the music.

'I really thought I could trust you,' he continued. 'What you have done is irresponsible and dangerous ... Anything could have happened to you. Where you have been is unstable ... Those sandstone rocks are rotten, and can easily break away and crush you to death, or at least break a leg ... You may not have felt it, but the glacier moves ... There are unseen crevasses everywhere ... The ground is tricky, and you could easily have twisted your ankle. It would not be easy to find you in your green tweeds — you'd be completely camouflaged ... I must remind you that even the bright colours of today are not easy to detect when people are any distance ... I just can't believe you've done this! You promised you would never do anything silly, and do exactly as I told you! ... If you behave like this on the mountain, then I won't accept the responsibility ... '

Warren now joined in: 'David is quite right — it's dangerous up there. I check on every guy who goes up there, and rigorously always make sure they don't go solo ... '

There was a long pause while David nodded about four times, which is a habit of his when he is confirming a point. Jeff stood still, like the Rock of Gibraltar, and said nothing.

I was the Incredible Shrinking Man — about one and a half inches tall, and getting smaller by the minute. With my mind digging a hole in the ground with an imaginary shovel, I waited, hoping to be let off the hook. It never came, and David strode off with Jeff following, to attend to more important matters.

I headed for my tent utterly ashamed of myself. After about half an hour, I was aware of J.P. by my side. He had a flask of coffee and poured some into my plastic mug, at the same time giving me a handful of delicious chocolates from the Fortnum's hamper. 'You've been a naughty boy, Big Yeti!' he whispered. 'And I should really give you a lot of lines to learn. On second thoughts, I'll leave the flask of coffee with you. Remember, you must keep drinking. See you at supper.'

Two hours later I joined the chomping gang as they enjoyed gorgeous soup, mouth-watering cheese, fresh bread and omelettes. As chocolate pudding was being served, and fresh coffee was brewing in the background, the dining area hummed with anticipation and happiness. I took advantage of the moment and apologized to David and everyone else for my irresponsible behaviour.

It was generously accepted by all, and David viewed me with a long, measured smile and nodded four times, in that strange way of his. He then broke his silence, by requesting me to imitate George C. Scott, as General Patton, in one of our favourite films, *Patton: Lust For Glory*. He liked the moment when Patton wins a tank battle against Rommel, and shouts, 'You magnificent bastard! I read yer book!'

Much to David's delight, I then recited the last speech in the film.

Later that night, snug in my sleeping bag, as my eyes closed I saw David's face. He was nodding in that strange way of his and smiling at my rendering of General Patton, confirming that I had indeed been forgiven for my ill-advised stroll up the glacier.

At breakfast the next day I was jokingly chastised by Margaret for not making use of the shower tent that had been painstakingly erected by Wongchu and Phuli. The technique of using it was elementary: you simply carried a large, hot bowl of water, placed it inside, stripped off and washed yourself all over. I shunned this activity, feeling that I would lose my body oils. At ground level, I passionately love taking a bath at any opportunity, but at high altitude I found I didn't sweat. Besides, I have a keen nose and didn't detect anything untoward. Of course, I washed my hands, face and hair, but nothing else. It was like some superstition. So far I hadn't had a headache or a cold. In fact I hadn't even sneezed and I felt very well and fit. I just didn't want to disturb my metabolism unduly, but there was no convincing Margaret, who insisted that I was too lazy to bother.

J.P. had arranged for us to film the lama, the nuns and monks during a Buddhist service at the Rongbuk Monastery. At the same time he was arranging for a *puja*. This sacred ceremony would be conducted by the lama, for it was absolutely essential that we should be blessed by the dear old man. Without it, the Sherpas would refuse to climb higher.

Our expectations of peace as we approached the gate to the courtyard of the monastery were shattered by a dog that would have rivalled Cerberus, the three-headed canine that even Hercules had difficulty in controlling. Dogs are no strangers to me. I've kept them all my life and have six at the time of writing, but nothing in all my experience of them had prepared me for this character. He was obviously possessed by the goblin Srin-Po, who devours the limbs of men. His black wiry fur stood up like bristles on a yard broom, and his red gums and pronounced white teeth were in keeping with his boiling, bloodshot eyes.

Jeff, big as he was, was the first to be bitten, which gave me time to form my defences. That trusty friend, the British umbrella, proved infallible, and I stuck it firmly in the brute's mouth. Try as he might, he couldn't get past it, giving everybody else time to climb up the nearby walls.

Then the old lama arrived and gave a sound like a weasel, whereupon the goblin-dog became like an angel. Sweet accord was again returned to the monastery.

Instantly the lama indicated that he wanted the favour returned by displaying his open mouth and emphasizing that his five remaining teeth were giving him hell. Could he have some aspirins? J.P. gave the old boy a month's supply, and we were admitted to the monastery.

Swanee was soon rolling the camera. It was a strange, captivating experience to be sitting there in the last remaining small central hall with the old lama and his ten monks and two nuns, as they chanted and played their ancient instruments.

One could not help but be moved by their devotion. Outside, the wind seemed to bemoan the loss of so many mystical and enchanting buildings. In 1922 there were hundreds of monks and nuns at Rongbuk, resplendent in ceremonial robes and fantastic masks as they danced for hours in honour of Mallory and his companions. Thank God that Captain Noel had put it all on film for future generations to see.

The lama of the monastery in 1922 was one of the holiest Hermit Monks of Tibet, and the incarnation of the god Chongraysay. The monastery was the shrine dedicated to Chomolungma, and the lama was the High Priest of the mountain, who communed with the Goddess Mother of the Earth.

According to Tibetan legend, Rongbuk Monastery was built two thousand years ago. The great Indian saint, Padmasambhava, after travelling the Himalayas, rested a while at the monastery on his mission to bring Buddhism to Tibet. It is said that he ascended Everest, sitting in his chair and transported by a sunbeam. There he sat, enthroned on the summit of the world, many centuries before Hillary and Tenzing's ascent.

Our filming lasted for an hour or so. My thoughts and feelings fluctuated between the images of the twenties and the present day.

Of all the places on this beautiful planet of ours, this highest-situated of lamasaries is surely the fabled Shangri-La. And what a privilege to be a part of this rare ceremony. At its conclusion we presented the lama with a splendid Tibetan *thangka*, signifying long life, that J.P. had brought from Bhuton.

The lama was deeply touched, and bestowed white scarves of blessing around our shoulders. His face was dark, almost purple, and strong and criss-crossed with deep lines, while his eyes were full of kindness and merriment. He was a splendid little fellow, whose face lit up even more when Wongchu translated to him the message that J.P. would give the monastery all our surplus food when the expedition was over.

The dreaded Tibetan tea was then served. This appalling brew is terribly sweet, and topped with rancid butter. To refuse a cup would be, at the very least, impolite. To reduce the agony, I gulped mine down quickly, not realizing that if you do so, your cup is immediately refilled. The lama wouldn't let me off the hook, insisting on further cups, and showing great interest in my twenties clothes.

J.P. said that the old boy probably remembered me from a previous incarnation, and mistook me for General Bruce. Incidentally, in 1922, when the general was offered buttered tea in the same circumstances, he declined, saying, with some inspiration, 'Tibetan buttered tea is the most delicious tea in the world, but I have taken a vow not to drink it until I have climbed Mount Everest.'

The lama's joy knew no bounds when J.P. loaded him with big fat bags of popcorn, his favourite treat!

The last shot of the day was of the monks and the lama doing a ritualistic dance outside in the small courtyard. It was very commendable but a bit lethargic. J.P. tried to energize them into something more exciting, by giving a demonstration of some rare dance performed in Bhutan. They were completely mystified by it all. J.P.'s efforts to convince them became more and more dramatic and elaborate, as he turned round and round in his vibrant Berghaus padded jacket, looking like a cross between a whirling dervish and the Michelin Man, doing the Mexican hat dance. He was a lovely mover, and we applauded him accordingly.

We were all laughing so much and having such a good time, that we almost forgot Cerberus, tied up by the door. We gave the snarling beast a wide berth, and went on our way, exchanging waves and goodbyes with our delightful hosts.

One of the most striking features of the Captain Noel film is that the monastery, for all its glory, was very modest in design. Had it have been a giant edifice, it would have ruined the natural grandeur of the valley, with its own natural cathedral, Everest.

Of course, only a few buildings remained now, and the large *chorten*, which once had emblems of the sun and moon, symbolizing the light of Buddha's teaching illuminating the world, was in a sorry state, and collapsing by the day.

Still, there were welcome signs of restoration, for elderly nuns painstakingly applied their skills to painting the bare, broken rooms. Above the monastery, there are numerous hidden rock-hewn caves dotted all over the hillsides. In 1922 each one was inhabited by a hermit, and these men lived their entire lives there. Here, they fasted and meditated, evolving towards freedom, so that when they died their soul might escape from the cycle of earthly birth, death and rebirth.

I have described how cold it is up there, so you can imagine what these hermits endured in their hillside cells. David found us one that went deep underground. We lit the old wax candles that were down there, and were riveted by the Buddhas and other holy relics that were revealed in every corner. There we were, filming in a dark, holy cave, right under Everest itself!

Before General Bruce departed from the monastery in 1922, he and Captain Noel were granted an audience with the great 'God Lama'. They found themselves walking up a narrow, dark stairway to his shrine in the upper part of the monastery. A long, deep trumpet call heralded their arrival. Captain Noel told me that other trumpeters held the note, blowing in relays. They came to a small, simply furnished room. Inscriptions in Tibetan were on the walls, and before them were two lamas holding a screen of cloth, which they then slowly lowered.

A figure sat cross-legged, in the Buddha posture, absolutely motionless and still. They saw the face of an elderly man of extraordinary personality. His Mongolian features had a singular cast of thought and beauty. Captain Noel told me, 'He seemed to look over us, and yet through us ... There was something vastly observant, and yet impersonal about his gaze ... The screen of cloth was raised, and our audience was at an end.'

Outside, General Bruce said, 'Gee, that chap is either the holiest saint, or the greatest actor on earth!'

To end this account of our day's filming, I should add that as Swanee completed the last shot in the cave the fiendish Mr Ping appeared like a hobgoblin from behind a boulder, demanding more dollars. J.P. rose above his impolite sneers, and handled him charmingly.

The following morning I was amazed to find the lama outside our mess tent, stuffing his face with porridge and pancakes, and drinking with relish the Fortnum's Blue Mountain coffee. I sat down with him and nodded him a 'Good morning', and in between mouthfuls he said, 'Aaalooo, Bed Yeti!'

He had obviously heard J.P. call me 'Big Yeti', and thought it was my name. When the old boy was suitably fed, he ascended the small hill overlooking our camp, and joined us for the sacred *puja*.

Wongchu and all the Sherpas had done a lovely job fixing all the pretty, coloured prayer flags to string attached to poles and ski sticks. It was good to see Krisna there too, giving a hand and arranging the offerings. A steady, cold breeze blew from the mountain, emphasizing that she, Chomolungma, was what it was all about. When everything was in order, and the whole of our expedition comfortable, the lama, with the help of a young smiling monk, began.

It was a short but immensely moving ceremony, with the lama and the monk taking it in turns to chant out the prayers. At the climax we all stood and threw rice into the air. This action was repeated several times, and unfortunately, each time the strong wind sent it straight into the lama's face. This forced the young monk to hide his face with a smile, as the quiet expletives from the old boy were not part of the ceremony. When the *puja* was over, we all nodded and shook hands. With the mountain looking ominous in the background, we were all deeply grateful to make our peace with the goddess.

I embraced the lama tightly and his purple face cracked into a smile. Within twenty minutes he was enjoying more food and coffee, then he trundled off with his disciple towards the Peace Climb, to perform the same ceremony.

Base Camp was now becoming rather overcrowded. A youthful Californian group arrived, finding the choice camping areas taken up by the other four expeditions, namely a group of New Zealanders, Habeler's group, us, and also the lone climber, the German-Armenian Mischa Saleki, who was attempting a solo ascent of the West Ridge.

The Californians had been given permission to attempt Everest's North Peak, Changtse, which is over 24,000 feet high. They were an easygoing, fast-moving bunch, and one felt that they intended to achieve their objective quickly, and get off the mountain. They seemed to have selected a particularly fluorescent set of colours to wear, which dazzled the eyes. I found them fun to talk to, though I sensed that David Breashears was far from enamoured.

Mischa Saleki, everyone informed me, was a madman, and to be avoided at all costs. His abode, twenty yards above us in a rocky enclave, was not a tent. He had built it up with numerous stones, and I found it movingly cosy. I had stolen into this stone room to have a look. It was set out carefully with two old, red sleeping bags on the floor; one was for his Japanese girlfriend. There were plastic bottles filled with water, and a cooking stove and a well-stocked and varied larder. In addition there was a large blue towel, and fat candles artistically placed in crannies protected from the wind. Instinctively I already liked this man. When I asked members of the Peace Climb about him, they confirmed that he was crazy and had a gun, and was threatening, when he came down from the mountain, to shoot Mr Ping.

That evening at dinner the flap of our tent opened and in strode a figure of heroic majesty. The noble forehead, glittering blue eyes, high cheek bones and well-formed beard suggested the conquistador Cortés. The handsome, smiling face exuded confidence and good cheer. It was the great climber, Peter Habeler.

Immediately, I rose to greet him and he took my hand and shook it vigorously. Alongside him was the powerful Basque climber, Martín Zabaleta, smiling, with his dark eyes and black hair.

Slightly behind was Todd Burleston, the young, slim American who had organized their expedition.

'So you're following in the footsteps of Mallory?' smiled Habeler. Wonderful!'

Introductions completed, we settled down for a filmed dinner that was out of this world. There, in front of me, at Everest Base Camp, was Peter Habeler, who in 1978 had climbed Everest with Messner, without oxygen. He was now forty-eight and as fit and as strong as ever.

Martín said that Habeler's form in the Alps, before coming to Everest, had been staggering.

'He's strong!' he laughed. 'Very difficult to keep up with uphill.'

During the course of three hours or so, the conversation seesawed backwards and forwards, as the camera took in everything. Habeler and I got on wonderfully.

'You must come to Austria, Brian, with your wife, and join me with mine, and I will take you on some beautiful, easy rambles. You will love it! You say things about climbing that I love and believe in ... We all love and admire Mallory − he is a great hero for me − but how can I advise you about Everest? ... Jesus Christ! What can I say? ... Jesus Christ! ...'

'Don't do it!' interrupted Todd.

Hebeler laughed at this, and then, becoming serious, he said, 'You must listen all the time to your body ... If you hear anything strange going on, like your heart hurting, or your lungs making strange gurgling sounds, then you must come down ... Don't ever consider going on! ... High up there, symptoms of sickness can be followed by complete collapse, but you seem well, and you have David and Jeff to look after you ... You couldn't be in better hands!

'Your previous experience on mountains should give you a fair chance of getting up the [North] Col. You seem very happy, which is all important, and I feel that you will do very well.'

Now that Habeler was sitting directly under the bright light of the lamp, I could see his features more closely. He and Martín, but not Todd, who had been at the lower camp, had suffered the torments of hell, at 25,000 feet on the West Ridge. The storms had been terrible, and I was astonished to see how sore and red

The seemingly interminable climb, with our thirty yaks, up the East Rongbuk Glacier towards Camp II, at 19,800 feet.

The Via Dolorosa, from Camp II to Camp III. 'Hard Drill' was how Bonington described it. I called it 'Pure Hell'.

Opposite: Everest changes shape as we round Changtse at 20,000 feet.

Camp III, at 21,300 feet.

The Fairy Kingdom of Ice, where the temperature rose to 40°C. 'The White Rabbit himself would have been bewildered here,' as Mallory observed.

Everest from the Sharks' Fins of the East Rongbuk Glacier.

The base of the North Col. One slip and you're heading for a crevasse at fifty miles an hour.

Climbing the North Col at 23,000 feet.

Looking towards the summit and the North-East Ridge from the North Col.

'There's no air here.' My high point at 25,400 feet.

Habeler's face was. The skin looked as though it had been flayed by the terrible wind.

This is a very tough man! I thought.

There's no doubt at all that Messner, Habeler, Doug Scott, David Breashears and the like are all a bit special in this world.

By the end of the evening I felt very close to this great climber and his friend Martín. I'm afraid Todd gave me the pip. Throughout the evening he had been a prophet of doom.

'If you are fortunate enough to get up the North Col, which I doubt,' he said, 'then you'll be well advised not to go any further. If the altitude doesn't kill you, then the winds will. I tell you now, my friend, if you go up there ... you will die!'

I nodded and thanked him for his advice, and quietly said, 'Bollocks', at the same time remembering the northern comic who used to say, 'It's being so cheerful that keeps me going!'

Nevertheless, the evening cemented some fine friendships, and I expressed my warmest thanks to Habeler for his kindness and encouragement.

The following day, as we completed filming, Everest looked haunting and blood-red in the fading light. My brain had been humming with fear all day, not because of Todd's gloomy prediction — I couldn't give a damn about that — but because I'd heard Habeler was going home. The terrible weather he had suffered on high had taken its toll, and he had pneumonia.

God! I thought. If a Titan like that can be hit, what chance do I have? J.P. sensed it, and was determined to film my reactions. I was in a strange mood.

'What the hell am I doing here?' I shouted. 'My daughter could lose a father, and Hildegard a husband! Not to mention my mum and dad, and other loved ones! Look at it! ... Look at that damn mountain! ... It draws people on like the white whale in *Moby Dick*... Yes! It's true! Just like the sailors in the story, with their harpoons and ropes, the climbers approach Everest with their axes and ski sticks and pitons, which they stick into its sides!

'Does she weep, the goddess? Does she cry with the pain of the blows?

'Why, Mallory and Irvine are up there, too, with so many more! Where's the sense of it, eh? I ask you? ... The answer, J.P., is very simple: I am being utterly selfish, as Bonington maintained!

'Can you imagine the scene when Mallory's wife, Ruth, was told that he was dead? And she went for a long walk with her friends? Just think of it! ... They were young and wonderfully in love ... Bloody hell, J.P.! ... It doesn't bear thinking about!

'His children! ... Just think of his children ... Just wee tots! ... Imagine Ruth standing in the doorway of her house ... And her three children, aged between seven and three, noticing her red eyes ... And asking when Daddy's coming home ...

'What does it all mean, eh?

'Irvine was such a young man when he died ... Twenty-two years old! ... I don't know, J.P. ... What do you make of it, eh? ... Some people say climbers are mad. What was it Cervantes said? ... Ah, yes!

> Who knows where madness lies?
> Too much sanity may be madness,
> And maddest of all to see life as it is,
> And not as it should be!

'Well, J.P., me old cock, I have to come down on the side of adventure. Without it, the quality of life would be a poor thing! We need challenges and quests and frontiers to cross, and horizons to love and marvel at ... It is completely natural, this feeling for adventure ... Looking here at Everest, and the universe beyond, fills us with awe ... It is in that awe that we each discover our own dream!

'The image of Mallory and Irvine, disappearing in the mists in 1924 on this great mountain, has thrilled the souls of generations, of lovers of adventure. Sitting here tonight in the twilight, there is no feeling of death ... Those two fine young men point the way to limitless landscapes ... As Ruth said: "It is not difficult for me to believe that George's spirit was ready for another life, and his way of going to it very beautiful."'

6

Onward and Upward

Two days later, on 21 April, we received the news that we would be moving up the mountain to 19,800 feet. On this auspicious occasion J.P. would have to stay at Base Camp to arrange a hundred and one things, including the yaks for Camp III. There would be no filming – it was all part of our gradual acclimatization.

We were going to Camp II, which David, Veronique, Jeff and the Sherpas had set up days ago. The same people would take Margaret, Graham, Swanee, Jules and me up, and establish more stores. Everyone would go down the same day, except for Jeff and me, who would stay the night to acclimatize further.

I shall resist the temptation to write of this climb in detail, as I shall cover extensively our second ascent. Suffice it to say, we were all feverish with excitement.

David was concerned that Swanee had a bad cough and cold, although he appeared to have it under control. Jules was still having the occasional headache, but was otherwise fine. David himself had suffered from a slight cold, which he had cleared days before by putting a towel over his head and inhaling various potions. Jeff had decided to take a drug called Diamox, to aid acclimatization. Margaret and Veronique seemed in good shape, and I too shared their condition.

Of the three Sherpas, Chuldim and Nawang seemed fine, but Phuli complained of a headache. Krisna, our gallant cook, would remain for the rest of the expedition at Base Camp. To our great relief, he was much better.

The only person who really concerned us was our sirdar, Wongchu. Our 'Tiger Sherpa', he was expected to go high and urge me on. He had a lousy cough and spat loudly and continuously. It was just as well that he was staying at Base Camp with J.P., as this would give him time to shake it off.

So, early on that morning, we intrepid mountaineers set off. We covered the first mile, barely gaining a couple of hundred feet, but then the rise became appreciable and we suddenly felt it, with one steep section hitting us hard and making us wonder, if we felt like this now, how would we be higher up. For another half a mile it levelled out and we felt relieved, but then we dipped down into a valley and started up another steep incline. Our hearts were pounding and our legs felt like lead.

Where are all the weeks of acclimatization? I thought.

On and on, higher and higher we went. At times we were in agony, and had to pause frequently to rest. Our progress was terribly slow, and I had serious doubts of ever getting up high at all. Jeff was just behind me, and sensed this. His kind words reassured me and calmed me down.

'It's all right, Brian ... You're going at precisely the right pace. Don't try and increase it. I'm in just as much agony as you!'

David and Veronique were way ahead, almost out of sight. They wanted to have a brew ready for us when we arrived there, which would be hours yet.

An ascent from 17,000 to 19,800 feet sounds fine as the crow flies, but we were zigzagging for miles, and suddenly being shocked by yet another steep pitch. We were getting slower by the minute, and the rests were longer and more frequent.

We stopped by a stream that was acknowledged as safe for drinking, and filled our water bottles. Of course, we welcomed any opportunity to stop, for then we could get some respite from the violent panting and the heavy hammering of the heart. When we stood still, the throbbing ceased, only to start up again as we pressed on.

We were hot and cold by turns. The air was sharp, freezing and rarefied. A sudden gust of wind would force you to put on your windproofs, and the next moment you would find yourself claustrophobically sweating and confused, as the tropical sun, almost vertical above, scorched down with ferocity. Yet over a period of an hour or so, we had noticeably begun to gain height.

'How high are we now, Jeff?' I muttered.

'Oh, about 19,000 feet, Brian,' came back the answer.

Below Jeff, I could see Swanee and Jules grimly struggling on, their bodies bent over in pain, and their faces set and resolved to reach Camp II. Jeff's information was relayed to them and received with pride and satisfaction by both. It was the highest they had ever been before.

Margaret was just in front of me, having difficulty in deciding what style she should adopt as the terrain became more steep and difficult. Eventually she bent over, almost on all fours, like Quasimodo, the Hunchback of Notre Dame.

'Margaret,' I asked with a smile, 'why do you do that?'

'It gives me some bloody relief from the agony of being upright! I feel better climbing this way!' she replied.

From that moment on, the scenery for me became Margaret's rear end, as, like everyone else, she groaned her way up. Maybe Margaret had introduced something new to mountaineering, that all budding Everesteers might take up.

'I'm going to finish this climb if it's the last thing I do!' she grunted.

The word 'finish' reminded me of her father Magnus Magnusson's catchphrase on the quiz show *Mastermind*: 'I've started, so I'll finish.'

How proud of her he would have been now. What guts she had – all the more commendable since she had been frighteningly ill when we had climbed together on Kilimanjaro a couple of years before.

After a further half-hour of delicate manoeuvring we came to the steepest part of the route. We stopped and drank, and climbed and rested and drank again. It was some kind of purgatory. You felt your heart bursting with the effort and, try as you might, your legs would not respond efficiently to the call of the brain. Yet throughout it all, there was a feeling of being wonderfully alive. As Mallory put it, when writing to his wife: 'This is a thrilling business altogether. I can't tell you how it possesses me, and what a prospect it is, and the beauty of it all!'

As we approached the hardest bit of all, I spotted Veronique two hundred yards away, shouting down encouragement: 'You're nearly there – it's just round the corner and in the valley!'

Her words were just what the doctor ordered, and we renewed our efforts with happy determination. Mountaineers have an awful habit of glossing over the difficulties. So I'll just say that after what seemed an interminable climb we at last reached Camp II, at 19,800 feet.

We all threw ourselves to the ground, clapped out.

God! I thought. If it's going to be like this now on the so-called easy section, what's it going to be like further up, when the going gets really tough?

I harboured serious doubts in my mind.

'Well, Big Yeti!' David smiled. 'How was that?'

'Tough, David. Tough. I'd love to have a crack at the next camp!'

David nodded in that strange way of his, and didn't believe a word of it.

'Nineteen thousand eight hundred feet, eh, Margaret? ... Eh, boys?' I said, looking at Jules and Swanee, who lay on their backs almost comatose.

They managed the weeniest of smiles, and that said it all.

Chuldim, the largest of our Sherpas, and the smaller Nawang, looked knackered but happy too as they busied themselves on the stove with the coffee.

An hour later, at 1 p.m., Jeff and I wished them cheerio, and our good friends set off back to Base Camp.

The breeze had subsided, and there was an uncanny stillness. There we were, two men alone at 19,800 feet. This was the highest I had ever been, and I was thrilled to bits.

Even though our tent was up, there was plenty to occupy our minds, as we prepared the evening meal, unrolled our sleeping bags and arranged things inside the tent. I say the evening meal, but our appetites were small, and all we could manage was some pea soup, which was delicious, some chocolate and lots of tea. We were enclosed by mountains, with Everest way out of sight. The sun very quickly left the sky, and we turned in early, wrapped in our sleeping bags with the flap of the tent open, as we peacefully watched the mists descend and light snow fall.

Jeff and I were perfectly at ease together, and in his own quiet way he described how he was writing a book about the Chinese invasion of Tibet. He had amassed a tremendous amount of information on the subject, and his research had yielded some frightful facts that were distressing to hear. As he paused, I mentioned that the Dalai Lama had once said that the hardest task for him was to love the Chinese.

'If I meet him, Jeff, I'll ask him if he succeeded!' I promised.

Then Jeff asked me about different aspects of the Mallory story.

'You know, Brian,' he said later, 'this mountain is like a vampire, sucking out your life's blood ... Altitude is invisible, that's what makes it so dangerous ... You look out and the sky is blue and the day fine, and to all intents and purposes it looks exactly like a day at sea level ... Not so ... The invisible enemy is gradually taking the life out of you ... Just like a vampire!'

With that, he fell asleep.

The next day we collapsed our tent to protect it from the wind, and secured it with a lot of extra stones. We then moved off downhill with Jeff leading.

Back at Base Camp we were greeted by the Soviets, who had come to see us and to ask whether we had any fresh fruit. Feeling very pleased with myself after my night at Camp II, I embraced them like a Siberian bear as fellow mountaineers.

In the tent the cameras rolled and lunch was served to us all by the healthy, bouncing Krisna. The Soviets were a colourful set of gents, and full of fun. Their names were Slava, Victor and Sasha.

Slava was the eldest, at forty-two and the other two were in their twenties. Sasha was handsome and tall, and smiled all the time. Slava, of medium stature, gave the impression that his mouth was always semi-open, ready for a laugh, whereas Victor was quiet but as cheerful as the other two, just not as extrovert.

Going up the North Col, Victor had developed advanced signs of pulmonary oedema. His condition was under control, but he did appear distinctly unwell. The great thing was that he was enjoying the meal and the fun.

I had them singing 'The Song of the Volga Boatmen' with me, with them singing marvellously in Russian. Their English was good, and Slava, when talking about Everest, loved to say, 'No problem!'

He described how, in Odessa where he lived, the ladies were very beautiful. To which I replied that I was delighted to hear it, as Mrs Brezhnev's moustache, over the years, had put me off Russian women. They laughed, and Slava informed us that Brezhnev had decorated himself over the years, finally becoming a five-star general.

They were all fascinated by Mallory, Slava expressing his admiration by saying, 'For me, yes, Mallory is a gero! For all Russian climbers, a gero!'

The filming and lunch finished, my happy Soviet friends gave me a big hug, and went off to visit the New Zealanders. The following day, J.P., with a mischievous glint in his eye, informed me that I was to meet, and be filmed with, Mischa Saleki, the wild Armenian, who had solo'd many of the Himalayan giants. He had recently climbed Cho-Oyu and had been on Everest for weeks, having just come down from the West Ridge.

The wily, ever-present, grasping, spawny-eyed git, Mr Ping, was after him. He wanted Mischa off the mountain, apparently, for it appeared his visa was about to expire.

Mischa had threatened to shit and piss on the Chinese flag, and shoot Mr Ping. There was little doubt that if he wished to carry out his threat, there were precious few who could stop him. J.P. and everybody had met this extraordinary Armenian. The scale of what he'd achieved as a climber was astonishing. The mountaineering world is full of the most varied and colourful personalities, and here was a man who was King of the Eccentrics.

When I set eyes on Mischa in the mess tent, guzzling coffee and devouring large chunks of bread and cheese, I thought he was a cross between Ben Gunn and Ivan the Terrible.

Just my cup of tea! I thought.

'Ah! So you're the wild man who's going to shoot Mr Ping! ... Come here, you crazy bastard!' I roared at him.

David Breashears, who was watching, was vastly amused.

'You are doing the Mallory story, I teeenk?' Mischa replied.

'I am indeed!' I shouted, and we embraced like long-lost brothers.

'I am glad!' he continued. 'Dis man, I tell you, Mallory is big hero ... He understand me!'

For an hour he bubbled and fermented like a yeast-filled Vesuvius, erupting periodically like King Lear on the heath, to rage at all forms of bureaucracy.

'Those bloody bastards!' he foamed. 'I would really, Brian, like to twist their bloody heads off! ... I tell true! ... I stick Mr Ping's head on goddamn bloody pole, or use it for a football!'

'Thees Peace Expedition ... I call it Piss Expedition ... They cheat us! ... Yes! ... They cheat the human spirit! ... All dis talk of peeece, when all these countries are invading others! China in Tibet, Russia in Afghanistan, America in Panama ...

'Diss Mallory, I only theenk he interested in climbing ... I tell you diss, I want to climb with you ... I take you up North Col, with me! You can do it! ... Soon you must climb with me on Cho-Oyu ... Yes, I take you ... I see you eyes ... You make me want to say "Shit!" to Chinese and go climb again!'

'Yes!' I urged him. 'Defy the Chinese, and go, man, go!'

'You fire me up, Brian, to climb everything! I go soon with my girlfriend ... You like her? She is nice! ... And cross Lo La, into Nepal, and climb Everest South Side. I pick up my equipment on Rongbuk Glacier — I have expensive cameras!'

This conversation went on for hours, and the small sample above shows what a gorgeous eccentric he was. During the course of the next few days, he disappeared with his Japanese girlfriend up the central Rongbuk Glacier.

I felt responsible for this, and was quite worried about him. Later we were to find out that the Chinese sent the police to fetch him, and he was imprisoned, escaped and made a daring solo of Cho-Oyu (26,906 feet) before going over the border into Nepal. J.P. describes him perfectly: 'His independent nature, and quasi-mystical attachment to the mountains, does not find favour with the climbing authorities, who like to patrol and cost every route up a peak.'

I agree with J.P. In a materialistic world, how refreshing it is to meet such an individual ... Our paths will cross again.

What follows is in no way fanciful. It happened, and that was that, and it was recorded on film. I had this dream about Mallory; I mean it was a horrible dream. It was a nightmare, it wasn't just a dream; it was so vivid, it was a vision. I woke up at about three or four o'clock in the morning in the tent, and it was kind of fuzzy at the sides, and there was this magnetic picture of Mallory, and he was coming down the road towards me, and he was running, steaming ahead, saying, 'I hate what you're doing! I hate it! I hate it!'

And his eyes were so piercing, and I was shocked that he hated me so much. He came towards me at speed, and he was reknowned for his grace in movement, but it was easy to sidestep him, and he went through this wooden fence. Then he stuck his hands through and tried to grab me, so I grabbed his wrists, and said,

'Stop it! ... Stop it! ... '

And he said, 'Well, I hate it! I hate what you're doing! I don't want publicity! I don't want the filming!'

And I said, 'Stop it! You're a hypocrite! ... Winthrop Young always said that you wanted a label! You always wanted to be well known, and that's why we're telling your story! ... Nobody knows about your marvellous story! ... What I am doing is good! It's pure! It's true!'.

And he went still, and his eyes, they were still horrible, they were still piercing, and then he lowered his head and his hands went slack in my grip and he seemed to reluctantly accept what I was saying ... It was a shock to me, considering my love for the man and the subject-matter. It left me feeling awful and has haunted me ever since.

As I'm in the mood, I might as well relate the second dream-like experience, which actually happened higher on the mountain, at the now-established Camp II.

Again, it was about three in the morning, and I found myself in a small study, with an old upright piano and a few armchairs covered in flowered chintz. There was a lady in the corner, in her early forties, painting pottery. I recognized her as Ruth Mallory. She had a little plaited band on her head, to keep her hair in place.

The door opened casually, and in strode Mallory, in a faded brown tweed jacket with protective leather patches on the elbows. He was about fifty, with distinguished-looking, greying hair. At a glance, he took me in, and nodded a polite 'Hello'. Then he stared happily through the windows at some pine trees outside. Ruth smiled at me, and Mallory confessed he'd never been happier. He was teaching, he informed me, and positively enjoying it. I asked him where Irvine was, and he replied, 'Oh, he's gone on to new adventures.'

I watched him as he gracefully reclined against the piano, the picture of happiness, and then the image faded.

It was now 22 April, Earth Day 20, and celebrations to mark the twentieth anniversary of the auspicious occasion were ringing throughout the USA. Organizations from Seattle to Costa Rica, covering acid rain, toxic waste, ozone depletion, global warming, marine pollution, alternative energy and related issues, were to take the lead in the Earth Day 20 International Scientific Symposium.

Jim Whittaker, much to the relief of the Peace Climb, was now back at their Base Camp, bristling with health and ambition, with the fear of a possible clot on his leg being diagnosed as 'non-fatal'. The climax of these celebrations, on the magical day of the 22nd, was the placing of one climber from each nation – China, the USA and the Soviet Union – on the summit of Mount Everest. This accomplishment would be filmed live by satellite to all three nations, with communication between the summit team and political leaders of the three nations. All lovely stuff! But Everest had other ideas. The proposed ascent was postponed because of hazardous weather conditions. Also, the satellite apparatus at Base Camp was defunct.

The skills of our very own sound man, Graham 'Dogbollock' Hoyland, were called for. There, in the blustery cold, with his red nose spreading across his face and quivering in the wind, he applied his expertise to save the day, and make it possible for the lads to speak to the US president, George Bush.

After many hours, Graham gave a satisfied nod. His industry had paid off, much to the delight of the whooping Americans. The interview would take place at four in the morning, and we were invited to film it. None of this remotely appealed to me – I simply couldn't relate to it at all. But J.P. rightly felt that it was all part of the film and we should include it. This would prove a complete contrast to the twenties expeditions.

J.P. woke me at 3 a.m. and with Swanee and Jules we trundled through the freezing cold to the solitary, well-lit tent that housed the delightful Warren Thompson and the communications equipment. Warren was always kindness itself to us, and on this occasion, even more so, as he loaded us with hot, steaming mugs of coffee.

Big Jim Whittaker was there, equally kind, but seemingly nervous about talking to President Bush, as he constantly patted his face and fidgeted. There was a tremendous tension in the air, and a fear that the satellite apparatus would not function properly. Swanee assured them, after several tests, that everything was in order, but the fidgeting continued.

Dr Kurt kept popping his head through to ask if there was any news. With Jim, Warren and the camera crew, and J.P. and myself, packed in the tent, there wasn't even enough room for a gnat on Dogbollock's nose. Therefore, each time Kurt popped his head through the lower flap of the tent, letting in the cold, his face was pushed back like a squashed prune by Jim or Warren.

Time went by, and the tension mounted. Jim and Warren were beside themselves with concern, checking the time and pressing the odd button.

'What do you think, you guys? Is this thing gonna work?' asked Jim.

'Sure! … Sure, Jim. It'll work!' comforted Warren, biting his lip.

Kurt was now popping his head through like a demented jack-in-the-box, with a rapid 'Any news?'

On receiving a shake of the head from Warren, he instantly removed his face to avoid it being squashed again. Then there was a loud pip, and the sound equipment crackled into life, and the forty-first President of the USA was on the line, loud and clear.

Jim gripped the phone tightly, and spoke. Warren quietly shook with pride, and Kurt, poking his head through the flap, was finally tolerated. J.P. was recording the conversation, and said that it sounded as if it were coming from next door. Jim informed President Bush that they had made good progress on the mountain, and that all was well.

It was amusing to think that the president was phoning and being filmed fishing in the heat of Florida, while Big Jim's arse was freezing off at Base Camp.

The conversation lasted about ten minutes, and when it had ended we offered our congratulations to the delighted Americans. Grinning with relief, Jim told Warren that they would be visiting the White House, and would probably have tea with 'Mr President' in his beautiful back garden, to which Warren wistfully replied, 'Ah, I've always wanted to see that garden!'

We were cordially invited into the cooking area, where breakfast was served. I really wasn't hungry, but I accepted an omelette made from powdered eggs. Ten minutes later I made my apologies and beat a hasty retreat. I was in bloody agony! My stomach appeared to be swelling like a Yorkshire pudding!

Within minutes I had put a hundred yards between me and the Peace Camp. It was still dark, with a half-moon that lit the barren landscape and highlighted Everest's brooding form. In all my fifty-three years, I had never been so ill. I became feverish and fell on my knees, vomiting ... Then I became aware of the other trouble. It was now completely unavoidable ... I had the shits!

No! I thought. Not in these sub-zero temperatures at five in the morning!

Now I found myself totally agreeing with Mischa's description of the Peace Climb as the 'Piss Climb'.

'What have they done to me?' I wheezed. 'Bloody hell! This is the end of the expedition for me ... I'm going to die! ... '

I was perspiring and dizzy, and on the point of exploding. Oh, the embarrassment!

What the hell! I thought. If I don't give in, I'll lose my bloody life!

Through the longest five minutes of my life, I removed my Alpinex baby suit, windproofs, trousers, socks and boots, and let nature take its course. At over 17,000 feet, the combination of my weird condition and the lack of air pressure resulted in my bowels exploding in all directions! The jet shot out everywhere, to a distance of fifteen feet. I was now naked – I had to be, as my clothes would have been ruined and I needed them for filming. During a temporary lull in my crisis, I tied them all together like a long rope so that they were kept out of harm's way, then I dragged them in a straight line.

The cold was unbelievable! What the hell does it matter about frostbite to my toes! I thought. My dick will probably fall off!

167

Then it started again, and I still had half a mile to go. My voice throbbed out in pain, in an effort to keep my spirits up.

'I am the original shitbag! ... Please, God in Heaven, help me!'

More yards gained, then another attack. I was covered in the awful stuff ... Oh, never was a human more mortified! I just didn't know what to do!

By some miracle the clothes were spared, but there I was, with a penis the size of a ferret's, covered in shit, and exploding and vomiting. It must have been twenty below, or something like that – I don't bloody know! Covered in frost and crap, who cares?

During a pause before the next storm, I attacked the ice of a stream two hundred yards outside our Base Camp. My desire to clean myself was wild, and paramount. Smashing the ice with my boots and ski stick, I managed to make a hole big enough to partially submerge my body.

It's impossible, I thought, to get any colder ...

I was wrong.

Within seconds, I was singing 'Auld Lang Syne'. Oh, man alive! What screaming tremors of hell penetrated my body.

Keep living! I thought. Rub! Bloody hell, man! Rub the stuff off! ...

I succeeded, and somehow managed to avoid fainting. Singing helped – Andrew Lloyd Webber songs ... anything! I walked on all fours, and estimated I would get to Base Camp in twenty minutes ... I was wrong again.

I was hit with another tremor, which appeared to rejoice in the low atmospheric pressure. The newly washed Everesteer was a shitbag again. Three more times I visited the frozen stream of perpetual delight, before I stumbled into camp, and collided with a furry beast outside my tent. The creature was as surprised as I was ... No, it wasn't a yeti ... Our yaks had arrived.

'Hello, yak ... the iceman cometh!' I said.

An hour later, after incessant rubbing, I zipped myself into my Alpinex baby suit and shivered my way back to life again, in my big green sleeping bag, relieved and happy that I was, at last, a *clean* English gentleman.

I told the story to everyone the next morning, and Margaret laughed the loudest. Apparently the Magnussons are partial to the odd joke about the basics. Extraordinarily, despite a slight feeling of weakness, I had made a complete recovery, which was just as well, as David and Jeff had decided to take us close to the Rongbuk Monastery, for some climbing lessons. When we arrived they had fixed up some ropes on a huge boulder, about a hundred yards high. We spent about two hours ascending and descending, until they were satisfied that we were proficient in our handling of the jumars and descenders.

If two days before it had been World Earth Day, now it was Yak Day. Scores of them surrounded the tents. Dear animals, their colours range from black to various shades of brown, to even the occasional white. Swanee had already struck up a sweet relationship with a small, fluffy, light-brown female, and was always feeding her lumps of sugar. In personality, they seem to be a curious mixture of docility and passionate arrogance. They carry great burdens, and are amazingly sure-footed — a fine example of how to move on the mountain, slowly and easily. Yaks travel at about a mile an hour, and watching them move, you think they'll never get there, but the next minute, you raise your head, and they're already disappearing on the horizon.

The yak herders, as you can imagine, are as tough as old boots. Their clothing is made of woven yak wool and the skin of yaks imbued with oils, and with their furry hats they give the impression that their dress has not changed for centuries.

They whistle a variety of sounds, and give the occasional cry, all of which the yak understands perfectly.

I would not recommend getting too close to them, and certainly avoid sitting downwind of them ... It is also advisable to lock up your daughters, zip up your tents, and keep your hands in your pockets! The herders have a reputation for being the thieving magpies of the mountain. It wasn't a question of morals — simply an age-old tradition that had been handed down from father to son. But our light-fingered friends were cheerful companions, singing and laughing all day long.

Krisna wouldn't tolerate them for one minute in his kitchen area, and, with Wongchu, would chase them away with strange, guttural cries.

In a similar fashion to the cattle in Switzerland, the yaks had endearing bells tied round their necks. Jules once complained that he had not slept a wink all night, because several of the musical animals had been tethered around his tent. It was the only time that I ever heard Jeff raise his voice, saying, 'David, are those yaks staying there?'

Which signified that he had suffered the same fate as Jules.

The time had come for us to make our big move, to Camp III, at 21,300 feet. Everyone was quiet and serious, each locked in his or her own world, wondering how he or she would get up high.

Taking stock of our little team, Wongchu did not seem to be improving – his cough was definitely getting worse. If he couldn't go high, it would be a serious blow. Swanee had a very bad chest cold, and for him to get up to any height would call for a lot of guts. Jules was still prone to bad headaches, but he shared with Swanee great courage and determination. J.P. had a slight cough, but appeared to be in excellent health. David and Veronique were marvellously fit, and Margaret seemed in fine fettle.

Jeff was still taking Diamox to help him acclimatize, and although he was as strong as a bull he was unnervingly quiet. Graham had a bad cough, yet seemed very strong. Of our happy band of Sherpas, only little Phuli seemed out of sorts. I was relieved that my stomach was functioning normally, and I felt fit and raring to go.

David and J.P. decided that there would be an advance party comprising the Sherpas, David, Veronique, Jeff, Graham, J.P. and me. Besides his duties as climbing leader, David would also have to do the filming, aided by J.P. and Veronique. Also, there was the task of getting up and establishing Camp III. This was to be of considerable size, and for this purpose David had supplied a large green tent.

Though disappointed, Swanee, Jules and Margaret would be given the opportunity to go up in a few days' time. Nevertheless they would accompany us and film right up to the point where the East Rongbuk Glacier begins. It was essential that Margaret, as assistant producer, should remain at Base Camp to handle any eventualities.

The night before our big push I was far too excited to sleep properly, and ached for the dawn. At last I was going up the mountain, to heights that I'd never reached before!

On the morning of 27 April I put on my Alpinex baby suit, plus-fours and tweed jacket. My boots were very old; they were the pair I'd used on Kilimanjaro in 1988. Soaked in waterproofing, they were blissfully comfortable. High up, I would use the green plastic boots that Luigi had designed especially for my feet.

Weeks before, in Bhutan, on the Chomolhari trek, I had broken the big toes on both feet. A small boulder had fallen on them. At the time I didn't let on, as I was determined that nothing would jeopardize the expedition. I had experienced a broken toe before – they soon heal up – but I think the ever-perceptive Margaret had noticed my discomfort at that time. Now, at last, they were completely healed, and, thank God, my feet were fine.

I put on my Homburg and twenties Elliot glasses, and tied round my neck the white sacred scarf that the lama had given me. David looked at me happily, and imitated George C. Scott as General Patton, shouting, 'You magnificent bastard!'

And I recited lines from *Henry V*, but with a slight difference:

'I see you stand like greyhounds in the slips, straining upon the start, the game's afoot! ... Follow your spirit, and upon this charge cry! ... "God for David, England and George Mallory!"'

Then we moved.

Thirty yaks, spurred on by their herders, were laden with tents, equipment, tripods, camera boxes and film crates. It had started snowing, and we all put on our windproofs. David nodded all the time with satisfaction, roaring with laughter as I started to sing the words from the old TV series, *Rawhide*:

Rolling, rolling, rolling, keep them dogies rolling!
Rolling, rolling, rolling, Rawhide! ...

As I reached the climax, screeching in a peculiar falsetto:

Move 'em in, move 'em out ... ride 'em in, ride 'em out ...
David totally collapsed with the giggles. All the time, J.P. grinned and looked like a leprechaun king.

We were in great spirits, and moving joyously across the plain, towards the terminal moraine of the Central Rongbuk Glacier. Everest, which had been hidden from view because of the swirling snow, suddenly revealed itself, bringing to mind more of Mallory's words: 'The curtain was withdrawn. Rising from the bright mists, Everest above was imminent, vast, forceful ... No fleeting apparition of elusive dream form; nothing could have been more set and permanent ... More terrific ... More unconquerable ... '

Swanee and Jules, panting with their exertions, endeavoured to capture the ever-changing light and scenery on film.

'Don't go so fast, Big Yeti!' said David, holding my shoulders.

Jeff nodded in agreement, and I exercised greater caution, but my God! I was so thumpingly happy!

My breathing was easy, yet my heart skipped a beat with the thrill of it all. We were now at 17,500 feet, a quarter of a mile up the glacier.

Messner had told me to trust my instincts, and everything in my being felt that the mountain would be good to us. As this feeling grew in intensity, the snow stopped and the weather became clear. Now the great glacier, with its myriad shapes, surpassed itself with beauty as the newly fallen snow and morning sun dazzled our senses. The wind blew itself out, and we could hear the tiny, tinkling sound of the yak bells. Gradually, the sound disappeared as the animals pressed on.

We stopped to film. In that uncanny stillness I became aware that the mountain *was* a goddess. It was a strange, certain feeling that it was a living entity, and positively female. I may sound vain, but I felt the Old Gal liked me!

With the shot completed, we moved on. J.P. had not been here before, and he was quite overwhelmed by it all. On these occasions I usually hugged him ... Now he returned the gesture.

On and on we went, deeper into the gigantic glacier, until at last we arrived at the historic point, the entrance to the East Rongbuk Glacier. There, in that stupendous scenery, I gushed at the camera: 'Look at it! This is the Central Rongbuk Glacier! Mallory said that it runs up to the base of the mountain, like the Charge of the Light Brigade. Just think! Mallory and his companion Bullock explored it all for weeks, desperately trying to find a way to the North Col.

'This was a colossal effort, working their way up the sides of the glacier, and then on it for miles up there. They suffered the ferocious winds, and the terrible heat of the sun reflecting off the glacier, the insidious, debilitating, short-wave, ultraviolet rays.

'Then they came down, and have often been criticized for missing the entrance to the East Rongbuk Glacier, which leads finally to the North Col. That little trickle of water there, and the small amount of ice, is the entrance. It appears actually to lead away from the mountain.

'You'd have missed it! ... I'd have missed it! ... And Mallory and Bullock came down in a blizzard! ... Anyway, they came all the way down to Base Camp, and went right round, 150 miles, to the Kharta Valley, and reached the Lhakpa La, Windy Gap, and found a way from there! ... But what courage! ... What tenacity! ... And that's where I'm heading now, by way of the East Rongbuk!'

Sadly, we had to say goodbye to our BBC camera team, and with Margaret leading the way, they departed. At this point, on the previous ascent, I had found the going pretty awful. The hill you have to surmount is very steep, for about three hundred feet. I could see the pain on J.P.'s face as the effort hit him. He, of course, had not had the luxury of going to 19,800 feet days before. It was interesting, but now I found it fifty percent easier. Nevertheless, I moved slowly, and conserved energy.

This respite from the dreadful panting and thudding of my heart gave me time to take in the landscape. Once on the hill, I looked two hundred yards down on J.P. making his way up. My view was now restricted, because I was at the beginning of a two-mile valley.

An interesting fact about the tropical sun is the way in which eastward and westward-flowing glaciers have their southern sides melted back into ice cliffs, the East Rongbuk tributary being an example.

I looked to the sides of the cliffs around me, and as I had been informed, they were made up of metamorphosed and crystalline limestone, which rested on granite. This giant landscape belonged to the Jurassic and Eocene period, when dinosaurs roamed the earth.

The spectacle of Everest and her surrounding peaks was now blocked from our view. My eyes followed the twisting trail of the valley, twelve miles further up the glacier, and I thought I might see the North Col and Everest, as I'd never seen her before.

David and Veronique were, between them, carrying the Arriflex

camera and the equipment that went with it; a hell of an undertaking. We were now at 18,000 feet, yet this load didn't seem to
bother them, for they were amazingly fit. Jeff, like the Sherpas,
was carrying a considerable load, and Graham, as well as the
burden of his increasingly bulbous nose, also had the extra task of
carrying the DAT sound machine. As for me, I simply carried my
nutritious 'power bars' and sleeping bag in my twenties rucksack.
J.P.'s pack was not dissimilar, except I suspected his contained
chocolate and cigars. He was now going through the hell that we
had already suffered, yet he always managed a smile and continued to be smitten by the beauty of it all.

After a slight descent into the valley, we arrived again at our
friend, the stream. Here, everybody drank their fill and topped up
their water bottles. Seduced by the scenery, I failed to do this and
feasted my eyes on the increasing size of the glacier, in particular
the strange 'cryoconite holes', or dust wells. These were intriguing.
Here, in the high-altitude tropical sun, stones and particles had
melted their way very deep down, making weird ice flowers of
black, blue and white, not unlike a giant honeycomb with a pond
of deep green at its base.

The glacier, even at this height, revealed tiny grasses and lichen
on its sides, and the occasional tortoiseshell butterfly. We had to
balance our way delicately across the sea of punctured ice to get to
the other side. This was a tricky operation and David led the way,
with me following and the rest behind. Underneath, the ice torrent
roared dangerously ... It was not a place to hang about! Once this
obstacle had been overcome, we meandered round many more
dust wells, which required great care, before reaching the crucial
hills leading to Camp II.

Though I was more acclimatized, I still found this tough going.
It is extraordinary how the hammering of the heart seems to carry
the same rhythm to the brain, and the whole lot pounds at you
unnervingly. We simply had to stop frequently to rest.

Jeff, again, was right behind me, giving encouragement and
saying that my pace was just fine. David and Veronique, with
Graham, had gone ahead to set up some shots. J.P. was a little
behind, fighting for breath. Jeff advised me to continue, saying
that he would stay with him.

On I went for another half-hour, with the broken path and the odd cairn erected by previous expeditions showing the way. The sky was free of clouds and a brilliant blue. Higher I went, skirting alongside the glacier and panting feverishly in the tropical midday sun.

I was now approaching 19,000 feet and struggling. Why was I struggling? I'd had weeks of acclimatization and I was fit. No colds! No headaches! No sore throat! What was the matter? Was I too old after all? Instinctively, I knew this wasn't the case. Nevertheless my performance wasn't as good as on the previous ascent to that height. If I failed now, all those bloody boring sceptics would be proved right! Todd's doom-laden words came to mind: 'If you are fortunate enough to get up the North Col ... '

Bollocks! I thought. I'm not packing in now! Yet I was confused, and depressed at my form. Of course, I wasn't going to let on how weak I was. For the moment there was nobody around to witness my shambling gait and deterioration.

Up, up I went, moving lamentably on all fours on the steeper sections. The heat was stifling and I had stripped down to the essentials. If I was suffering like this now, what would I be like when I entered the dank and dead air of the ice region of the trough at 20,000 feet or more? I cast the thought aside and moved on.

I was suddenly aware of David, in front of me, waving his arms and shouting. He wanted to do a shot of me among some yaks, as I approached the brow of the hill where he was standing. The yaks belonged to another expedition, and even at one mile an hour, they were gaining on me. My condition was getting worse by the minute, and I was quietly despairing. Also, the ground was loose, and stepping aside for the animals so that I could follow behind as instructed, I momentarily stumbled and the shot was lost. David entreated me to run after them, but it was quite beyond me.

This was the worst moment in the expedition for me. My behaviour was appalling, and completely unjustified. I raved at David, shouting, 'What the bloody hell do you want me to do? Waving your arms about like a bloody lunatic!'

Then I became a baby who wants his lollipop: 'Where's J.P.? I want J.P.! You don't know what you're doing! The whole bloody film is a waste of time ... Stand up! Go there! Keep still! The whole thing is a bloody great joke! I don't know what you want, or where that bloody stupid sod of a yak is going! ... '

David was white with shock, Veronique had tears in her eyes, and Graham was sitting on a rock, his head slumped in despair. My eyes became glazed, and I wound down like an old clock. David, as always, was authoritative and eloquent. His words were quiet and measured: 'I am trying to shoot my first scene in the film. I work in a different way to Swanee and Jules. Also, I'm carrying out J.P.'s exact instructions. This is where he wants the next shot ...

'I am horrified at your outburst! You've removed all the respect I had for you. God Almighty, man! What's the matter with you? What's happened? Where's the lovely Brian gone? Perhaps you never were nice! Everyone is hell-bent on getting you up the mountain, and you behave like a prima donna!'

Veronique tried to interrupt, but David continued.

'I just can't begin to understand what's the matter with you! But understand this: on the mountain there's no margin for error. If you behave like this, then you're on your own! I will wash my hands of you! Do you hear me? ... Do you hear me, Brian?'

I remained silent, in a strange, almost drunken state.

'What is the matter with you?'

'I'm buggered if I know!' I replied.

David came closer and noticed that my speech was slurred and that I was foaming at the mouth.

'God, Brian! You're completely dehydrated! When did you last drink?'

I looked at him and pondered for a while, and said, 'At Base Camp ... '

'Base Camp!' he gasped. 'God, man! I've drunk two litres since then!'

Within minutes he had poured me a huge mug of water, and when I had knocked it back, he filled it again, and I drained the second mug. Then I sat down, with my head slumped against my chest like Graham, and closed my eyes. It was the oddest sensation: I could feel the liquid running round my body and completely restoring me.

Now I started to remember how quickly I had become dehydrated on Kilimanjaro two years earlier. There is a long-held view that Everest will always find out your weakness. I always thought it was my feet, but it was not so. I was very prone to dehydration, and it needed to be watched. Now my energy started to return, and my brain ticked over.

'Sorry, David ... Sorry, Veronique ... Dogbollock ... That was not me. Please forgive my behaviour ... Tell me, David, what I must do.'

David nodded in that strange way of his and accepted my apology, and began to explain his simple filming technique.

'I hold my arms wide, for action, Brian ... And cross them when it's a cut ... '

From that moment on, we worked splendidly as a team, and we never had a cross word again. My exuberance had made me forget the basics. On a mountain like Everest, this can be very dangerous. Mallory himself had his dark moments on the mountain. In 1921, he wrote to a friend: 'I sometimes think of this expedition as a fraud from beginning to end, invented by the wild enthusiasm of one man, Younghusband ... The prospect of ascent in any direction is almost nil, and our present job is to rub our noses against the impossible in such a way as to persuade mankind that some noble heroism has failed once again ... '

The incident with David was forgotten. We were too close as friends for it to scratch remotely the love we had for each other. Fifteen minutes later we were lying in the sun on a steep slope, looking across the glacier to a wonderful dark rock face that was part of Mount Kellas.

'Is that the wonderful mountain that Mallory climbed, called Ri-Ring, David?' I whispered.

'I'm not sure, Big Yeti,' he replied. 'I think it is only named Kellas.'

As he spoke he poured me some more water, giving me a waspish smile. We were on the move again, and filming with quiet determination. The valley started to widen to over a mile, the glacier growing to embrace it and rising majestically as the beginnings of the most amazing ice kingdom on earth.

Our Camp II was situated on a hill overlooking a glacier stream, and far enough from the avalanche-prone rock cliffs on our right. We walked on a circular route below these intimidating cliffs, and then down two hundred yards, finally arriving in good spirits at our camp at 19,800 feet.

Shortly, J.P. and Jeff arrived, and we all pitched in to erect the tents. As it was for me, this was the highest that J.P. had ever been, and he was delighted.

My fitness had returned, and after some soup and tea, and as it was still only three in the afternoon and everybody felt full of energy, J.P. decided to do some more filming. As fortune would have it, a team of yaks was going down the valley, to emerge on the other side and ascend on the rocky moraine a few hundred feet higher, and then press on to join the Peace Climb at 21,300 feet.

In a flash I was with them, and David and Veronique started filming. J.P. said it looked absolutely wonderful, and I could believe him. From where I was, the call to go on and on was irresistible.

I was now on the glacier proper. Giant white ice fins, a hundred feet high, were on my right and left. Then there were subsidiary glaciers reaching down towards us from their respective peaks. At the base of each, almost in military formation, were blocks of frozen ice that reminded me of the terracotta knights found in Beijing.

My eyes were drawn scores of miles up the glacier, towards the fabled kingdom of ice that Captain Noel had so often told me about. Could I just have a teeny, weeny peek? ... No! ... The fading light and descending mists obscured my view. Anyway, to see more would be greedy. I was now at 20,000 feet, and I was astonished to see a large lammergeyer gliding above me, beckoning me on. David's voice rang out, 'Come back, Big Yeti!'

I obeyed instantly. I had given that young man enough hassle for the day.

J.P. was thrilled with the filming, and we settled down in the evening light around a roaring gas fire, and enjoyed more soup and omelettes. Everyone smiled with contentment. The Sherpas had carried thirty-pound loads, and had performed wonderfully. The yak herders were a few yards away, smiling broadly and eating, with relish, something that looked like black pudding. Their delight increased as J.P. gave them goodies from the bottomless Fortnum's hamper.

Later that night, I shared a tent, for the first time on the expedition, with J.P. As always, we laughed and giggled for a couple of hours like schoolkids: 'Peter Pans!' as Margaret would say. We got her on the radio, and she was obviously missing J.P. David and Veronique could be heard laughing together, and Graham and Jeff got on like a house on fire, chatting nineteen to the dozen.

There is no doubt at all that J.P. is terribly clever and highly educated, and is Sir Galahad to boot. But never, in the entire history of Everest, has anybody broken wind so often! It even astonished the yak herders, who became quite partial to him!

Dawn heralded a day that was to prove to be one of the most astonishing in my life. The Californians, who were going to make their push for the North Peak, Changtse, arrived and immediately began to erect their tent alongside ours. This was simply not on. David, Jeff, Veronique and the Sherpas had sweated blood to clear the area to make it habitable, and they didn't take kindly to the interlopers. Besides their garish, discordant outfits did not bring much serenity to the mind.

David was highly emotional and very funny, yet always in control of himself and the proceedings. He described, in no uncertain manner, how he had travelled across the world to get away from the likes of them, and no way would he tolerate them in such close proximity.

For a while, the Californians stood their ground, stubbornly insisting that it was a free world. At that point, David quietly advised them that if they insisted on staying he would throw their tents down the hillside. Observing David's obvious fitness and strength, and that Jeff was also looming large in the background, the 'Rednecks', as David called them, beat a hasty retreat, and camped fifty yards away.

David, the Bostonian, had triumphed at another historic 'tea party', aided by the sheriff from Denver, Colorado, Jeff, and not a single shot had been fired. With laughter breaking out from all quarters, we gathered ourselves in readiness for the filming and the climb.

We did a repeat of the shot the night before, with me walking up the rock-strewn glacier, and, in company with the yaks, along the wide ridge. After a while the crew joined me, and Wongchu, the Sherpas and the yak team were given leave to proceed on to Camp III. Soon, they were out of sight, and we were alone in the haunting scenery.

The glacier had twisted and broken into a belt some two miles wide. As the fine mist of the morning started to clear, the giant sharks' fins of ice, over a hundred feet high, became amazingly more numerous. Fissures over fifty feet deep appeared. Crevasses – some narrow, some wide – would bar our way, forcing us to make a detour. David knew the terrain very well, as he had been there before, and he watched our reactions with great interest.

The seductive route drew me on, the scenery bewitching my eyes. On all sides ... mountains! Oh, what monoliths of splendour surrounded us, their striking, pristine, symmetrical forms releasing, at their bases, huge, energized glaciers. Their ribbed blue flutings whispered far-away songs in the gentle breeze, as the resulting drops of ice delicately showered our bodies.

The brain, in its rarefied state in that sparse air, together with the heart, sent messages of thanks upwards to the throne of the great goddess Chomolungma.

'Thank you, sweet lady!' I found myself whispering.

I caught my companions' gaze; we felt very close to each other.

On, on, the winding rough path went through the region of blue and green bergs, and seracs. Could the senses take in more? We were at 20,000 feet and moving in a dream. How discourteous of me to question the reality of it all, but I did. My thoughts went to the M4 motorway years before, when I was driving at night, utterly tired. My hands, although holding the wheel solidly, appeared to float through it in a ghostly fashion. For a while I didn't know what was real and what was not. Of course, I got off the motorway and rested for a few hours.

Was this real now? Was I on the East Rongbuk Glacier where Mallory, Irvine and Captain Noel had previously been? Or was I still in my garden, dreaming in the wicker chair on a summer's afternoon?

I held my pulse, and gripped my old-fashioned black ski stick.

This had to be real! It had to be! Nature couldn't be so cruel as to fool me.

'Look! Look!' I shouted to J.P.

Several choughs and a single lammergeyer flew above us, showing the way to Chomolungma. My mind hummed happily, the camera hummed, and the beckoning fair one drew us on.

'Steady, Big Yeti!' interrupted David. 'You're going too fast.'

His common sense confirmed that all was real. Then we came upon the empty tents of Camp II of the Peace Climb, situated on a mound, or moraine. These mounds vary in size, from the large to the small, and comprise small stones and, frequently, large boulders. The East Rongbuk Glacier used to be much larger and longer. Throughout its long history, it has eaten its way into the innermost recesses of the mountains, to form numerous cirques and corries, depositing these mounds in the process. It is evident that the glaciers in the region are shrinking back from their gigantic size, into the recesses of their birth. You could feel that Everest rules all, drawing back to her womb the children of her creation.

We sat down for half an hour and ate a little, and drank a large amount of water. The sun was now directly overhead. Nothing I had experienced compared to its power here, not even in Kenya or Tanzania. We were now moving into a landscape of glaring sun and ice. The twenties expeditions used to avoid travelling in it around the middle of the day, reserving their efforts for the early mornings and late evenings. It is hard to conceive, but the brightest of sunlight in England would be dusk by comparison. To take your glasses off in this region would, within minutes, result in serious sun blindness, for the white-hot rays reflect torturously from the amazing ice formations.

Any exposed part of the body was instantly covered up, and oodles of cream were ploughed into the face, neck, ears and nose. You even had to push cream up your nostrils, otherwise the intense light would burn up towards the pituitary gland. Despite this extreme need for protection, what a stunning, magical world the Fairy Kingdom of Ice is!

The fantastic shapes entranced us as we moved into an inner sanctum rather like an ice palace. Here, ice pinnacles of iridescent green, blue, black, white and crystal-clear soared all around us. We stood on a white lake of frozen enchantment, and time stood still. Here, nature was at its most sublime and dangerous. The cobalt-blue sky shimmered, with its unseen, deadly ultraviolet rays, and the equally dreaded cosmic variety. As Mallory observed, 'The White Rabbit himself would have been bewildered here!'

It was time to leave these graceful spires, and make our way to the famous trough. At this point, we were passed by the Californians. They were steaming ahead, and anyone could see that they were going too fast.

After a further half-hour we entered the trough at about 1 p.m. The trough is a depression, or a natural snow and ice causeway, that runs for two miles up the East Rongbuk Glacier. Imagine a corridor fifty feet deep, and about a hundred feet wide, with steep sides of blue, green and white ice. At intervals, there are lovely glacial lakelets to delight the eye. It is a remarkable feature, and is the last obstacle to surmount before arriving at Camp III, at 21,300 feet. As I looked at it, I thought how glorious it looked, but what a task in the midday sun.

This region is renowned for its stagnant, dead air and its fiery heat. The sky was clear, and there was no cooling breeze; the stillness was frightening. Everest is situated at a low latitude, 28°N, and the tropical sun was now at its zenith, beating down remorselessly.

I found I was stumbling about at the start of the trough, with David and Jeff shouting instructions to me from behind the camera. The reason for this was that there is a great deal of concealed ridging of ice at the base of the trough, caused by the immense pressure from above. Once over this, I was on my merry way. We filmed for an hour over half a mile or so, until J.P. was satisfied.

David decided that we now needed to get up to Camp III before it was dark. Then the agony started. Despite the liberal amounts of cream administered to our faces, we were cooking like roast chickens. J.P. and the crew suddenly found that they had to stop, as they spied some enticing shot. Therefore Graham and I continued up together. Even though I was suffering, I was out of my

mind with happiness, to think that I was actually climbing in that
historic trough. I felt sure that Captain Noel was thrilled, and
watching me. And Chris Bonington's words came to mind: 'The
East Rongbuk Glacier is Hard Drill.'

It certainly was.

Looking down, I could see J.P. and the others as little dots.
Graham and I were labouring like ninety-year-olds, for there was
no respite from the heat, and the dreaded glacier lassitude forced
us to move in slow motion. And yet the scenery never ceased to
inspire us. Gradually and painfully, we were getting there. Or were
we? ...

After climbing a hill of snow, we found another to ascend, and
another, and another, and another. We longed to get out of the
trough. I could no longer see J.P. and the others, and the weather
was cooling rapidly, as it was now about 4 p.m. We simply could
not rush it, for we were approaching 21,000 feet. After a hundred
feet, we would sit down and rest a few minutes, our hearts pulsating with the effort. Graham moved ahead of me as we crested
the umpteenth hill, and shouted back, 'We're out of the trough,
General!'

He always called me by this name, and within seconds I was
breathlessly by his side.

'Look! ... Look! ...' he whispered. 'There's the Lhakpa La,
Windy Gap, which Mallory climbed in 1921.'

We moved on with renewed vigour, and after wading in deep
snow for fifty yards found ourselves rounding a shoulder at the top
of the trough. Suddenly we sank in the snow with emotion and
hugged one another. For there, in front of us, two miles away, was
the legendary North Col.

'The North Col!' we madly shouted.

'Jesus, Graham! We're here! ... We're here! Man alive! We're
here at last!'

Our speech became disjointed, insane and feverish.

'See! ... See! ... The Col leading on to the North Ridge, and the
summit behind!' I rasped. 'And this is the huge North-East Ridge,
five miles long, man! ... Where Tasker and Boardman are, and
somewhere up there are Mallory and Irvine!'

In our excitement we quite forgot there was still half a mile to go to Camp III, the site of which Mallory and his companions had called the 'Snowfield Camp'. Pacing ourselves carefully, we arrived to find our yaks grazing on their hay, and the yak herders cooking in their tents. The Sherpas were busy putting up the tents, and there was a feeling of achievement and pride. The North Peak, Changtse, looked forbidding and loomed over us. The North Col, that ancient, frozen, gigantic fossil of ice, looked cold and treacherous in the evening light.

Suddenly Jeff arrived, and instantly applied himself, with serious determination, to every task in sight. The remaining tents shot up quickly, and then David and Veronique came into view. Like Jeff, they had carried a lot of gear; theirs was a terrific performance. I looked down on the snowfield and made out J.P. a couple of hundred yards away. His too was a smashing effort, for he hadn't had the benefit of acclimatizing to Camp II days earlier.

The last hundred feet were proving tough, and he kept sitting down in the snow, admiring the scenery. Finally he stumbled over to me and shouted, 'I'm completely shagged, Big Yeti!'

'You magnificent bastard!' I whispered. 'We've got to 21,300 feet, J.P.!'

His tired, crumpled face slowly took it all in, and he smiled with a far-away look. Although we were tired, David barked out insructions to keep us on our mettle.

'It's going to plunge to twenty degrees below zero in half an hour. Get into your tents and blow up your mattresses, and get in your sleeping bags, and eat chocolate or power bars, and drink till it comes out of your ears!'

The large green mess tent had been erected, and was to prove such a success that the other expeditions would be attracted to it like bees around a jam pot. It started to snow heavily, and it was lovely to see the yaks huddled together in the shelter of some large boulders, their thick coats impervious to the cold.

Soon, we were all snug in our sleeping bags. J.P. and I shared a little green tent, which was a cheerful abode. Two hours later Veronique woke us. Miraculously, a meal was being prepared in the mess tent.

We sat round the two gas fires, which burned cheerfully, cooking the food and warming us at the same time. The flaps of the window were shut tight, and the gas lamps hung from cords, and lit up our happy, worn faces. Little was said. We ate and drank, and stared at the flames. After two hours we braved the short distance to our tents, and once more enjoyed the warmth of our sleeping bags. We used our head torches to check that all was well, closed the inner zip and switched off the lamps. It was instantly pitch black. Outside, the wind howled on the mighty North Col, and we snuggled deeper into our efficient sleeping bags.

'Well, J.P.,' I whispered. 'Don't worry about the Col ... You're only on holiday, aren't you?'

'Yes, Big Yeti,' he replied. 'Goodnight. Sweet dreams!'

The next day was a sleepy, lazy day, as approved by J.P. and ordered by David. After the effort of the previous day, it was imperative to allow our bodies to adjust to this extreme height.

Both J.P. and I felt splendid – quite tired, but fit. We had been woken by the appalling sound of Wongchu, coughing and spitting. This he did all day long, and we found it repulsive. He really wasn't well at all. Dogbollock appeared to have been up for some time, and was deep in conversation with Veronique. The topic was, of course, food. Veronique always seemed to include the word pumpernickel in her conversation, so we named her the 'Pumpernickel Yeti'.

Our needs were basic, and it is fair to say that we were reduced to a rudimentary state. The only food I could still tolerate was porridge, eggs and plain dishes. Just the thought of anything spicy made me feel ill. Yet David, Veronique and J.P. adored spicy meals! I passionately loved jam, and any kind of soup.

At great height, the blood thickens incredibly and the glands, heart and lungs are affected. For instance, a symptom of disorder in the thyroid gland is a distaste for meat.

It was important to move about slowly and smoothly, as any quick action resulted in the body being convulsed by violent panting, followed by the heart beating like a hammer, although it soon returned to normal, once rested. David said he could not stress enough how important it was to relax as much as possible during the day.

After several mugs of tea, I lay on top of my sleeping bag with the lower part of the tent open, and stared for hours at the staggering five-mile North-East Ridge of Everest. Then I stared hard at the steep North Col.

'Can you see the Russians on it?' David shouted.

I looked long and hard, and after a great deal of help and pointing from Jeff, spotted what looked like tiny ants below an ice field. God! It looked intimidating! Captain Noel called it the 'Terrible Ice Cliff'.

J.P. sat beside me in an almost comatose state, and said that the Col looked horrible, and that he feared for my life. He maintained that though there were fixed ropes on it, the place was extremely dangerous, and capable of avalanching.

'It looks bloody vertical, Big Yeti!' he muttered. 'It gives me nightmares ... If anything happened to you, I just wouldn't know what to say to Hildegard ... You must watch it up there, and promise me not to let your emotions run away with you ... '

I nodded and patted his back. We were totally devoted to each other. It had been a long, hard journey for us to get here and be in striking distance of the 'Ice Cliff'. It rises from the top of the East Rongbuk Glacier for about two thousand feet. Near the top is a particularly tricky section that includes a rather daunting, long traverse, with a sheer drop of a thousand feet below it. Still, there were ropes there, which would prove a great help.

The North Col is connected to the North Ridge, which eventually joins up with the North-East Ridge to the First Step, at 28,000 feet, and then the Second Step, at 28,250 feet, then on to the Final Pyramid, and the Summit, at 29,028 feet.

I longed to have a go at the North Col; I felt sure I could climb it! What must the view be like from there, of the whole North Face? I thought. For now, I must put away all such thoughts ...

It would be days before I was presented with the opportunity. Far to the right, we could hear the occasional sound of an avalanche thundering down mighty Changtse's western flanks. It really did make a sound like distant artillery.

'Bloody hell!' I whispered.

'I told you,' replied J.P. 'This place is bloody dangerous and horrible!'

We turned over on our backs and carried on reading. J.P. was reading a book by Isabel Allende, and I, *Lost Horizon*. It was amusing to think that Mallory and Somervell, over sixty years before, had been reading *The Spirit of Man* on the same spot. Chris Bonington had always said that if he'd been on the expedition, we wouldn't have caught him reading such stuff. He'd have brought a good selection of thrillers!

The World Peace Climb was now manoeuvring for positions on the mountain, in the hope that there would be a window in the weather that would give them a chance of success. They deserved it: they had suffered and fought for weeks and had established a camp at over 27,000 feet. We would keep our fingers crossed for them.

The New Zealanders were now on the other side of the mountain, pushing their way slowly up the North Face. They were my favourites, and I passionately wanted them to succeed. 'The Whizkids', the Californians, were on Changtse. God knows how they would fare! And our little band would be trying soon.

The ascent to 21,300 feet had reduced my weight to about twelve and a half stone, and I was getting thinner by the hour. That evening J.P. and I chatted about our affection for the BBC, and after the customary bouts of giggling, fell asleep. I was awakened by awful groans from my companion. His pee bottle had spilled all over him. Poor J.P., wet and cold. I told him to strip off completely and put on dry clothes, and his padded jacket and trousers. This done, I zipped open my sleeping bag and cuddled him to sleep.

J.P. remembers clearly: 'As I lay snuggled up against the big bear snoring next to me, I was fearful for our ascent. Even with the fixed ropes the Peace Climb had put up there, there was no guarantee of safety. There are objective dangers you have to live with. I remember Messner's words: "If the rock smells bad, don't go!"

'It sounded simple, but how did you smell the rock? He said that it took a lifetime to know that. I would have to trust David and his experience. Luckily I knew that, if anything, he would err on the side of caution. The American climbers are reputedly the most cautious in the business, and David had an excellent reputation for safety. The margin of error at these heights is, of course, very slim. With these thoughts, I sank into a fitful sleep.

'It was sunny in the morning, thank God! The snow was a foot deep, but that didn't impede our plans. In a trice, the sleeping bag was soaking up the sun, and I was warm in our big mess tent, the thunderous roar of the pressure cookers telling me that vats of tea were being prepared. Gradually the team emerged, and we would take stock of the situation.

'David was bustling away as usual. Jeff looked a bit the worse for wear: he was still not acclimatizing very well. He had a headache and had not slept well, so the Diamox didn't seem to be helping him much. Phuli was still in bed feeling lousy. Chuldim and Newang seemed fine, and were busy hacking ice from the glacier to melt. Wongchu, somewhat to our relief, seemed to have lost his voice. We thought it was nothing more than a sore throat, the common affliction of altitude climbing, caused by cold air damaging the larynx. However, it was to have serious implications for the climb.

'Graham and Veronique were fine, and full of energy. Brian had survived my night's embrace with no ill effects, so I figured it was time to shoot some more sequences. We decided to venture up on to the glacier. It would not be a long trek — no more than an hour — but would give us a chance to gain an additional five hundred feet.

'We set off up the glacier, passing on our way the Peace Climb's advance Base Camp. It was nowhere near as nice as our own, and was nearly deserted, the majority of climbers having gone up the Col and beyond, to set up the high camps. We continued on past the debris of other expeditions. The crevasses were full of old gas cannisters, cartons of old food and cookers. It was not an attractive sight.

'The glacier, at this point, was still strewn with rocks and boulders, and felt quite safe, but soon we approached the sleek ice of the main glacier. Graham and I went on ahead across the ice to recce a spot in which to film Brian. It did not seem dangerous, true, for the glacier sloped away at an angle of about fifteen degrees for about two miles, and although there were countless crevasses, we felt quite secure as we plodded in our hiking boots to the centre of the ice. David called us back, furious. He was very agitated in a way that I had never seen before.

'"Don't ever do that again!" he warned us. "One slip and you're dead! Before you have a chance to grab hold of anything, you'll be swishing down that slope at fifty miles per hour and plop into a crevasse, and that'll be the last we ever see of you! It doesn't look dangerous, I know, but it is. Gore-tex on that ice is lethal. Put on your crampons, take an ice axe, and don't stray!"

'So we all put on our crampons for the first time, and with greater respect made our way across the ice to the centre of the glacier. Jeff went out on point to probe for crevasses, for with the recent fall of snow they could easily be hidden, and some went down a few hundred feet. This was a big glacier!

'We set up the camera, and Jeff took Brian some way down the glacier so we could film his approach to the camera. Suddenly the clapperboard fell out of Veronique's hand. She tried to grab it as it started its inevitable slide down the slope, and in a split second she too was sliding down after it. David and I, who had been setting up the tripod, lunged for her legs and stopped her slide. It all happened in a flash, and could so easily have been fatal. We all knew what David was talking about now.'

The weather was now beginning to deteriorate. With Jeff just below me in case I slipped, I walked carefully towards the camera, and exploded with genuine passion about an avalanche that had taken place in 1922 near where I was now standing. Seven Sherpas died in it, and Mallory, like the great man that he was, accepted the blame. He didn't pass the buck for one minute. It was simply that, at the time, they had no real knowledge of Himalayan conditions. There seemed to be nothing to suggest that the snow-field on the North Col would avalanche. Mallory and his companions spent hours trying to save the Sherpas and find their bodies. Captain Noel came up and helped.

'I pulled on a rope,' he told me back in England. 'There was a man on the end with tons of snow on him. I couldn't pull him up, I remember it distinctly. It always makes me cry when I think about it ...'

There I was, on the glacier, at the base of the North Col, at about 21,700 feet, in 1990, reliving the whole scene. It was a part of the story I particularly wanted to do. Captain Noel's description of the events had been so vivid that I could easily get into

Mallory's frame of mind. I had brought with me on the expedition the vacuum flask that the captain had taken up there with him, filled with soup to take to Mallory as he was trying to rescue the Sherpas ... A tangible link with the 1922 expedition.

At the time, my emotions were positively raging. I wasn't acting for one moment, but simply being myself. It was bizarre! My feelings were almost out of control, and at times I didn't make any sense. My brain throbbed and felt as though it were ever widening under unknown influences. Never, in my entire life, have I experienced such astonishing feelings. I felt free and unfettered ... Never to be the same again. It was as if, all my life, I had been imprisoned, and was now sweeping far and wide in every direction, with limitless being.

The camera crew were shocked, but there it was, recorded on film. Sweet Jesus! I shake as I write about it! Altitude was always noted for reducing emotions. Not so with me: they grew ... They expanded!

After the filming we raced back down to our camp, to avoid the coming storm. Then we sat down, all of us radiant, and the Sherpas heaped kindness and mugs of tea on us. The storm raged outside, and our breath steamed out with convulsive shudders. I roared and shouted and laughed totally ... You know what I mean. In our complicated modern life, you rarely see people laugh fully. I'm quite a strong laugher, but in that mess tent I roared out with joy like I'd never known! Everyone bounced up and down on their rock in a strange, happy rhythm.

'God, David!' I throbbed out. 'I can't control my feelings – I'm so happy and free!'

It was a colossal, earth-thumping sensation of never-ending expansion. My heart thudded, and felt like a galaxy! My brain sang in chords of refined music, and reached out beyond time and space!

It went on for hours! Would I ever come down again?

It was 30 April. Of course! Certain groups and churches were sending me their prayers ... I could feel it! I hate charlatans who play at the esoteric game. What I am writing about happened!

The next morning it was still with me, but quieter. It was time for us all to descend to Base Camp. It seems crazy, after such an effort to get to Camp III, but it was essential if one was to hope to go higher still. You have to descend to recuperate. If we stayed for days at 21,300 feet, we would quickly deteriorate. We were all delighted with the filming, and relieved that so far we had realized our objectives.

Down we plunged ... Down, down, down ... I felt absolutely possessed, and I raced down with Dogbollock, seeing if I could keep ahead of him. In what seemed like a moment we had reached the base of the trough, and then it was round the meandering pathways to the Fairy Kingdom of Ice, and on to the ridges of moraine above our Camp II. It all seemed like a film in reverse. We two had set off long before everybody else, and there was no one in front of us.

Down, down, still further, to the lip of the East Rongbuk Glacier, where the lovely vision of Margaret was there to greet us. Out came flasks of coffee, and she poured us mugs of the refreshing brew ... How kind and thoughtful of her. Half an hour later the rest joined us, and J.P. positively beamed with delight at his new wife's presence, and they hugged and kissed till the cows came home.

We arrived back at Base Camp at 9 p.m. The descent had taken only five and a half hours. There was tiny Krisna, completely recovered and smiling happily, with a feast prepared for us. It was great to see Jules and Swanee again, who were full of questions about the climb. That evening we ate masses of eggs and chips ... Krisna had done us proud.

It is doubtful, in the history of climbing, whether there has ever been a happier Base Camp, and in the middle of all this excitement we toasted Jeff, Wongchu, Phuli, Chuldim and Nawang, who were still up at Camp III, improving it and guarding our supplies. Their health and well-being were being tested to the full.

In five days' time we would be heading back up. It was definitely getting warmer; one or two people were even sunbathing. Everywhere there was a feeling of spring and expectancy. The World Peace Climb team were on the point of making their first summit bid, and the New Zealanders were also making good progress. Would Everest be kind and give us good weather?

We were to be given only a few days on the mountain, and we had to be careful not to hinder the Peace Climb. I wondered if any team had ever been given such a short time on the mountain. If the weather was bad during that time we would not be allowed to wait it out like the other expeditions. The Peace Climb had been up there for weeks, and a suitable break in the weather had still not occurred. Despite these restrictions, we were happy and hopeful. In my heart, I always felt that the Goddess Mother of the Earth would be kind to us.

As you have probably gathered, I was not inspired by the ideals of the Peace Climb. Politics is quite alien to me.

During the time on the mountain, I had the good fortune to meet most of the members of the Peace Climb, and to a man (and woman) I found them kind and a pleasure to be with. Their performances on Everest were outstanding, their courage was phenomenal and I totally respected them. Americans in particular often come in for a great deal of stick, but this is something I do not agree with. I like them. David Breashears, Jeff and Veronique are fine examples of that race. Jim Whittaker, who has the honour of being the first American to climb Everest, is another gentleman I admire. He told me how much he feared going through the dangerous ice wall on the South Col route of the mountain, yet he still went into the deadly region and saved the life of a Sherpa, carrying him back to safety.

To come back to politics, I come down on the side of my Armenian wild man, Mischa Saleki, like him regarding the ideals of the Peace Climb as dubious. I may be wrong, but there it is.

While I'm in a light-hearted mood, I must mention that it was J.P.'s birthday on 4 May, and also, Stephen Evans, our executive producer, had arrived from Lhasa, and was visiting us and embarking on a trek that was ultimately going up to Camp III. Everyone was invited to J.P.'s party, including the Kiwis and anybody from the Peace Camp. J.P. explains: 'Jules and Graham set to, with professional zeal, rigging the lights and sound machine into a disco in the mess tent. Champagne and smoked salmon were opened, Krisna and Veronique busied themselves making cakes, and party dresses were brought out.

'It was the best birthday party I've ever had. Jules was the DJ, hip and MC Hammer-like, a cool dude in his shades and head torch. The lights flashed, the corks popped and the yaks tinkled their bells as we boogied past midnight. No problem with the altitude now ... We were ready for the mountain ... '

7

Goddess Mother of the Earth

It was 6 May and the final push was on.

When Mallory was about to embark on his final, fatal climb in 1924, these were his words: 'The issue will shortly be decided. The third time we walk up the East Rongbuk Glacier will be the last ... For Better or Worse ... '

With Mallory's words ringing in my ears, I took my 'first important step', as Messner calls it, and moved off with the remaining half of the team.

The Peace Climb team were going for the summit, and the New Zealanders were pushing up higher on the North Face. Of the Californians on Changtse, we had no news.

I will not dwell on our ascent again to Camp III. Suffice it to say that Swanee, Jules and Margaret were marvellous. We filmed all the way and stopped again at Camp II, before proceeding towards Camp III. Swanee was in agony, and had a frightful chest cold. His breathing was heartbreaking to listen to, but on he struggled in that graceful style of his.

Jules was suffering too, from a terrible headache. The lack of atmospheric pressure was also giving Julian the further complication of piles. Uncontained, they protruded out and gave him untold misery. At times he appeared to weep quietly with pain, but then he would control himself and move on with great courage.

Margaret seemed to be in perfect health; except, of course, she often moved like Quasimodo. With the filming completed, I moved on a little to the Peace Climb's Camp II. A solitary figure came out to meet me: the young Soviet climber, Victor Volodin.

He looked frightful, and was still suffering from the after-effects of pulmonary oedema.

My God! I thought. You shouldn't be here, at 20,000 feet!

He was such a sweet lad, and greeted me with a weak smile. How sad for him: his comrades were way up the mountain, but in his condition he hadn't a hope in hell of going much higher.

I advised him to go down, but then I became aware that he had come all this way to bring an oxygen regulator up, for someone who was ill on the Californian climb. I thought this was a wonderful gesture by this young man, but he was now forced to admit that he couldn't get any higher, and would I take it up? I packed it in my rucksack, shared a coffee with him and went on ahead.

Near the beginning of the trough, I met a dismal gang of Californians coming down. Their lead climber, a young man in his mid-twenties, was a grim sight. He was suffering badly from the one thing that I dreaded: cerebral haemorrhage. This simply means that his brain was bleeding and badly damaged. Poor lad! He was completely incoherent and being led down at a snail's pace. I held out little hope for his survival.

I quickly brought out the oxygen regulator, and the Americans applied it to an oxygen bottle they had. Instantly you could see that he was getting some relief, if only from the pain. Tell-tale specks of dried blood were round the edge of his nostrils. I gently stroked his cheeks, murmuring encouragement. I could detect in him the will to survive.

It was the first time I'd really looked at the Californians. They were a good set of lads. Then, unbelievably, Victor arrived, and they all went down in a sick, huddled heap. I was shaken by it all, and gripped the white scarf given to me by the lama, and chanted. '*Om Mani Padme Hum.*'

Yet the feeling that I was being looked after never left me; it was almost as if I were in a protective bubble. The beckoning 'Fair One' in my mind's eye appeared to be smiling, calling me up ... She felt friendly.

The weather was good, with a slight breeze, which made the ascent of the trough more bearable. David and Veronique kept pace with Swanee and Jules, with J.P.'s head lolling from side to side, as he watched over his beloved Hunchback.

Halfway up the corridor of ice, I met a character coming down from the Peace Climb, who explained to me that the glacier moved downwards three to five inches a day. I nodded my thanks, and thought, Not a lot of people know that!

Two hours later I was greeted by a white-faced Jeff at Camp III. Another hour later Margaret clambered into the camp area, muttering hoarsely, in words that my mother would have described as 'pit language', that the climb had been hell. J.P., behind her, agreed, and joined me in congratulating her.

Later still, Jules and Swanee, with David and company behind watching over them, finally made it. They were worn out, and were quickly given lots of fluid. They received our congratulations with weary smiles. A fine achievement!

J.P. takes up the story: 'The day after arriving, everyone was pretty dead, but it was necessary to start setting up our high camps. The Sherpas, along with David, Jeff, Veronique and Graham, made an initial dump on the North Col. We would have three tents there, and enough food for a week.

'From the Col, there was a possibility that we could make the highly dangerous ascent to the North-East Ridge, the only factor to our advantage being that there were fixed ropes there from the Peace Climb. From the juncture of the North Col and the North-East Ridge, the going would be tough, over slabs of icy granite. We could use any oxygen supplies left by the Peace Climb, but Brian was determined to go as high as possible without oxygen. Both David and I were in agreement that it was better this way, for not only did it save a great deal of weight while climbing, but it also looked better for the film. If Brian's face was covered with a mask, it would be impossible to hear him, and I wanted as much real emotion, sound and fury as high as possible. It was possible to sleep with the oxygen, but Brian was acclimatizing so well that this hardly seemed necessary. He was of less concern than the Sherpas.

'They were essential to the success of the climb, and already two of them were looking pretty bad. Wongchu's throat had not cleared up. He was permanently hoarse, and more worryingly, was now coughing up blood. He was not going to make it to the Col in that condition. Phuli was also suffering with headaches and throat problems, but more from debilitating and severe diarrhoea.

'Jules was in the most pain, with haemorrhoids. The poor chap could hardly walk. Swanee's cough was still dreadful, and had it not been for his iron determination to keep going, he would have been sent back down to Base Camp. Jeff seemed a bit better, but was not going as well as he had hoped. All in all, we were hardly in peak condition. Margaret was suffering from the altitude badly enough to pose the question of whether she should go higher. As for me, it was the usual sore throat, but nothing more. I hadn't even had a headache yet. Brian seemed immune to it all; luckily he didn't seem to have any problems.

'After the first dump had been made, it was decided that we should split up into two groups. Swanee and I would film the first stage of the ascent of the Col, while David and Graham would handle the ascent to the top of it. That way, we could maximize our shots, using our long lens to dramatic effect. I would follow the next day with another load and the Sherpas. Jules, dignified to the end, even had to admit that his condition now prevented him from going any higher. It was obvious that he was upset, but put a brave face on it as we hugged him goodbye, with tears in his eyes, and headed off for the Col.

'It was 8 May. The Peace Climb had put their first group on the summit, and there were more waiting in the wings. We watched them bravely set off, tiny figures groping their way towards the Final Pyramid. We passed their big mess tent. Two Tibetans and two Americans had already returned, and were slowly recovering from their ordeal. We congratulated them, and headed on up. The weather was perfect: clear blue skies and hardly a breath of wind.

'By the time we reached the base of the Col, it must have been 40°C, and the radiant heat of the sun scorched our skin. It was too hot to wear anything more than a t-shirt, and the glare from the snow made it uncomfortable to take our snow-goggles off, which was a pity, as Brian was obliged to do all his speeches with them on.

'We made some solid progress, crossed the crevasse safely and did some great shots of the lone figure of Brian heading up the glacier. His profile looked terrific – you could easily imagine it was Mallory or Norton ... Brian had now lost nearly forty pounds, and his trousers threatened to fall off his bum!'

My adrenalin was overflowing, and my long-held belief that the weather would be good was now confirmed. Right at the base of the North Col, in the grip of the miracle of it all, I spoke Mallory's words to camera: 'It's an infernal mountain, cold and treacherous. Frankly, the game is not good enough; the risks of getting caught are too great; the margin of strength when men are at great heights is too small ... Perhaps it's mere folly to go up again, but how can I be out of the hunt?'

'Cut,' said J.P., and a strange silence followed. It was broken by my friend Slava, arriving after his successful summit attempt. He looked exhausted and happy, and on seeing me, surprisingly said, 'I theenk of you, Mr Mallory! Hello, how are you?'

Throughout all this, Swanee was filming away, and Doctor Kurt was testing Slava's reactions. The Russian's heart and mind seemed fine, and I embraced him.

David Breashears announced that it was getting late, and that we needed to get a move on up the North Col. His words made me nervous, and at the same time thrilled me.

This is the crunch! I thought. The acid test!

I looked around at my gallant companions – J.P., Margaret and Swanee – shouted a farewell, connected my yellow jumar to the rope, adjusted my sling, and I was off.

Directly above me was David, filming my progress, assisted by Veronique; a tremendous task. Slightly above them were two strong Sherpas, Chuldim and Nawang, and alongside them was Graham with his sound machine. What would his great-uncle, the famous Howard Somervell, have thought of him now, following in his footsteps? There was a marvellous feeling of occasion to it all.

Jeff was immediately below me, guarding my every move. The big loss was Wongchu, our sirdar and Tiger Sherpa, who was very ill and in danger of losing his life.

Already J.P. and the BBC team were growing smaller, and they filmed our progress from below.

In the name of heaven! I thought. I was actually on the North Col, like Mallory and Captain Noel!

What a shock, though! It was murderously hard for me. My relative ease at ascending the East Rongbuk Glacier had fooled me into thinking that the rest of the climbing would be the same. I was now awake to the horrible reality of it all. It was steeper than I'd anticipated, with slopes of seventy degrees or more commonplace.

My breathing became rapid, and frightening. My heart, which had felt so elated the other day, was employing every last ounce of strength to pump my blood, which was the consistency of glue, around my body. Thump! thump! thump! it went, deafening my ears until they felt fit to burst.

'Where's the air?' I gasped. 'And where are my lungs?'

I slumped in the snow, shocked and frightened. Surely I would have a haemorrhage or heart attack at this rate?

'Jeff? ... Jeff? ...' I whispered. 'I feel as though I'm going to die ... I thought the mountain liked me ... '

'It does!' Jeff said. 'But she's also a bloody great sow! ... So don't be afraid of her, and kick her in the ribs! ... But do it, Brian, in a controlled manner ... Go slower and relax a little.'

I did what he said.

'That's it, Brian! ... Very good. Nice and easy. Rhythmic ... You'll make it to the top of the Col, you'll see ... '

Dear Jeff, my giant minder, was so kind. His calming influence continued to steady my nerves, and fill me with periods of confidence. But the panic would return, as my heart seemed to change gear, staying for a moment in suspended animation, and then thump on as the crisis passed ... But I *was* getting higher! It was painfully slow, to be sure, but I was moving up ... An hour or more passed ...

'How high now, Jeff?' I groaned.

'Maybe 22,500 feet.'

It was reassuring to see that my companions were also having a tough time, and of course, they were carrying cameras and gear as well, whereas my load was very light: sleeping bags and so on.

What was concerning everybody was that I appeared to be slowing down. The day had been intensely hot, and now it was rapidly cooling. I was in my Alpinex gear, and I was getting near to the point where I needed to put some additional clothing on. The sun was beginning to go down, and we still had five hundred feet to go, including the exposed traverse and vertical finish.

David and the others, as well as Jeff, moved ahead of me to fix the cameras for a tremendous shot. For the past half-hour I'd been having trouble with my harness, which kept coming loose. In Kathmandu, when it was fitted, I was sixteen stone, whereas now I was nearer ten. I just couldn't adjust the bloody thing!

The temperature suddenly plummeted and a breeze sprang up. I announced very calmly that I felt depressed, which I realized was the first stage of deterioration.

'I need to get warmer, gentlemen ....'

David and Jeff descended to me in a flash, and pulled out my Berghaus thermal underjacket — I didn't need the full high-altitude one — and helped me on with it. I immediately felt better, and after their expert adjustments to my harness, I was ready to continue. David had his reservations, though, saying that if I showed any more signs of deterioration he would have to order me down.

'Not on your nellie!' I replied. 'I'm fine!'

We started upwards again, and the breeze had disappeared. My heart now seemed to be more even in its beat, though it was still tough going. Captain Noel was strongly in my mind, and I could feel him close, urging me on.

'Captain Noel would never forgive me if I stopped now!' I shouted out.

There was no echo. My voice, which had lost its resonance days ago, was lost in the white folds of the colossal ice wall. The ice now started to turn an old-gold colour, as the sun hastened to leave us. Jeff and I were now on the vertical traverse.

'You can do it!' David shouted. 'You're getting closer, Brian!'

His shouts were augmented by roars of encouragement from all quarters.

Great! I thought. I'm over the tricky pitch!

And the only thing that stood between me and the top of the Col was a fifty-foot vertical wall. David was above me, filming for all he was worth, and in unison with Veronique, was encouraging me also.

I pulled on the rope strenuously, and felt good.

'Go on, man!' whispered Jeff below. 'Go, Brian! ... Go, man! Go! ... Yes! You're there!' he shouted.

It was a narrow, knife-edged ridge of ice, and I placed myself on it, straddling my legs either side of it. I was, at last, on top of the North Col, at 23,100 feet. The realization devastated me, and I cried like a baby. So many years of endeavour were encapsulated in that moment! So many sacrifices and efforts of so many people over the years to the present moment ... This was their climb ... Their reward ... Their fulfilment ...

'Captain Noel!' I roared out, at the same time weeping. 'I'm here! ... I've done it ... '

As I ripped my goggles off, my rampaging emotions ebbed and flowed amid showers of tears. My voice was asthmatic and choked as I poured out my feelings.

'I thought I was finished halfway up! Oh, God!' I whispered to myself. 'I thought I was done for! ... All the bloody bureaucracy of borders and soldiers in Kathmandu, and India! ... And people telling me I couldn't do it! ... Well *I'm* here! ... Here! ... '

I roared out again and again, 'Captain Noel! ... Captain Noel! ... I'm here! ... '

David interrupted me, just as emotionally, shouting, 'Come over here, Big Yeti, and see the greatest sight in the world!'

Walking along the ridge, I came to a wide snow slope and stopped alongside my friends. We looked down and up, left and right, and our eyes glistened in the setting sun. There was the whole North Face of Everest, directly in front of us! It is the most awesome and stupendous sight on earth! In that thin air you felt as though you could touch it. The silence and stillness was alive and holy.

Dear Goddess Mother of the Earth! I thought. Your ethereal qualities transcend beauty ...

Wide and high and towering is her grandeur. From her white head and powerful shoulders sweep down gigantic ridges and fiery spurs. Couloirs of cold snow pour down her Spartan dress of sandstone and granite, and absorb her brother the sun's radiance.

As children of nature we stood, hardly daring to breathe, for fear that the noise might disturb the hallowed figure in front of us. After a passage of time, Chomolungma herself gave us the cue to move: her eyes blinked sleepily as the sun left her forehead.

David led the way quietly to our three tents, firmly placed in a snow hollow. One for Chuldim and Nawang, one for David and Veronique and one for Jeff, Graham and myself. Our whispering continued as we hurriedly zipped ourselves in, and began the long job of boiling water.

It was dark now, and while Graham was preparing tea and soup, I popped my head out to look at the night sky. What stars! Stars of a spring night on Chomolungma. The Milky Way, with its gracious curve, enfolded the goddess in its dense tapestry of glowing lights. Lights of blue, gold, green, white, yellow and red. Orion and his outriders lit the blanket of the night with their dazzling brightness. Rejoicing and cascading meteorites lent their brief, fiery sparks to the heavenly scene, and Chomolungma slept.

Inside the tent, the fiery orb of Graham's nose increased in intensity as he coughed dreadfully, and, grinning from ear to ear, presented me with a huge mug of soup.

Tea, soup and tea again. We drank for hours. Jeff was very quiet, and did not look at all well. Placing my hands on both men's shoulders, I thanked them for getting me up. My voice went further afield, to thank David and Veronique. Their hearty, 'You're welcome, Big Yeti!' made me smile, as did Chuldim's and Nawang's. The two Sherpas had worked their guts out, yet always managed to smile.

There was plenty of room in our tent for three men, and as the evening wore on and the correct amount of liquid was taken, we settled in our sleeping bags, and watched the tent accumulate the severe frost.

I felt fine, with just a slight light-headedness. Graham's face was now redder than his nose, and he looked completely different from the clean-shaven lad I'd met in India. He had a terrible cough, yet he was cheerful and strong.

There was something wrong with Jeff's breathing, and he dozed off continually, making the most nightmarish gurgling, guttural sounds. Graham and I had to wake him up regularly, as we feared that he was getting pulmonary oedema. It was all very worrying.

Captain Noel had told me that in 1924 he felt overpowered with exhaustion when he first arrived on the North Col. He felt paralysed and lolled about aimlessly. He maintained that at such an altitude one's mental capacity becomes dulled and one's memory hazy, and this leads easily to nervous tremors upsetting the heart, lungs and stomach. He also said that you feel as though you are being suffocated by some invisible, poisonous gas. Jeff was certainly displaying all the symptoms.

His disturbing, moaning, groaning sounds reminded me that we were in the 'death zone' now, and could all expect to deteriorate appreciably. J.P. came through on the walkie-talkie, sending love and congratulations. After this message I closed my eyes and slept soundly. I woke the next morning, and found myself looking into Graham's swollen red face.

'God, you're an ugly bugger!' I said. 'Make some tea!'

He nodded obediently, lit the gas fire and melted some snow. Dogbollock was such a sweet character.

'I always have to obey you,' he said.

'Yes,' I replied. 'Because I'm a star and sexy!'

Our minds were slow, and our humour basic.

It was about 8 a.m. and the weather was absolutely delightful. David emphasized that we should take it very easy, and film at our leisure. I sat in the snow, in my green high-altitude clothes, and stared, as if in a trance, at the scenery. The North Ridge was directly in front of me ... The next day, unbelievably, I would be trying to ascend it. It was all icing on the cake from here on.

The Col had been our objective. But could I get higher?

Most of the Peace Climb had used oxygen from here on up, and they were conditioned mountaineers. I was to go on without it. At fifty-three, there was every chance that I would break down within the first hundred feet.

On his first attempt, in 1922, Mallory had climbed without oxygen. I would do my best. We were now without Wongchu, who could have carried the cylinders up for us. Also, there weren't any spare regulators. The BBC had paid the Peace Climb a great deal of money for oxygen, and they were not being that helpful.

From my viewpoint, I could see the First and Second Step clearly. The famous Second Step, where Mallory and Irvine were last seen, looked inviting and accessible. The Russians informed us that the ground between the two steps was steep, exposed and dangerous. It had given one of their climbers a fright.

During the day, I peered down the Col to where the New Zealanders were located on the lower slopes of the North Face. David filmed me singing the song of the All Blacks rugby team, 'The Haka', to cheer them up ... I doubt whether they could hear me.

In the late afternoon, we observed a bulbous figure coming down the North Ridge and on to the Col. It was a Russian, and he looked as though he'd got the entire Peace Climb on his back, tents and all. He was heaped up like a mountain. As he came alongside me, I helped release the load from his shoulders. It was a colossal weight!

He explained that he had a climbing shop in the Soviet Union, and that his equipment was old and worn. With all the stuff he had now acquired, he could replenish his stocks. We gave him food and lots of coffee, and he descended down the Col, a very happy Russki.

Towards the late afternoon I filmed a scene with the North Face behind me, describing how in 1924 Norton and Somervell, on their momentous climb, reached 28,000 feet. Here, the redoubtable Somervell stopped, and shortly afterwards coughed up part of his larynx, which was obstructing his breathing. Norton then continued up for another 126 feet. This attempt was without oxygen.

We continued filming and I spoke of Mallory and Irvine's assault. They used a primitive form of oxygen apparatus, and ascended the North Col in fast time, and the next day proceeded up to Camp V at 25,000 feet, and settled down for the night. This height was to be attempted by me the next day.

That evening David gave me an encouraging pep talk, and we settled down for our second night on the Col. Despite the fact that he was suffering, Jeff concerned himself totally with my well-being, checking that my crampons were sound and making sure that I drank the necessary quota of fluid.

It was hard to reciprocate his kindness, as he was a self-sufficient and private giant. Both he and Graham were splendid lads to be sharing a tent with. J.P. and Margaret came through on the walkie-talkie, and wished us good luck. It was comforting to hear their voices. Then it was lights out, each of us feeling uptight about the morrow's climb.

I was awake long before dawn, and couldn't get out of my head how weak I had felt halfway up the Col the day before. If that had happened then, at that height, what chance had I now of going higher? Without oxygen, wasn't I challenging fate?

Lord Hunt's words came back to me: 'All my life, it would have been pointless climbing if there hadn't been that element of danger.'

I smiled at my fears, and attempted to sleep a little more. Two hours later Graham was melting snow in the cooking pot. With the best intentions in the world, it still takes several hours to be ready to go. Water boils so slowly at these altitudes, and getting your high-altitude boots on is a major operation that starts up the alarming hammers of the heart again.

I was amazed that three hours had passed. The early morning sun was peeping up below us, heralding a lovely day. Eventually, two hours later, our tiny group was almost ready to commence the climb.

Jeff, who had suffered another bad night, came up to me to check my crampons and harness again. He appeared to be fumbling with his fingers, and not concentrating.

'Brian,' he said quietly. 'I won't be coming with you today. I'm going down the North Col on the fixed rope with a couple of Americans to guide me ... I've gone blind.'

We were all stunned.

'Blind! Jeff! How? What? ... Snow-blind, do you mean?' I said.

'No. Kurt says I've haemorrhaged behind the eyes.'

God, I thought, this is terrible!

The man could also develop a cerebral haemorrhage!

'Jeff! Jeff! Jeff!' I sighed, sitting down with the shock. 'I don't know what to say ... '

Then that fine giant held me tightly by the shoulders.

'You concentrate all your mind on the climb. I'll be fine ... There's nothing to regret. I am content,' he said calmly.

Twenty minutes later he disappeared out of sight, and down to Camp III. David radioed down to J.P. so that help could be at hand. We were then dealt another body-blow.

J.P. wired to say that the Peace Climb had sent our yaks up. Apparently Warren Thompson was concerned about us, as the Chinese, in the person of Mr Ping, wanted us off the mountain immediately, otherwise that sneering four-eyed pillock wanted another $200,000 from the BBC. His orders were to come down immediately.

In addition, the Peace Climb, having achieved its objectives, was stripping the mountain of its tents. Then the most horrible thing happened. That fine doctor, Kurt, who had looked after everybody so well, and who was with us and the recuperating climbers on the North Col, received orders from below to start burning the tents.

We looked on stunned as one of the tents burst into flames. The pollution was awful as the plastic materials bubbled and spread in the snow.

'No! Stop it!' we all shouted.

He stopped instantly. Poor Kurt! The Sherpas were bewildered by it all. That thousand-dollar tent was a whole year's wages to them. David Breashears' face tightened with disgust at this sacrilege ... Why, even Captain Ahab, in *Moby Dick*, would not have started a fire on the white whale's back!

These actions only strengthened our resolve to press on. Screw pissy Ping, and all of 'em!

David set up the tripod, adjusted the camera, and I moved away from the Col, following the line of fixed ropes. To begin with, I descended a little way, then I started to ascend and found myself at the foot of the North Ridge. Pausing to enjoy the moment, I looked back and David waved me on. I took another step, and I was alone on that famous ridge.

Imagine my delight when I found my heart to be beating steadily, and my breathing easy and smooth. There, to my left, seemingly going on forever, was the staggering North-East Ridge.

Easy now! Take it easy now! I kept telling myself.

My steady rhythm felt comfortable, and I was gaining height. David, from below, didn't make any sign for me to stop, as it was obvious that the shots were out of this world. Each stop revealed more features of the landscape.

It was a wonderful feeling to look across to my right and see the summit of the fabulous pyramid-shaped mountain, Pumori, at

23,000 feet, now below me. I could hardly believe my eyes – was I actually higher than Pumori?

In fact, I was now looking down on the North Col, with the torturous moments of that ascent the day before behind me. Those thundering emotions that I had felt on top of the Col contrasted completely with my present condition. All was smooth and peaceful.

In and out my breath went, and on and on and on I ascended. We had started the climb late, because of our set-backs, and now it was midday, and the sun shone gloriously on the whole North Face. What a spectacle of wonder it was! Oh, my! Oh, bliss!

Ancient voices and sounds, far, far away, seduced my mind with their haunting tones. Gently, I shook with happiness as the reality of my situation penetrated my being. I was alive, awake, real, tangible, my veins throbbed with blood, and I was on the North Ridge of Everest!

Higher and higher I went.

Now, God in Heaven! I was joined with the mountain!

My ant-like form looked up and across, unable for a moment to comprehend the sheer size of the massive structure that shredded my senses with its primordial form. Though millions of years old, the great mountain was still young and growing. You could feel it pulsating with energy.

The Goddess Mother of the Earth was born in the dark geological night, by the thrust of the mighty Gondwanaland. Her supremacy was total, yet in those moments she felt kind and friendly to me. There was no ferocious wind to lift me yards into the air on the fixed rope. Only awareness and stillness. As she enveloped me with her size, I felt myself being drawn on. Maybe the impudence of it all amused her.

The thought made me laugh, and I buzzed as if kissed by angels. The mighty North Face appeared to breathe in and out in gigantic breaths, with me joining in the frolic. Now came the moment when many people will claim I hallucinated. It didn't feel like it though. There they were! General Bruce and all the members of the 1922 and 1924 expeditions. All smiling away, sitting in the snow!

The general was in shorts, standing with his legs wide open. All the rest of the men were gathered round, drinking from mugs of tea, and dressed in their twenties gear. There was Somervell, Norton, Irvine, Beetham, Finch, Odell, Captain Noel and all the rest. Mallory was very comical, grinning like a schoolboy and blowing on his tea to cool it. They chatted and waved, saying I would be fine and to keep on going. After a while, they announced that they were buzzing off for luncheon, and gradually faded away ...

Throughout this experience I had looked away to my left, and the vision had not followed me. On turning back, there they were. Their departure left me feeling lonely.

David had shouted for me to stop, before this, and the team were slowly climbing towards me. It was quite a wait, and I felt a little cold in my static position. David wanted to get above me to take shots. It was a tremendous performance by the team: the Arriflex camera alone weighs twenty-five pounds, and the rest of the gear even more. Their faces resembled astronauts undergoing 'G-Force' stress.

Breashears has the attributes of a superman. The way he moved around, placing the camera here and there, at that height, was astonishing. Veronique's fitness, too, was admirable. The two Sherpas bent their backs with effort and will-power. Graham, too, had a surplus of energy.

How much easier it would have been if we could have simply concentrated on the climbing, but we were making a film as well. J.P. had the camera focused on me from far below, at Camp III, so that, for the moment, he was with us.

The going started to get harder, and I was surprised how steep certain sections proved to be. Sometimes I found myself looking directly up at Graham's rear end. Then I was up in front again, driving myself on, as David contorted his body in an effort to get a dramatic shot.

It was ferociously hard, and I found myself suddenly in deep snow and up to my waist. Stopping a second to blow away the ice from my jumar so that it would grip properly and not slip, I turned and viewed our progress.

The North Col was now way below us, and the figures moving on it looked like tiny dots. David insisted that I clip off the rope, and manoeuvre myself on to a shelf of snow. I didn't like this at all, not one little bit, yet what a view!

My eyes could now look down on a large part of the North Face. Down it plunged, steeply, towards the Central Rongbuk Glacier. The valiant New Zealanders were down there somewhere.

Directly across from my eyeline was the North Peak of the mighty Changtse, its enormous bulk impressive and dominating. Then I realized with a thrill that I was almost as high as its summit, at 24,780 feet. Following the immense, long North-East Ridge, our eyes focused with delight on the Lhakpa La, which Mallory and his companions first climbed, *en route* to the North Col, on the 1921 reconnaissance.

Then David pointed over to our left, beyond Pumori, and past the region of the West Rongbuk Glacier, to majestic Gyachung Kang, at 25,990 feet, and further still to white and dazzling Cho-Oyu, at 26,880 feet. A titanic landscape on the roof of the world, composed of winding glaciers, yawning crevasses, knife-edged arêtes and stupendous ridges. On and on, this blue and white panorama stretched, highlighted magically by the sky, as it followed the curvature of the earth. Our minds marvelled and our hearts melted in awe at the life-force behind it all. We turned again to Chomolungma and continued our ascent.

It was now 3 p.m., and our momentum was forceful and our progress good. Up, up, up. As Mallory said, 'We are going to sail to the top this time, God willing! Or stamp to the top, with our teeth in the wind ...'

I was allowed to go ahead again, and I pitched in with all my strength up a sixty-degree slope. It was extraordinary, but my lips kept sticking together in the cold and dry air, and when I used my tongue to clear them, that stuck to them too!

I was aware that I was becoming slightly dehydrated: my known weakness. After another fifty yards I felt a sharp pain in my stomach. It was time for me to take in more liquid. While waiting for the others to join me, I rejoiced at the sight of the Second Step below the Final Pyramid. My emotions grew and grew, now even more so, as was to be expected at this height. Again and again, Mallory's words zizzed in my mind: 'To refuse the adventure is to run the risk of drying up like a pea in its shell ... '

'Adventure' ... The word reverberated in my head. I turned, and was looking down on Changtse's Peak. We were at 25,000 feet. This was beyond my wildest dreams!

I swayed from side to side to stop the numbing pain in my stomach, but it wasn't anything serious. Then I became aware of a figure on my left, sitting upright, looking up at the summit. It was a young Frenchman, and he was as dead as a doornail. He had died of exhaustion on a previous expedition. The Peace Climb found him looking the other way, and had turned him to face the summit. Then I remembered Messner's words about living on a knife edge between life and death, and that the object of the exercise was to survive.

The importance of picking up my daughter, Rosalind, from school, entered my mind.

The crew went ahead a hundred yards to the top of the snow slope of the North Ridge. They shouted 'Action!', and I climbed up and stopped in front of the camera, and poured out my appreciation to them.

For the last half-hour I had not taken note of the weather. Mist was rolling in at an alarming rate. We climbed higher, with Camp V of the Peace Climb on our left. We were now free of the fixed ropes, and moving on rock. The camera rolled again, and I roared out, 'Look! There's the Second Step!'

For the mist had obscured it ... It looked so close! I could see every feature. To think I was here!

'Do you see it?' I shouted, struggling to free my frozen lips. 'That's where they were last seen! ... Mallory and Irvine! ... How high are we, David?'

'About 25,400 feet,' he said. 'And we must go down ... '

Graham immediately disagreed, maintaining that we could go to Camp V, rest there for the night, and go for Camp VI the next day, at 27,400 feet.

David told him that it would be suicide, saying that there would be no food, cooking utensils or sleeping bags. Also, the tent at Camp VI had had its guy-lines cut and was, in all probability, floating down the face.

'The Peace Climb have abandoned the mountain,' he added.

David also said that he'd had another call on the walkie-talkie, saying that unless we came down immediately the Chinese would fine us $100,000. Graham looked to me for my opinion.

Breashears is a great leader, and despite my yearning to go on, I immediately agreed with him. God! We'd lost Wongchu and Jeff. David was the only climber among us. Veronique was only just learning the ropes. The two Sherpas were really cooks, I was a greenhorn, and Graham had only Himal Chuli to his name. David alone was responsible for all of us!

Against all the odds, we had put up a marvellous show. Then, as if the goddess frowned on our decision, she suddenly hit us with a storm of epic proportions. We rushed like hell to get our high-altitude gear on, and found ourselves fighting for our lives.

God, it was awful! I hate descending at the best of times, but this was ghastly. What was the matter with my lovely goddess? Why was she so angry? It became freezing cold. Mallory and Irvine had been caught in a squall after they had last been seen in 1924, but it didn't compare to this. The wind roared and tore at us. Everybody was motoring down as fast as their legs could carry them.

Throughout my training I had concentrated on going slowly, and this speed didn't agree with me at all. We were all connected to the fixed ropes, and I slid all over the bloody place. Twice I fell upside down, and I was getting very tired. After such a long day, to be using so much of my reserves of energy was devastating me.

Down, down, down … Faster, faster, faster …

In a short space of time we had descended a thousand feet. Wow! What was the matter with me? I was beginning to feel as if I were dried up! The fury of the wind increased and pounded us, flattening me to the ground for the umpteenth time. I looked towards the summit, and the visibility was only a dozen yards. Then, for a few seconds, there was a slight lull, and I was aware of a gathering force of awesome energy, and the hurricane suddenly moved at tremendous speed and made a deep rumbling sound, as it unleashed itself with an earth-shattering bang against the North Face.

'You must move quickly, Brian!' roared David. 'Or you're in real danger! Move, move, move! For God's sake, move!'

I was in agony, absolutely doubled over in pain from stomach cramps. Twenty more minutes of hell, and I was now five hundred feet from the Col. Down, down, down ... Another hundred feet, and as quickly as the storm came, it left us. It was ridiculously unnatural. My condition was appalling. I had virtually come to a standstill ... It was serious!

God knows how, but with the help of David and Graham to get within a hundred feet of our tents, I was now mustering everything in my being to place one foot in front of the other.

'I'm not going to die! ... I'm definitely not going to die, yet! ... I've got to get home! ... '

My mind was haunted by the image of the dead Frenchman above me. My body felt as though it were made of cardboard. David was being wonderfully kind and solicitous, and I was being supported between him and Graham, otherwise I would have collapsed.

'Up the hill, Big Yeti!' David said. 'And then you're there! ... '

The Sherpas came towards us with oxygen, and for the only time in the whole expedition, David swore: 'No fucking oxygen! ... He needs water, you bloody fools!'

Then he held me on his own, as there was no space for three people, as we negotiated a sharp arête with vertical walls on either side.

'Watch it, Big Yeti! ... Don't collapse here! ... '

Another slight hillock to climb, and we were beside the tents. I was incapable of getting inside, or undressing myself. What followed was one of the kindest scenes in my life. Veronique, David and Graham carried me in bodily, and undressed me down to my baby suit, then wrapped me in my sleeping bag. David poured about two litres of water down my throat. After this, he adjusted my sleeping bag, fluffed up a spare duvet and lifted my head, gently placing the duvet underneath it, and immediately put a big mug of sweet, milky tea in my hand. I said nothing ... His face was close to mine, and our eyes locked in friendship. We stared at one another for ages, and I finally said, 'Thank you for saving my life ... '

From that point on, everything is a haze in my memory, like a film in reverse, a kaleidoscope of images ... Morning ... Tea

...Porridge ... Faces ... Fatigue ... Doziness ... Descent ... Down ... Down ... Ropes ... Traverse ... Down ... North Col behind me ... on, on to Camp III ... Margaret ... J.P. ... Love ... Affection ... Blindness ... Jeff ... Trough ... Ice Kingdom ... Descent ... J.P. ... Margaret with me ... Down ... Down ... All slow ... All a dream ... Camp II ... Yaks ... Americans ... Base Camp ... Ah! Krisna ... Wongchu ... Jules ... Swanee ... David ... Life ... Veronique ... Graham ... Kindness ... Delights ... Sunsets ... Lama ... Monks ... Land-cruiser ... Rough roads ... Shekar Dzong ... Tingri ... Tibetan Plains ... Prayer flags ... Hills ... Colours ... Pink ... Beige ... Brown ... Land-cruisers ... On, on, on ... To rocky grandeur ... Border ... Chinese ... Friendship Bridge ... Tea shops ... Nepal ... Smiles ... Yetis ... Ducks ... Hens ... More tea ... Valleys ... Streams ... Rivers ... Villages ... Fields ... Sunshine ... Beautiful ladies ... Dresses of blue ... Green ... Yellow ... Red ... Smiles ... Kathmandu ... Temples ... Fruit bats ... Yak and Yeti Hotel ... Swimming pool ... Bedroom ... Mirror ... 'Mirror, mirror on the wall, who is the skinniest of them all?' ... Thin ... Emaciated ... Taxi ... Ticket ... Kathmandu airport ... J.P., Margaret, Jeff ... Wongchu ... Comfortable ... Care and friendship ... Plane ... Long journey ... All too fast ... Unreal ... Heathrow, London ...

Only days ago, I had been high on Everest. My blood was still thick, and I was in a world of my own.

'No, Mr Customs! I have nothing to declare! ... Nothing!'

I moved on.

'Brian! ... Brian! ... Brian, look at me, darling! ... It's me, Hildegard!'

Oh, it was so good to see my wife again. We embarrassed everybody at the airport with our unabashed embraces.

She drove me to Sunningdale, and I had cheese on toast at Anne Marie's café. A sweet lady called Barbara cooked it. She cried when she saw me.

Afterwards Hildegard drove me to school to pick up Rosalind. There she was, leaning against a fence, as pretty as a picture. She was fifteen and so grown-up. We embraced long and gently.

'Hello, darling Daddy ... '

'Hello, sweetheart ... '

Hildegard bit her lip in the car.

Off we went home, and there was Josie, my cheerful mother-in-law, hugging me with lots of energy.

'I've cooked you a meat and potato pie,' she said.

The dogs mobbed me again and again. The oldest one, fifteen-year-old-Jessie, who was dearest to my heart, held back till the commotion was over, and then licked me profusely.

And then, as I sat down by my koi-carp pond and drank tea, she wrapped herself around my legs …

Epilogue

In the autumn of 1990 I found myself in Nepal, sharing a room with J.P. at the Everest View Hotel – at 13,000 feet, the highest hotel in the world. We were there with Veronique and David, to film aerial shots of Everest for our film *Galahad of Everest*.

Astonishing to think that it had taken years to make our film on Everest from the Tibetan side, and now here we were, as easy as you like, about to experience the 'Pegasus factor' and fly over the great mountain.

The two of us sat drinking coffee on the veranda and looking at the miraculous night sky lit up by a continuous display of shooting stars, with Everest close by, brooding in the background.

A few hours later we were flying in a single-engined Pilatus plane with David in tow, filming as only he knows how, the dawn breaking on the Goddess Mother of the Earth. We were strapped in, and appropriately dressed, as David opened the door wide when we were at 28,000 feet, risking life and limb in his task. Actually we nearly lost J.P. when he suddenly realized that his oxygen wasn't properly connected. All's well that ends well, and fortunately the mistake was rectified.

It was haunting to see again the terrain where we had been in the spring. The autumn weather was clear and fine, and the filming was a great success. It was absolutely delightful to be with J.P., Veronique and David again.

J.P. writes: 'We married Veronique and David on a hill above the Dhaulikhel Restaurant. Brian played Spencer Tracy as a priest, booming, "With the power invested in me, I proclaim you man and wife."

215

'I nudged him, saying he had no power whatsoever invested in him, read a poem and blessed them with cognac from a Tibetan teacup. Wongchu threw rice into the air, and some Tibetan friends chanted and made the couple exchange vows with *chang*, the potent Tibetan beer. It was a great wedding, even if the US Government wouldn't accept our credentials. Veronique cried, David looked as pleased as punch and the sun set on the most spectacular view in the world, with the entire range of Nepal Himal laid out before us.

'The newlyweds kissed, and just so they wouldn't think that life was going to change because they were married, I got them to film the mountains, as the last rays of pink glow ebbed from their snowy flanks. They didn't bat an eyelid.

'We filed down the hill in darkness, and celebrated in style down in the restaurant: curry and Iceberg beer. It was the perfect end to a great expedition ... '

Several weeks after the reunion in Nepal, Hildegard told me that a relative of hers, walking up a *koppie* (a little hill), in the Transvaal in South Africa, had met a sweet, grey-haired man of seventy. The relative gave us his phone number, and I picked it up and phoned him. There was a pause, and then a clear and haunting voice said, 'Hello, Mallory here ... '

It was John Mallory, George Mallory's son. He was delighted to hear from me, and we spoke for twenty minutes. He described with emotion how he had twice been to Everest Base Camp.

Here, in June 1991, as I write in my study, I am pleased to tell you that the giant Jeff Long's eyesight is on the mend. That fine young man has recovered the sight of one of his eyes, and the other improves daily. It is only a matter of time before he makes a complete recovery.

Jules, Swanee and Blackie are all well and kicking. The bobby-dazzler herself, Margaret, much to everybody's delight, not to mention J.P.'s, is having a baby, due sometime in January.

Wongchu, Krisna and Nawang, Chuldim and Phuli are all happy and well. Graham ('Dogbollock') is now producing that lovely radio programme, *Down Your Way*. In fact, I've guested a programme with him.

The Russian climber, Victor, made a complete recovery from his pulmonary oedema, and has sent me a book about General Zhukov.

The New Zealanders got to 28,000 feet on Everest's North Face: a tremendous achievement.

Stephen Evans valiantly climbed to Camp III, at 21,300 feet, on his trek, when visiting us, and the Californian with a cerebral haemorrhage, whom I met on the East Rongbuk Glacier, is making a slow recovery. I'm also pleased to report that the Californians successfully climbed the North Peak, Changtse.

In retrospect, we all look back on the expedition with love and pride. Thank you to everyone who made it possible.

The question of whether Mallory and Irvine climbed Everest is a mystery, and as I've stated in the book, we, as an expedition, wholeheartedly embrace the mystery.

J.P., that father to be, and most excellent human being, will always be Sir Galahad in my heart. Without his extraordinary gifts, it would all have been impossible. David Breashears and Veronique, those two amazing souls from the New World, excelled far beyond the call of duty. They will join J.P., Graham and myself on a BBC yeti expedition.

We all plan to return to Everest in the post-monsoon season of 1993, to attempt to climb it by the South Col route, in celebration of the successful first ascent by the British, led by Lord Hunt forty years ago. On this auspicious occasion, Nick Mason, the man with the glint in his eye, will lead the expedition. The Goddess Mother of the Earth is calling us back again.

Several months ago, J.P. miraculously managed to arrange for us to have an audience with the Dalai Lama in Dharamsala. It is an integral part of our film. His Holiness explained that Everest had always been known to his people as the Blue, or Turquoise Mountain.

As I received his blessing, he asked me if I would put his sacred scarf on the summit of Everest in the name of peace, and also, that I should chant the mantra, 'Om Mani Padme Hum' – 'Hail! Jewel in the Lotus Flower'.

His Holiness then added a more complex and private mantra, for me to chant in homage to the Goddess Mother of the Earth.